Cram101 Textbook Outlines to accompany:

Transnational Management

Bartlett, Ghoshal, Birkinshaw, 4th Edition

An Academic Internet Publishers (AIPI) publication (c) 2007.

You have a discounted membership at www.Cram101.com with this book.

Get all of the practice tests for the chapters of this textbook, and access in-depth reference material for writing essays and papers. Here is an example from a Cram101 Biology text:

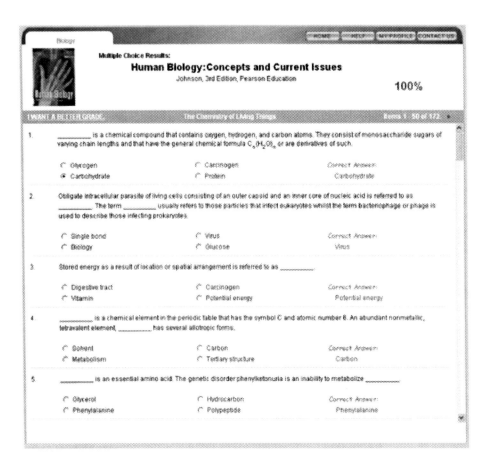

When you need problem solving help with math, stats, and other disciplines, www.Cram101.com will walk through the formulas and solutions step by step.

With Cram101.com online, you also have access to extensive reference material.

You will nail those essays and papers. Here is an example from a Cram101 Biology text:

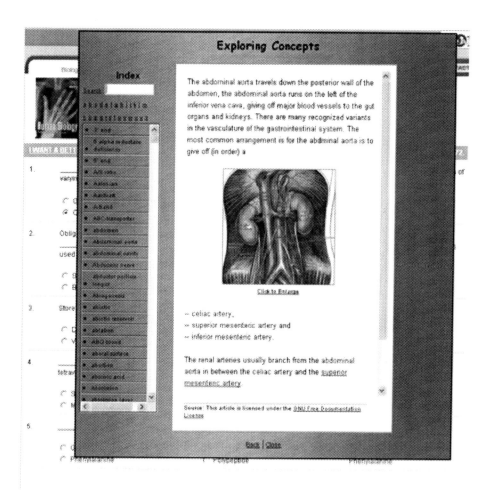

Learning System

Cram101 Textbook Outlines is a learning system. The notes in this book are the highlights of your textbook, you will never have to highlight a book again.

How to use this book. Take this book to class, it is your notebook for the lecture. The notes and highlights on the left hand side of the pages follow the outline and order of the textbook. All you have to do is follow along while your intructor presents the lecture. Circle the items emphasized in class and add other important information on the right side. With Cram101 Textbook Outlines you'll spend less time writing and more time listening. Learning becomes more efficient.

Cram101.com Online

Increase your studying efficiency by using Cram101.com's practice tests and online reference material. It is the perfect complement to Cram101 Textbook Outlines. Use self-teaching matching tests or simulate in-class testing with comprehensive multiple choice tests, or simply use Cram's true and false tests for quick review. Cram101.com even allows you to enter your in-class notes for an integrated studying format combining the textbook notes with your class notes.

Visit **www.Cram101.com**, click Sign Up at the top of the screen, and enter **DK73DW3353** in the promo code box on the registration screen. Access to www.Cram101.com is normally $9.95, but because you have purchased this book, your access fee is only $4.95. Sign up and stop highlighting textbooks forever.

Transnational Management
Bartlett, Ghoshal, Birkinshaw, 4th

CONTENTS

Domestic	From or in one's own country. A domestic producer is one that produces inside the home country. A domestic price is the price inside the home country. Opposite of 'foreign' or 'world.'.
Operation	A standardized method or technique that is performed repetitively, often on different materials resulting in different finished goods is called an operation.
Market	A market is, as defined in economics, a social arrangement that allows buyers and sellers to discover information and carry out a voluntary exchange of goods or services.
Option	A contract that gives the purchaser the option to buy or sell the underlying financial instrument at a specified price, called the exercise price or strike price, within a specific period of time.
Internationa-ization	Internationalization refers to another term for fragmentation. Used by Grossman and Helpman.
International Business	International business refers to any firm that engages in international trade or investment.
Merchant	Under the Uniform Commercial Code, one who regularly deals in goods of the kind sold in the contract at issue, or holds himself out as having special knowledge or skill relevant to such goods, or who makes the sale through an agent who regularly deals in such goods or claims such knowledge or skill is referred to as merchant.
Scope	Scope of a project is the sum total of all projects products and their requirements or features.
Corporation	A legal entity chartered by a state or the Federal government that is distinct and separate from the individuals who own it is a corporation. This separation gives the corporation unique powers which other legal entities lack.
Direct investment	Direct investment refers to a domestic firm actually investing in and owning a foreign subsidiary or division.
Investment	Investment refers to spending for the production and accumulation of capital and additions to inventories. In a financial sense, buying an asset with the expectation of making a return.
Export	In economics, an export is any good or commodity, shipped or otherwise transported out of a country, province, town to another part of the world in a legitimate fashion, typically for use in trade or sale.
United Nations	An international organization created by multilateral treaty in 1945 to promote social and economic cooperation among nations and to protect human rights is the United Nations.
Enterprise	Enterprise refers to another name for a business organization. Other similar terms are business firm, sometimes simply business, sometimes simply firm, as well as company, and entity.
Asset	An item of property, such as land, capital, money, a share in ownership, or a claim on others for future payment, such as a bond or a bank deposit is an asset.
Policy	Similar to a script in that a policy can be a less than completely rational decision-making method. Involves the use of a pre-existing set of decision steps for any problem that presents itself.
Integration	Economic integration refers to reducing barriers among countries to transactions and to movements of goods, capital, and labor, including harmonization of laws, regulations, and standards. Integrated markets theoretically function as a unified market.
Management	Management characterizes the process of leading and directing all or part of an organization, often a business, through the deployment and manipulation of resources. Early twentieth-century management writer Mary Parker Follett defined management as "the art of getting things done through people."
Open market	In economics, the open market is the term used to refer to the environment in which bonds are bought and sold.

Go to **Cram101.com** for the Practice Tests for this Chapter.

Parent company	Parent company refers to the entity that has a controlling influence over another company. It may have its own operations, or it may have been set up solely for the purpose of owning the Subject Company.
Affiliates	Local television stations that are associated with a major network are called affiliates. Affiliates agree to preempt time during specified hours for programming provided by the network and carry the advertising contained in the program.
Service	Service refers to a "non tangible product" that is not embodied in a physical good and that typically effects some change in another product, person, or institution. Contrasts with good.
Sony	Sony is a multinational corporation and one of the world's largest media conglomerates founded in Tokyo, Japan. One of its divisions Sony Electronics is one of the leading manufacturers of electronics, video, communications, and information technology products for the consumer and professional markets.
BMW	BMW is an independent German company and manufacturer of automobiles and motorcycles. BMW is the world's largest premium carmaker and is the parent company of the BMW MINI and Rolls-Royce car brands, and, formerly, Rover.
Points	Loan origination fees that may be deductible as interest by a buyer of property. A seller of property who pays points reduces the selling price by the amount of the points paid for the buyer.
Manufacturing	Production of goods primarily by the application of labor and capital to raw materials and other intermediate inputs, in contrast to agriculture, mining, forestry, fishing, and services a manufacturing.
Ford	Ford is an American company that manufactures and sells automobiles worldwide. Ford introduced methods for large-scale manufacturing of cars, and large-scale management of an industrial workforce, especially elaborately engineered manufacturing sequences typified by the moving assembly lines.
Amortization	Systematic and rational allocation of the acquisition cost of an intangible asset over its useful life is referred to as amortization.
Depreciation	Depreciation is an accounting and finance term for the method of attributing the cost of an asset across the useful life of the asset. Depreciation is a reduction in the value of a currency in floating exchange rate.
Revenue	Revenue is a U.S. business term for the amount of money that a company receives from its activities, mostly from sales of products and/or services to customers.
Profit	Profit refers to the return to the resource entrepreneurial ability; total revenue minus total cost.
Economy	The income, expenditures, and resources that affect the cost of running a business and household are called an economy.
Supply	Supply is the aggregate amount of any material good that can be called into being at a certain price point; it comprises one half of the equation of supply and demand. In classical economic theory, a curve representing supply is one of the factors that produce price.
Goodyear	Goodyear was founded in 1898 by German immigrants Charles and Frank Seiberling. Today it is the third largest tire and rubber company in the world.
Alcoa	Alcoa (NYSE: AA) is the world's leading producer of alumina, primary and fabricated aluminum, with operations in 43 countries. (It is followed in this by a former subsidiary, Alcan, the second-leading producer.)
Competitive advantage	A business is said to have a competitive advantage when its unique strengths, often based on cost, quality, time, and innovation, offer consumers a greater percieved value and there by differtiating it from its competitors.
Economies of scale	In economics, returns to scale and economies of scale are related terms that describe what happens as the scale of production increases. They are different terms and not to be used interchangeably.

Go to **Cram101.com** for the Practice Tests for this Chapter.

Nestle	Nestle is the world's biggest food and beverage company. In the 1860s, a pharmacist, developed a food for babies who were unable to be breastfed. His first success was a premature infant who could not tolerate his own mother's milk nor any of the usual substitutes. The value of the new product was quickly recognized when his new formula saved the child's life.
Bayer	Bayer is a German chemical and pharmaceutical company founded in 1863. By 1899, their trademark Aspirin was registered worldwide for the Bayer brand of acetylsalicylic acid, but through the widespread use to describe all brands of the compound, and Bayer's inability to protect its trademark the word "aspirin" lost its trademark status in the United States and some other countries.
Factors of production	Economic resources: land, capital, labor, and entrepreneurial ability are called factors of production.
Production	The creation of finished goods and services using the factors of production: land, labor, capital, entrepreneurship, and knowledge.
Competitive disadvantage	A situation in which a firm is not implementing using strategies that are being used by competing organizations is competitive disadvantage.
Tariff	A tax imposed by a nation on an imported good is called a tariff.
Labor	People's physical and mental talents and efforts that are used to help produce goods and services are called labor.
Product line	A group of products that are physically similar or are intended for a similar market are called the product line.
Household	An economic unit that provides the economy with resources and uses the income received to purchase goods and services that satisfy economic wants is called household.
Industry	A group of firms that produce identical or similar products is an industry. It is also used specifically to refer to an area of economic production focused on manufacturing which involves large amounts of capital investment before any profit can be realized, also called "heavy industry".
Product cycle	Product cycle refers to the life cycle of a new product, which first can be produced only in the country where it was developed, then as it becomes standardized and more familiar, can be produced in other countries and exported back to where it started.
Innovation	Innovation refers to the first commercially successful introduction of a new product, the use of a new method of production, or the creation of a new form of business organization.
Competitor	Other organizations in the same industry or type of business that provide a good or service to the same set of customers is referred to as a competitor.
Exporter	A firm that sells its product in another country is an exporter.
International trade	The export of goods and services from a country and the import of goods and services into a country is referred to as the international trade.
Economics	The social science dealing with the use of scarce resources to obtain the maximum satisfaction of society's virtually unlimited economic wants is an economics.
Journal	Book of original entry, in which transactions are recorded in a general ledger system, is referred to as a journal.
Developing country	Developing country refers to a country whose per capita income is low by world standards. Same as LDC. As usually used, it does not necessarily connote that the country's income is rising.
Firm	An organization that employs resources to produce a good or service for profit and owns and operates one or more plants is referred to as a firm.
International	Trying to create value by transferring core competencies to foreign markets where indigenous

Go to **Cram101.com** for the Practice Tests for this Chapter.
And, **NEVER** highlight a book again!

strategy	competitors lack those competencies is called international strategy.
Market opportunities	Market opportunities refer to areas where a company believes there are favorable demand trends, needs, and/or wants that are not being satisfied, and where it can compete effectively.
Product development	In business and engineering, new product development is the complete process of bringing a new product to market. There are two parallel aspects to this process : one involves product engineering ; the other marketing analysis. Marketers see new product development as the first stage in product life cycle management, engineers as part of Product Lifecycle Management.
Raw material	Raw material refers to a good that has not been transformed by production; a primary product.
Technology	The body of knowledge and techniques that can be used to combine economic resources to produce goods and services is called technology.
Positioning	The art and science of fitting the product or service to one or more segments of the market in such a way as to set it meaningfully apart from competition is called positioning.
Intervention	Intervention refers to an activity in which a government buys or sells its currency in the foreign exchange market in order to affect its currency's exchange rate.
Matching	Matching refers to an accounting concept that establishes when expenses are recognized. Expenses are matched with the revenues they helped to generate and are recognized when those revenues are recognized.
Factor cost	Factor cost is a measure of National Income or output based on the cost of factors of production, instead of market prices. This allows the effect of any subsidy or indirect tax to be removed from the final measure.
Cash cow	A cash cow is a product or a business unit that generates unusually high profit margins: so high that it is responsible for a large amount of a company's operating profit.
Leverage	Leverage is using given resources in such a way that the potential positive or negative outcome is magnified. In finance, this generally refers to borrowing.
Harvard Business Review	Harvard Business Review is a research-based magazine written for business practitioners, it claims a high ranking business readership and enjoys the reverence of academics, executives, and management consultants. It has been the frequent publishing home for well known scholars and management thinkers.
Marketing	Promoting and selling products or services to customers, or prospective customers, is referred to as marketing.
Value chain	The sequence of business functions in which usefulness is added to the products or services of a company is a value chain.
Liability	A liability is a present obligation of the enterprise arizing from past events, the settlement of which is expected to result in an outflow from the enterprise of resources embodying economic benefits.
Brand	A name, symbol, or design that identifies the goods or services of one seller or group of sellers and distinguishes them from the goods and services of competitors is a brand.
Franchise	A contractual right to sell certain products or services, use certain trademarks, or perform activities in a geographical region is called a franchise.
License	A license in the sphere of Intellectual Property Rights (IPR) is a document, contract or agreement giving permission or the 'right' to a legally-definable entity to do something (such as manufacture a product or to use a service), or to apply something (such as a trademark), with the objective of achieving commercial gain.
Gain	In finance, gain is a profit or an increase in value of an investment such as a stock or bond. Gain is calculated by fair market value or the proceeds from the sale of the investment minus the sum of the purchase price and all costs associated with it.

Uppsala model	The lack of knowledge of foreign markets is critical for most theories about internationalization. In behavioral models dealing with the internationalization process, such as the Uppsala Model, knowledge and learning have a profound impact on how the firm is seen to approach foreign markets.
Multinational enterprise	Multinational enterprise refers to a firm, usually a corporation, that operates in two or more countries.
Transnational	Transnational focuses on the heightened interconnectivity between people all around the world and the loosening of boundaries between countries.
Brief	Brief refers to a statement of a party's case or legal arguments, usually prepared by an attorney. Also used to make legal arguments before appellate courts.
Ad hoc	Ad hoc is a Latin phrase which means "for this purpose." It generally signifies a solution that has been tailored to a specific purpose and is makeshift and non-general, such as a handcrafted network protocol or a specific-purpose equation, as opposed to general solutions.
Foundation	A Foundation is a type of philanthropic organization set up by either individuals or institutions as a legal entity (either as a corporation or trust) with the purpose of distributing grants to support causes in line with the goals of the foundation.
Subsidiary	A company that is controlled by another company or corporation is a subsidiary.
Entrepreneur	The owner/operator. The person who organizes, manages, and assumes the risks of a firm, taking a new idea or a new product and turning it into a successful business is an entrepreneur.
Host country	The country in which the parent-country organization seeks to locate or has already located a facility is a host country.
Production efficiency	A situation in which the economy cannot produce more of one good without producing less of some other good is referred to as production efficiency.
Trade barrier	An artificial disincentive to export and/or import, such as a tariff, quota, or other NTB is called a trade barrier.
Standardized product	Standardized product refers to a product whose buyers are indifferent to the seller from whom they purchase it, as long as the price charged by all sellers is the same; a product all units of which are identical and thus are perfect substitutes.
Preference	The act of a debtor in paying or securing one or more of his creditors in a manner more favorable to them than to other creditors or to the exclusion of such other creditors is a preference. In the absence of statute, a preference is perfectly good, but to be legal it must be bona fide, and not a mere subterfuge of the debtor to secure a future benefit to himself or to prevent the application of his property to his debts.
Argument	The discussion by counsel for the respective parties of their contentions on the law and the facts of the case being tried in order to aid the jury in arriving at a correct and just conclusion is called argument.
Organization structure	The system of task, reporting, and authority relationships within which the organization does its work is referred to as the organization structure.
Local content requirement	A requirement that some specific fraction of a good be produced domestically is called local content requirement.
Economic efficiency	Economic efficiency refers to the use of the minimum necessary resources to obtain the socially optimal amounts of goods and services; entails both productive efficiency and allocative efficiency.
Multinational corporation	An organization that manufactures and markets products in many different countries and has multinational stock ownership and multinational management is referred to as multinational corporation.
Trend	Trend refers to the long-term movement of an economic variable, such as its average rate of increase or

Go to **Cram101.com** for the Practice Tests for this Chapter.

decrease over enough years to encompass several business cycles.

International division

Division responsible for a firm's international activities is an international division.

Expatriate

Employee sent by his or her company to live and manage operations in a different country is called an expatriate.

Appeal

Appeal refers to the act of asking an appellate court to overturn a decision after the trial court's final judgment has been entered.

Credibility

The extent to which a source is perceived as having knowledge, skill, or experience relevant to a communication topic and can be trusted to give an unbiased opinion or present objective information on the issue is called credibility.

Authority

Authority in agency law, refers to an agent's ability to affect his principal's legal relations with third parties. Also used to refer to an actor's legal power or ability to do something. In addition, sometimes used to refer to a statute, case, or other legal source that justifies a particular result.

Operations management

A specialized area in management that converts or transforms resources into goods and services is operations management.

Customer experience

The sum total of interactions that a customer has with a company's website is referred to as the customer experience.

Initial public offering

Firms in the process of becoming publicly traded companies will issue shares of stock using an initial public offering, which is merely the process of selling stock for the first time to interested investors.

Joint venture

Joint venture refers to an undertaking by two parties for a specific purpose and duration, taking any of several legal forms.

Acquisition

A company's purchase of the property and obligations of another company is an acquisition.

Senior management

Senior management is generally a team of individuals at the highest level of organizational management who have the day-to-day responsibilities of managing a corporation.

Special meeting

Meeting of shareholders to take action on specific proposals submitted by management and the Board of Directors for consideration and approval is a special meeting.

Margin

A deposit by a buyer in stocks with a seller or a stockbroker, as security to cover fluctuations in the market in reference to stocks that the buyer has purchased but for which he has not paid is a margin. Commodities are also traded on margin.

Advertising

Advertising refers to paid, nonpersonal communication through various media by organizations and individuals who are in some way identified in the advertising message.

Market research

Market research is the process of systematic gathering, recording and analyzing of data about customers, competitors and the market. Market research can help create a business plan, launch a new product or service, fine tune existing products and services, expand into new markets etc. It can be used to determine which portion of the population will purchase the product/service, based on variables like age, gender, location and income level. It can be found out what market characteristics your target market has.

Core

A core is the set of feasible allocations in an economy that cannot be improved upon by subset of the set of the economy's consumers (a coalition). In construction, when the force in an element is within a certain center section, the core, the element will only be under compression.

Fixed cost

The cost that a firm bears if it does not produce at all and that is independent of its output. The presence of a fixed cost tends to imply increasing returns to scale. Contrasts with variable cost.

Utility

Utility refers to the want-satisfying power of a good or service; the satisfaction or pleasure a

Go to **Cram101.com** for the Practice Tests for this Chapter.

consumer obtains from the consumption of a good or service.

Controlling	A management function that involves determining whether or not an organization is progressing toward its goals and objectives, and taking corrective action if it is not is called controlling.
Market share	That fraction of an industry's output accounted for by an individual firm or group of firms is called market share.
Franchising	Franchising is a method of doing business wherein a franchisor licenses trademarks and tried and proven methods of doing business to a franchisee in exchange for a recurring payment, and usually a percentage piece of gross sales or gross profits as well as the annual fees. The term " franchising " is used to describe a wide variety of business systems which may or may not fall into the legal definition provided above.
Capital	Capital generally refers to financial wealth, especially that used to start or maintain a business. In classical economics, capital is one of four factors of production, the others being land and labor and entrepreneurship.
Partnership	In the common law, a partnership is a type of business entity in which partners share with each other the profits or losses of the business undertaking in which they have all invested.
Franchise agreement	An arrangement whereby someone with a good idea for a business sells the rights to use the business name and sell a product or service to others in a given territory is a franchise agreement.
Closing	The finalization of a real estate sales transaction that passes title to the property from the seller to the buyer is referred to as a closing. Closing is a sales term which refers to the process of making a sale. It refers to reaching the final step, which may be an exchange of money or acquiring a signature.
Trust	An arrangement in which shareholders of independent firms agree to give up their stock in exchange for trust certificates that entitle them to a share of the trust's common profits.
Fund	Independent accounting entity with a self-balancing set of accounts segregated for the purposes of carrying on specific activities is referred to as a fund.
Equity	Equity is the name given to the set of legal principles, in countries following the English common law tradition, which supplement strict rules of law where their application would operate harshly, so as to achieve what is sometimes referred to as "natural justice."
Property	Assets defined in the broadest legal sense. Property includes the unrealized receivables of a cash basis taxpayer, but not services rendered.
Vendor	A person who sells property to a vendee is a vendor. The words vendor and vendee are more commonly applied to the seller and purchaser of real estate, and the words seller and buyer are more commonly applied to the seller and purchaser of personal property.
Management team	A management team is directly responsible for managing the day-to-day operations (and profitability) of a company.
Quality control	The measurement of products and services against set standards is referred to as quality control.
Brand awareness	How quickly or easily a given brand name comes to mind when a product category is mentioned is brand awareness.
Promotion	Promotion refers to all the techniques sellers use to motivate people to buy products or services. An attempt by marketers to inform people about products and to persuade them to participate in an exchange.
Startup	Any new company can be considered a startup, but the description is usually applied to aggressive young companies that are actively courting private financing from venture capitalists, including wealthy individuals and investment companies.

Project manager	Project manager refers to a manager responsible for a temporary work project that involves the participation of other people from various functions and levels of the organization.
Lease	A contract for the possession and use of land or other property, including goods, on one side, and a recompense of rent or other income on the other is the lease.
Cost structure	The relative proportion of an organization's fixed, variable, and mixed costs is referred to as cost structure.
Budget	Budget refers to an account, usually for a year, of the planned expenditures and the expected receipts of an entity. For a government, the receipts are tax revenues.
Business development	Business development emcompasses a number of techniques designed to grow an economic enterprise. Such techniques include, but are not limited to, assessments of marketing opportunities and target markets, intelligence gathering on customers and competitors, generating leads for possible sales, followup sales activity, and formal proposal writing.
Interest	In finance and economics, interest is the price paid by a borrower for the use of a lender's money. In other words, interest is the amount of paid to "rent" money for a period of time.
Preparation	Preparation refers to usually the first stage in the creative process. It includes education and formal training.
Business model	A business model is the instrument by which a business intends to generate revenue and profits. It is a summary of how a company means to serve its employees and customers, and involves both strategy (what an business intends to do) as well as an implementation.
Logo	Logo refers to device or other brand name that cannot be spoken.
Pizza Hut	Pizza Hut is the world's largest pizza restaurant chain with nearly 34,000 restaurants, delivery-carry out units, and kiosks in 100 countries
Precedent	A previously decided court decision that is recognized as authority for the disposition of future decisions is a precedent.
Concession	A concession is a business operated under a contract or license associated with a degree of exclusivity in exploiting a business within a certain geographical area. For example, sports arenas or public parks may have concession stands; and public services such as water supply may be operated as concessions.
Compromise	Compromise occurs when the interaction is moderately important to meeting goals and the goals are neither completely compatible nor completely incompatible.
Exchange	The trade of things of value between buyer and seller so that each is better off after the trade is called the exchange.
Credit	Credit refers to a recording as positive in the balance of payments, any transaction that gives rise to a payment into the country, such as an export, the sale of an asset, or borrowing from abroad.
Committee	A long-lasting, sometimes permanent team in the organization structure created to deal with tasks that recur regularly is the committee.
Human resources	Human resources refers to the individuals within the firm, and to the portion of the firm's organization that deals with hiring, firing, training, and other personnel issues.
Restructuring	Restructuring is the corporate management term for the act of partially dismantling and reorganizing a company for the purpose of making it more efficient and therefore more profitable.
General manager	A manager who is responsible for several departments that perform different functions is called general manager.
Consideration	Consideration in contract law, a basic requirement for an enforceable agreement under traditional contract principles, defined in this text as legal value, bargained for and given in exchange for an

	act or promise. In corporation law, cash or property contributed to a corporation in exchange for shares, or a promise to contribute such cash or property.
Quality assurance	Those activities associated with assuring the quality of a product or service is called quality assurance.
Per capita	Per capita refers to per person. Usually used to indicate the average per person of any given statistic, commonly income.
Advertising campaign	A comprehensive advertising plan that consists of a series of messages in a variety of media that center on a single theme or idea is referred to as an advertising campaign.
Marketing strategy	Marketing strategy refers to the means by which a marketing goal is to be achieved, usually characterized by a specified target market and a marketing program to reach it.
Turnover	Turnover in a financial context refers to the rate at which a provider of goods cycles through its average inventory. Turnover in a human resources context refers to the characteristic of a given company or industry, relative to rate at which an employer gains and loses staff.
Publicity	Publicity refers to any information about an individual, product, or organization that's distributed to the public through the media and that's not paid for or controlled by the seller.
Contract	A contract is a "promise" or an "agreement" that is enforced or recognized by the law. In the civil law, a contract is considered to be part of the general law of obligations.
Targeting	In advertizing, targeting is to select a demographic or other group of people to advertise to, and create advertisements appropriately.
Acer	Acer is one of the world's top five branded PC vendors. It owns the largest computer retail chain in Taiwan. Acer's product offering includes desktop and mobile PCs, servers and storage, displays, peripherals, and e-business solutions for business, government, education, and home users.
Shill	A shill is an associate of a person selling goods or services, who pretends no association to the seller and assumes the air of an enthusiastic customer.
Delegation	Delegation is the handing of a task over to another person, usually a subordinate. It is the assignment of authority and responsibility to another person to carry out specific activities.
Dealer	People who link buyers with sellers by buying and selling securities at stated prices are referred to as a dealer.
Warehouse	Warehouse refers to a location, often decentralized, that a firm uses to store, consolidate, age, or mix stock; house product-recall programs; or ease tax burdens.
Purchasing	Purchasing refers to the function in a firm that searches for quality material resources, finds the best suppliers, and negotiates the best price for goods and services.
Company culture	Company culture is the term given to the values and practices shared by the employees of a firm.
Licensing agreement	Detailed and comprehensive written agreement between the licensor and licensee that sets forth the express terms of their agreement is called a licensing agreement.
Product design	Product Design is defined as the idea generation, concept development, testing and manufacturing or implementation of a physical object or service. It is possibly the evolution of former discipline name - Industrial Design.
Negotiation	Negotiation is the process whereby interested parties resolve disputes, agree upon courses of action, bargain for individual or collective advantage, and/or attempt to craft outcomes which serve their mutual interests.
Licensing	Licensing is a form of strategic alliance which involves the sale of a right to use certain proprietary knowledge (so called intellectual property) in a defined way.

Unisys	Unisys was formed in September 1986 through the merger of the mainframe corporations Sperry and Burroughs, with Burroughs buying Sperry for $4.8 billion. The name was chosen after an internal competition. The merger was the largest in the computer industry at the time and made Unisys the second largest computer company, with annual revenue of $10.5 billion.
Trademark	A distinctive word, name, symbol, device, or combination thereof, which enables consumers to identify favored products or services and which may find protection under state or federal law is a trademark.
Securities and exchange commission	Securities and exchange commission refers to U.S. government agency that determines the financial statements that public companies must provide to stockholders and the measurement rules that they must use in producing those statements.
Security	Security refers to a claim on the borrower future income that is sold by the borrower to the lender. A security is a type of transferable interest representing financial value.
Shares	Shares refer to an equity security, representing a shareholder's ownership of a corporation. Shares are one of a finite number of equal portions in the capital of a company, entitling the owner to a proportion of distributed, non-reinvested profits known as dividends and to a portion of the value of the company in case of liquidation.
Chase Manhattan	The Chase Manhattan Bank was formed by the merger of the Chase National Bank and the Bank of the Manhattan Company in 1955.
Stock	In financial terminology, stock is the capital raized by a corporation, through the issuance and sale of shares.
Distribution	Distribution in economics, the manner in which total output and income is distributed among individuals or factors.
Estate	An estate is the totality of the legal rights, interests, entitlements and obligations attaching to property. In the context of wills and probate, it refers to the totality of the property which the deceased owned or in which some interest was held.
Swap	In finance a swap is a derivative, where two counterparties exchange one stream of cash flows against another stream. These streams are called the legs of the swap. The cash flows are calculated over a notional principal amount. Swaps are often used to hedge certain risks, for instance interest rate risk. Another use is speculation.
Business unit	The lowest level of the company which contains the set of functions that carry a product through its life span from concept through manufacture, distribution, sales and service is a business unit.
Incentive	An incentive is any factor (financial or non-financial) that provides a motive for a particular course of action, or counts as a reason for preferring one choice to the alternatives.
Administration	Administration refers to the management and direction of the affairs of governments and institutions; a collective term for all policymaking officials of a government; the execution and implementation of public policy.
Organizational structure	Organizational structure is the way in which the interrelated groups of an organization are constructed. From a managerial point of view the main concerns are ensuring effective communication and coordination.
Productivity	Productivity refers to the total output of goods and services in a given period of time divided by work hours.
Evaluation	The consumer's appraisal of the product or brand on important attributes is called evaluation.
Distribution channel	A distribution channel is a chain of intermediaries, each passing a product down the chain to the next organization, before it finally reaches the consumer or end-user.
Channel	Channel, in communications (sometimes called communications channel), refers to the medium used to

Go to **Cram101.com** for the Practice Tests for this Chapter.
And, **NEVER** highlight a book again!

convey information from a sender (or transmitter) to a receiver.

Mistake	In contract law a mistake is incorrect understanding by one or more parties to a contract and may be used as grounds to invalidate the agreement. Common law has identified three different types of mistake in contract: unilateral mistake, mutual mistake, and common mistake.
Management philosophy	Management philosophy refers to a philosophy that links key goal-related issues with key collaboration issues to come up with general ways by which the firm will manage its affairs.
Stock exchange	A stock exchange is a corporation or mutual organization which provides facilities for stock brokers and traders, to trade company stocks and other securities.
Organization model	The Stages of Organization Model provides a system-level language for understanding the evolutionary development of organizations. The model describes seven types of dynamic equilibrium, each of which can provide a coherent basis for action. They represent the increasing complexity possible when people learn the lessons of early stages of activity and incorporate this learning while tackling more advanced challenges.
Intellectual property	In law, intellectual property is an umbrella term for various legal entitlements which attach to certain types of information, ideas, or other intangibles in their expressed form. The holder of this legal entitlement is generally entitled to exercise various exclusive rights in relation to its subject matter.
Operating activities	Cash flow activities that include the cash effects of transactions that create revenues and expenses and thus enter into the determination of net income is an operating activities.
Decentralization	Decentralization is the process of redistributing decision-making closer to the point of service or action. This gives freedom to managers at lower levels of the organization to make decisions.
Compaq	Compaq was founded in February 1982 by Rod Canion, Jim Harris and Bill Murto, three senior managers from semiconductor manufacturer Texas Instruments. Each invested $1,000 to form the company. Their first venture capital came from Ben Rosen and Sevin-Rosen partners. It is often told that the architecture of the original PC was first sketched out on a placemat by the founders while dining in the Houston restaurant, House of Pies.
In transit	A state in which goods are in the possession of a bailee or carrier and not in the hands of the buyer, seller, lessee, or lessor is referred to as in transit.
Inventory	Tangible property held for sale in the normal course of business or used in producing goods or services for sale is an inventory.
Automation	Automation allows machines to do work previously accomplished by people.
Total cost	The sum of fixed cost and variable cost is referred to as total cost.
Product cost	Product cost refers to sum of the costs assigned to a product for a specific purpose. A concept used in applying the cost plus approach to product pricing in which only the costs of manufacturing the product are included in the cost amount to which the markup is added.
Logistics	Those activities that focus on getting the right amount of the right products to the right place at the right time at the lowest possible cost is referred to as logistics.
Competitiveness	Competitiveness usually refers to characteristics that permit a firm to compete effectively with other firms due to low cost or superior technology, perhaps internationally.
Configuration	An organization's shape, which reflects the division of labor and the means of coordinating the divided tasks is configuration.
Product management	Product management is a function within a company dealing with the day-to-day management and welfare of a product or family of products at all stages of the product lifecycle.The product management function is responsible for defining the products in the marketing mix.

Product manager	Product manager refers to a person who plans, implements, and controls the annual and long-range plans for the products for which he or she is responsible.
Focus group	A small group of people who meet under the direction of a discussion leader to communicate their opinions about an organization, its products, or other given issues is a focus group.
Users	Users refer to people in the organization who actually use the product or service purchased by the buying center.
Competitive market	A market in which no buyer or seller has market power is called a competitive market.
Icon Medialab International AB	Icon Medialab International AB provides interactive digital communication services including Internet, intranet, extranet and e-commerce solutions. The company's solutions are a mix of three components: programming, business consulting and creative market communications.
Board of directors	The group of individuals elected by the stockholders of a corporation to oversee its operations is a board of directors.
Case study	A case study is a particular method of qualitative research. Rather than using large samples and following a rigid protocol to examine a limited number of variables, case study methods involve an in-depth, longitudinal examination of a single instance or event: a case. They provide a systematic way of looking at events, collecting data, analyzing information, and reporting the results.
Siemens	Siemens is the world's largest conglomerate company. Worldwide, Siemens and its subsidiaries employs 461,000 people (2005) in 190 countries and reported global sales of €75.4 billion in fiscal year 2005.
Fortune magazine	Fortune magazine is America's longest-running business magazine. Currently owned by media conglomerate Time Warner, it was founded in 1930 by Henry Luce. It is known for its regular features ranking companies by revenue.
Advertising agency	A firm that specializes in the creation, production, and placement of advertising messages and may provide other services that facilitate the marketing communications process is an advertising agency.
Holding company	A corporation whose purpose or function is to own or otherwise hold the shares of other corporations either for investment or control is called holding company.
Holding	The holding is a court's determination of a matter of law based on the issue presented in the particular case. In other words: under this law, with these facts, this result.
Project management	Project management is the discipline of organizing and managing resources in such a way that these resources deliver all the work required to complete a project within defined scope, time, and cost constraints.
Management consulting	Management consulting refers to both the practice of helping companies to improve performance through analysis of existing business problems and development of future plans, as well as to the firms that specialize in this sort of consulting.
Team management	Team management teaches a number of techniques that aim at forming and managing teams.
Extranet	An extension of the Internet that connects suppliers, customers, and other organizations via secure websites is an extranet.
Intranet	Intranet refers to a companywide network, closed to public access, that uses Internet-type technology. A set of communications links within one company that travel over the Internet but are closed to public access.
Prototype	A prototype is built to test the function of a new design before starting production of a product.
Inception	The date and time on which coverage under an insurance policy takes effect is inception. Also refers to the date at which a stock or mutual fund was first traded.

Go to **Cram101.com** for the Practice Tests for this Chapter.

Hosting	Internet hosting service is a service that runs Internet servers, allowing organizations and individuals to serve content on the Internet.
Knowledge management	Sharing, organizing and disseminating information in the simplest and most relevant way possible for the users of the information is a knowledge management.
Chief knowledge officer	A chief knowledge officer is an organizational leader, responsible for ensuring that the organization maximizes the value it achieves through knowledge.
Virtual private network	A private data network that creates secure connections, or tunnels, over regular Internet lines is called virtual private network.
Management information system	A computer-based system that provides information and support for effective managerial decision makin is referred to as a management information system.
Information system	An information system is a system whether automated or manual, that comprises people, machines, and/or methods organized to collect, process, transmit, and disseminate data that represent user information.
Performance feedback	The process of providing employees with information regarding their performance effectiveness is referred to as performance feedback.
Consultant	A professional that provides expert advice in a particular field or area in which customers occassionaly require this type of knowledge is a consultant.
Commerce	Commerce is the exchange of something of value between two entities. It is the central mechanism from which capitalism is derived.
Outsourcing	Outsourcing refers to a production activity that was previously done inside a firm or plant that is now conducted outside that firm or plant.
Venture capitalists	Venture capitalists refer to individuals or companies that invest in new businesses in exchange for partial ownership of those businesses.
New economy	New economy, this term was used in the late 1990's to suggest that globalization and/or innovations in information technology had changed the way that the world economy works.
Business strategy	Business strategy, which refers to the aggregated operational strategies of single business firm or that of an SBU in a diversified corporation refers to the way in which a firm competes in its chosen arenas.
Accenture	In October 2002, the Congressional General Accounting Office (GAO) identified Accenture as one of four publicly-traded federal contractors that were incorporated in a tax haven country. Accenture is a global management consulting, technology services and outsourcing company. Its organizational structure includes divisions based on client industry types and employee workforces.
Boston Consulting Group	The Boston Consulting Group is a management consulting firm founded by Harvard Business School alum Bruce Henderson in 1963. In 1965 Bruce Henderson thought that to survive, much less grow, in a competitive landscape occupied by hundreds of larger and better-known consulting firms, a distinctive identity was needed, and pioneered "Business Strategy" as a special area of expertise.
Wholesale	According to the United Nations Statistics Division Wholesale is the resale of new and used goods to retailers, to industrial, commercial, institutional or professional users, or to other wholesalers, or involves acting as an agent or broker in buying merchandise for, or selling merchandise, to such persons or companies.
Venture capital	Venture capital is capital provided by outside investors for financing of new, growing or struggling businesses. Venture capital investments generally are high risk investments but offer the potential for above average returns.
Organic growth	Organic growth is the rate of business expansion through increasing output and sales as opposed to

Go to **Cram101.com** for the Practice Tests for this Chapter.

Go to **Cram101.com** for the Practice Tests for this Chapter.
And, **NEVER** highlight a book again!

mergers, acquisitions and take-overs. Typically, the organic growth rate also excludes the impact of foreign exchange. Growth including foreign exchange, but excluding divestitures and acquistions is often referred to as, core growth.

Euro	The common currency of a subset of the countries of the EU, adopted January 1, 1999 is called euro.
Merger	Merger refers to the combination of two firms into a single firm.
Mergers and acquisitions	The phrase mergers and acquisitions refers to the aspect of corporate finance strategy and management dealing with the merging and acquiring of different companies as well as other assets. Usually mergers occur in a friendly setting where executives from the respective companies participate in a due diligence process to ensure a successful combination of all parts.
Portfolio	In finance, a portfolio is a collection of investments held by an institution or a private individual. Holding but not always a portfolio is part of an investment and risk-limiting strategy called diversification. By owning several assets, certain types of risk (in particular specific risk) can be reduced.
Bull market	A rising stock market. A bull market exists when stock prices are strong and rising and investors are optimistic about future market performance.
Valuation	In finance, valuation is the process of estimating the market value of a financial asset or liability. They can be done on assets (for example, investments in marketable securities such as stocks, options, business enterprises, or intangible assets such as patents and trademarks) or on liabilities (e.g., Bonds issued by a company).
Downturn	A decline in a stock market or economic cycle is a downturn.
Bankruptcy	Bankruptcy is a legally declared inability or impairment of ability of an individual or organization to pay their creditors.
Default	In finance, default occurs when a debtor has not met its legal obligations according to the debt contract, e.g. it has not made a scheduled payment, or violated a covenant (condition) of the debt contract.
Drawback	Drawback refers to rebate of import duties when the imported good is re-exported or used as input to the production of an exported good.
Buyer	A buyer refers to a role in the buying center with formal authority and responsibility to select the supplier and negotiate the terms of the contract.
Senior executive	Senior executive means a chief executive officer, chief operating officer, chief financial officer and anyone in charge of a principal business unit or function.
Personnel	A collective term for all of the employees of an organization. Personnel is also commonly used to refer to the personnel management function or the organizational unit responsible for administering personnel programs.
Assignment	A transfer of property or some right or interest is referred to as assignment.
Managing director	Managing director is the term used for the chief executive of many limited companies in the United Kingdom, Commonwealth and some other English speaking countries. The title reflects their role as both a member of the Board of Directors but also as the senior manager.
International firm	International firm refers to those firms who have responded to stiff competition domestically by expanding their sales abroad. They may start a production facility overseas and send some of their managers, who report to a global division, to that country.
Forming	The first stage of team development, where the team is formed and the objectives for the team are set is referred to as forming.
Foreign	A company owned in a foreign country by another company is referred to as foreign subsidiary.

Go to **Cram101.com** for the Practice Tests for this Chapter.

subsidiary	
Ethnocentrism	Ironically, ethnocentrism may be something that all cultures have in common. People often feel this occurring during what some call culture shock. Ethnocentrism often entails the belief that one's own race or ethnic group is the most important and/or that some or all aspects of its culture are superior to those of other groups.
Financial control	A process in which a firm periodically compares its actual revenues, costs, and expenses with its projected ones is called financial control.
Polycentrism	Polycentrism is the principle of organization of a region around several political, social or financial centres. Today, the area is a large city that grew from a dozen smaller cities. As a result, the "city" has no single centre, but several.
Geocentrism	Geocentrism in marketing is a global orientation with marketing strategies adapted to local country conditions.
Contribution	In business organization law, the cash or property contributed to a business by its owners is referred to as contribution.
International management	International management refers to the management of business operations conducted in more than one country.
Financial manager	Managers who make recommendations to top executives regarding strategies for improving the financial strength of a firm are referred to as a financial manager.
Consumer good	Products and services that are ultimately consumed rather than used in the production of another good are a consumer good.
Global competition	Global competition exists when competitive conditions across national markets are linked strongly enough to form a true international market and when leading competitors compete head to head in many different countries.
Balance	In banking and accountancy, the outstanding balance is the amount of money owned, (or due), that remains in a deposit account (or a loan account) at a given date, after all past remittances, payments and withdrawal have been accounted for. It can be positive (then, in the balance sheet of a firm, it is an asset) or negative (a liability).
Economic nationalism	Economic nationalism is a term used to describe policies which are guided by the idea of protecting domestic consumption, labor and capital formation, even if this requires the imposition of tariffs and other restrictions on the movement of labor, goods and capital. Economic nationalism may include such doctrines as protectionism and import substitution.
Task force	A temporary team or committee formed to solve a specific short-term problem involving several departments is the task force.
Long run	In economic models, the long run time frame assumes no fixed factors of production. Firms can enter or leave the marketplace, and the cost (and availability) of land, labor, raw materials, and capital goods can be assumed to vary.
Expense	In accounting, an expense represents an event in which an asset is used up or a liability is incurred. In terms of the accounting equation, expenses reduce owners' equity.
Bureaucracy	Bureaucracy refers to an organization with many layers of managers who set rules and regulations and oversee all decisions.
Monopoly	A monopoly is defined as a persistent market situation where there is only one provider of a kind of product or service.
Professional development	Professional development refers to vocational education with specific reference to continuing education of the person undertaking it in the area of employment, it may also provide opportunities for other

Go to **Cram101.com** for the Practice Tests for this Chapter.

career paths.

Devise

In a will, a gift of real property is called a devise.

Honda

With more than 14 million internal combustion engines built each year, Honda is the largest engine-maker in the world. In 2004, the company began to produce diesel motors, which were both very quiet whilst not requiring particulate filters to pass pollution standards. It is arguable, however, that the foundation of their success is the motorcycle division.

Primary market

The market for the raising of new funds as opposed to the trading of securities already in existence is called primary market.

Arbitrage

An arbitrage is a combination of nearly simultaneous transactions designed to profit from an existing discrepancy among prices, exchange rates, and/or interest rates on different markets without assuming risk.

Declining industry

An industry in which economic profits are negative and that will, therefore, decrease its output as firms leave it is called declining industry.

Global citizenship

Global citizenship is a person's obligation to respect and protect their environment and people around them while thinking on a global scale. This can be related to globalization.

Trade flow

The quantity or value of a country's bilateral trade with another country is called trade flow.

Screening

Screening in economics refers to a strategy of combating adverse selection, one of the potential decision-making complications in cases of asymmetric information.

Nissan

Nissan is Japan's second largest car company after Toyota. Nissan is among the top three Asian rivals of the "big three" in the US.

Product strategy

Decisions on the management of products or services based on the conditions of a given market is product strategy. Two general strategies that are well known in the marketing discipline are marketing mix and relational marketing.

Market segments

Market segments refer to the groups that result from the process of market segmentation; these groups ideally have common needs and will respond similarly to a marketing action.

Peak

Peak refers to the point in the business cycle when an economic expansion reaches its highest point before turning down. Contrasts with trough.

Globalization

The increasing world-wide integration of markets for goods, services and capital that attracted special attention in the late 1990s is called globalization.

Product concept

The verbal and perhaps pictorial description of the benefits and features of a proposed product; also the early stage of the product development process in which only the product concept exists.

Trade union

A Trade Union, as we understand the term, is a continuous association of wage-earners for the purpose of maintaining or improving the conditions of their employment. They may organise strikes or resistance to lockouts in furtherance of particular goals.

Union

A worker association that bargains with employers over wages and working conditions is called a union.

Premium

Premium refers to the fee charged by an insurance company for an insurance policy. The rate of losses must be relatively predictable: In order to set the premium (prices) insurers must be able to estimate them accurately.

Gucci

Gucci, or the House of Gucci, is an Italian fashion and leather goods label. It was founded by Guccio Gucci (1881-1953) in Florence in 1921. In the late 1980s made Gucci one of the world's most influential fashion houses and a highly profitable business operation. In October of 1995 Gucci decided to go public and had its first initial public offering on the AEX and NYSE for $22 per share..

Consumer demand

Consumer demand or consumption is also known as personal consumption expenditure. It is the largest

Go to **Cram101.com** for the Practice Tests for this Chapter.

part of aggregate demand or effective demand at the macroeconomic level.There are two variants of consumption in the aggregate demand model, including induced consumption and autonomous consumption.

Synergy	Corporate synergy occurs when corporations interact congruently. A corporate synergy refers to a financial benefit that a corporation expects to realize when it merges with or acquires another corporation.
Frequency	Frequency refers to the speed of the up and down movements of a fluctuating economic variable; that is, the number of times per unit of time that the variable completes a cycle of up and down movement.
Commodity	Could refer to any good, but in trade a commodity is usually a raw material or primary product that enters into international trade, such as metals or basic agricultural products.
Complaint	The pleading in a civil case in which the plaintiff states his claim and requests relief is called complaint. In the common law, it is a formal legal document that sets out the basic facts and legal reasons that the filing party (the plaintiffs) believes are sufficient to support a claim against another person, persons, entity or entities (the defendants) that entitles the plaintiff(s) to a remedy (either money damages or injunctive relief).
Retailing	All activities involved in selling, renting, and providing goods and services to ultimate consumers for personal, family, or household use is referred to as retailing.
Dividend payout ratio	A measure of the percentage of earnings paid out in dividends; found by dividing cash dividends by the net income available to each class of stock is the dividend payout ratio.
Payout ratio	A measure of the percentage of earnings distributed in the form of cash dividends to common stockholders is referred to as the payout ratio. More specifically, the firm's cash dividend divided by the firm's earnings in the same reporting period.
Dividend	Amount of corporate profits paid out for each share of stock is referred to as dividend.
Financial statement	Financial statement refers to a summary of all the transactions that have occurred over a particular period.
Accounting	A system that collects and processes financial information about an organization and reports that information to decision makers is referred to as accounting.
Toshiba	Toshiba is a Japanese high technology electrical and electronics manufacturing firm, headquartered in Tokyo, Japan. It is the 7th largest integrated manufacturer of electric and electronic equipment in the world.
Consolidation	The combination of two or more firms, generally of equal size and market power, to form an entirely new entity is a consolidation.
General Electric	In 1876, Thomas Alva Edison opened a new laboratory in Menlo Park, New Jersey. Out of the laboratory was to come perhaps the most famous invention of all—a successful development of the incandescent electric lamp. By 1890, Edison had organized his various businesses into the Edison General Electric Company.
Diversification	Investing in a collection of assets whose returns do not always move together, with the result that overall risk is lower than for individual assets is referred to as diversification.
Cash flow	In finance, cash flow refers to the amounts of cash being received and spent by a business during a defined period of time, sometimes tied to a specific project. Most of the time they are being used to determine gaps in the liquid position of a company.
Late Movers	Late movers often imitate the technological advances of other businesses or reduce risks by waiting until a new market is established. The competitive advantage held by businesses that are late in entering a market.
Leadership	Management merely consists of leadership applied to business situations; or in other words: management

35

forms a sub-set of the broader process of leadership.

Gross margin	Gross margin is an ambiguous phrase that expresses the relationship between gross profit and sales revenue as Gross Margin = Revenue - costs of good sold.
Brand image	The advertising metric that measures the type and favorability of consumer perceptions of the brand is referred to as the brand image.
Samsung	On November 30, 2005 Samsung pleaded guilty to a charge it participated in a worldwide DRAM price fixing conspiracy during 1999-2002 that damaged competition and raized PC prices.
Target market	One or more specific groups of potential consumers toward which an organization directs its marketing program are a target market.
Market position	Market position is a measure of the position of a company or product on a market.
Caterpillar	Caterpillar is a United States based corporation headquartered in Peoria, Illinois. Caterpillar is "the world's largest manufacturer of construction and mining equipment, diesel and natural gas engines, and industrial gas turbines."
Benchmarking	The continuous process of comparing the levels of performance in producing products and services and executing activities against the best levels of performance is benchmarking.
Niche	In industry, a niche is a situation or an activity perfectly suited to a person. A niche can imply a working position or an area suited to a person who occupies it. Basically, a job where a person is able to succeed and thrive.
Gap	In December of 1995, Gap became the first major North American retailer to accept independent monitoring of the working conditions in a contract factory producing its garments. Gap is the largest specialty retailer in the United States.
Loyalty	Marketers tend to define customer loyalty as making repeat purchases. Some argue that it should be defined attitudinally as a strongly positive feeling about the brand.
Differentiated product	A firm's product that is not identical to products of other firms in the same industry is a differentiated product.
Oligopoly	A market structure in which there are a small number of sellers, at least some of whose individual decisions about price or quantity matter to the others is an oligopoly.
Complexity	The technical sophistication of the product and hence the amount of understanding required to use it is referred to as complexity. It is the opposite of simplicity.
Agent	A person who makes economic decisions for another economic actor. A hired manager operates as an agent for a firm's owner.
Currency risk	Currency risk is a form of risk that arises from the change in price of one currency against another. Whenever investors or companies have assets or business operations across national borders, they face currency risk if their positions are not hedged.
Openness	Openness refers to the extent to which an economy is open, often measured by the ratio of its trade to
Standing	Standing refers to the legal requirement that anyone seeking to challenge a particular action in court must demonstrate that such action substantially affects his legitimate interests before he will be entitled to bring suit.
Incidence	The ultimate economic effect of a tax on the real incomes of producers or consumers. Thus a sales tax may be paid by a retailer, but it is likely that the incidence falls upon the consumer.

International Business	International business refers to any firm that engages in international trade or investment.
Industry	A group of firms that produce identical or similar products is an industry. It is also used specifically to refer to an area of economic production focused on manufacturing which involves large amounts of capital investment before any profit can be realized, also called "heavy industry".
Scope	Scope of a project is the sum total of all projects products and their requirements or features.
Industrial revolution	The Industrial Revolution is the stream of new technology and the resulting growth of output that began in England toward the end of the 18th century.
Economies of scale	In economics, returns to scale and economies of scale are related terms that describe what happens as the scale of production increases. They are different terms and not to be used interchangeably.
Technology	The body of knowledge and techniques that can be used to combine economic resources to produce goods and services is called technology.
Economy	The income, expenditures, and resources that affect the cost of running a business and household are called an economy.
Production	The creation of finished goods and services using the factors of production: land, labor, capital, entrepreneurship, and knowledge.
Capital	Capital generally refers to financial wealth, especially that used to start or maintain a business. In classical economics, capital is one of four factors of production, the others being land and labor and entrepreneurship.
Domestic	From or in one's own country. A domestic producer is one that produces inside the home country. A domestic price is the price inside the home country. Opposite of 'foreign' or 'world.'.
Export	In economics, an export is any good or commodity, shipped or otherwise transported out of a country, province, town to another part of the world in a legitimate fashion, typically for use in trade or sale.
Market	A market is, as defined in economics, a social arrangement that allows buyers and sellers to discover information and carry out a voluntary exchange of goods or services.
Economies of scope	The ability to use one resource to provide many different products and services is referred to as economies of scope.
Consumer good	Products and services that are ultimately consumed rather than used in the production of another good are a consumer good.
Marketing	Promoting and selling products or services to customers, or prospective customers, is referred to as marketing.
Unit cost	Unit cost refers to cost computed by dividing some amount of total costs by the related number of units. Also called average cost.
Exporting	Selling products to another country is called exporting.
Service	Service refers to a "non tangible product" that is not embodied in a physical good and that typically effects some change in another product, person, or institution. Contrasts with good.
Credit	Credit refers to a recording as positive in the balance of payments, any transaction that gives rise to a payment into the country, such as an export, the sale of an asset, or

Go to **Cram101.com** for the Practice Tests for this Chapter.

Go to **Cram101.com** for the Practice Tests for this Chapter.
And, **NEVER** highlight a book again!

borrowing from abroad.

Factor cost	Factor cost is a measure of National Income or output based on the cost of factors of production, instead of market prices. This allows the effect of any subsidy or indirect tax to be removed from the final measure.
Supply	Supply is the aggregate amount of any material good that can be called into being at a certain price point; it comprises one half of the equation of supply and demand. In classical economic theory, a curve representing supply is one of the factors that produce price.
Michael Porter	Michael Porter is a leading contributor to strategic management theory, Porter's main academic objectives focus on how a firm or a region, can build a competitive advantage and develop competitive strategy. Porter's strategic system consists primarily of 5 forces analysis, strategic groups, the value chain, and market positioning stratagies.
Logistics Management	Logistics management refers to the practice of organizing the cost-effective flow of raw materials, in-process inventory, finished goods, and related information from point of origin to point of consumption to satisfy customer requirements.
Management	Management characterizes the process of leading and directing all or part of an organization, often a business, through the deployment and manipulation of resources. Early twentieth-century management writer Mary Parker Follett defined management as "the art of getting things done through people."
Logistics	Those activities that focus on getting the right amount of the right products to the right place at the right time at the lowest possible cost is referred to as logistics.
Economics	The social science dealing with the use of scarce resources to obtain the maximum satisfaction of society's virtually unlimited economic wants is an economics.
General Agreement on Tariffs and Trade	The General Agreement on Tariffs and Trade was originally created by the Bretton Woods Conference as part of a larger plan for economic recovery after World War II. It included a reduction in tariffs and other international trade barriers and is generally considered the precursor to the World Trade Organization.
International trade	The export of goods and services from a country and the import of goods and services into a country is referred to as the international trade.
Free trade	Free trade refers to a situation in which there are no artificial barriers to trade, such as tariffs and quotas. Usually used, often only implicitly, with frictionless trade, so that it implies that there are no barriers to trade of any kind.
Tariff	A tax imposed by a nation on an imported good is called a tariff.
Trend	Trend refers to the long-term movement of an economic variable, such as its average rate of increase or decrease over enough years to encompass several business cycles.
Globalization	The increasing world-wide integration of markets for goods, services and capital that attracted special attention in the late 1990s is called globalization.
Innovation	Innovation refers to the first commercially successful introduction of a new product, the use of a new method of production, or the creation of a new form of business organization.
Efficient scale	The quantity of output that minimizes average total cost is referred to as efficient scale.
Single market	A single market is a customs union with common policies on product regulation, and freedom of movement of all the four factors of production (goods, services, capital and labor).
Minimum efficient scale	The smallest output of a firm consistent with minimum average cost. In small countries, in some industries the level of demand in autarky is not sufficient to support minimum efficient scale.

Go to **Cram101.com** for the Practice Tests for this Chapter.

Manufacturing	Production of goods primarily by the application of labor and capital to raw materials and other intermediate inputs, in contrast to agriculture, mining, forestry, fishing, and services a manufacturing.
Restructuring	Restructuring is the corporate management term for the act of partially dismantling and reorganizing a company for the purpose of making it more efficient and therefore more profitable.
Product line	A group of products that are physically similar or are intended for a similar market are called the product line.
Operation	A standardized method or technique that is performed repetitively, often on different materials resulting in different finished goods is called an operation.
Labor	People's physical and mental talents and efforts that are used to help produce goods and services are called labor.
Standardization	Standardization, in the context related to technologies and industries, is the process of establishing a technical standard among competing entities in a market, where this will bring benefits without hurting competition.
Preference	The act of a debtor in paying or securing one or more of his creditors in a manner more favorable to them than to other creditors or to the exclusion of such other creditors is a preference. In the absence of statute, a preference is perfectly good, but to be legal it must be bona fide, and not a mere subterfuge of the debtor to secure a future benefit to himself or to prevent the application of his property to his debts.
Competitor	Other organizations in the same industry or type of business that provide a good or service to the same set of customers is referred to as a competitor.
Consumer behavior	Consumer behavior refers to the actions a person takes in purchasing and using products and services, including the mental and social processes that precede and follow these actions.
Competitive Strategy	An outline of how a business intends to compete with other firms in the same industry is called competitive strategy.
Global strategy	Global strategy refers to strategy focusing on increasing profitability by reaping cost reductions from experience curve and location economies.
Interdependence	The extent to which departments depend on each other for resources or materials to accomplish their tasks is referred to as interdependence.
Corporation	A legal entity chartered by a state or the Federal government that is distinct and separate from the individuals who own it is a corporation. This separation gives the corporation unique powers which other legal entities lack.
Fund	Independent accounting entity with a self-balancing set of accounts segregated for the purposes of carrying on specific activities is referred to as a fund.
Argument	The discussion by counsel for the respective parties of their contentions on the law and the facts of the case being tried in order to aid the jury in arriving at a correct and just conclusion is called argument.
Global village	Global village describes how electronic mass media collapse space and time barriers in human communication, enabling people to interact and live on a global scale. In this sense, the globe has been turned into a village by the electronic mass media.
Host country	The country in which the parent-country organization seeks to locate or has already located a facility is a host country.
Uncertainty	The extent to which people prefer to be in clear and unambiguous situations is referred to as

Go to **Cram101.com** for the Practice Tests for this Chapter.

avoidance	the uncertainty avoidance.
Power distance	Power distance refers to the degree to which the less powerful members of society expect there to be differences in the levels of power. A high score suggests that there is an expectation that some individuals wield larger amounts of power than others. Countries with high power distance rating are often characterized by a high rate of political violence.
Matrix organization	Matrix organization refers to an organization in which specialists from different parts of the organization are brought together to work on specific projects but still remain part of a traditional line-and-staff structure.
Management system	A management system is the framework of processes and procedures used to ensure that an organization can fulfill all tasks required to achieve its objectives.
Wage differential	The difference between the wage received by one worker or group of workers and that received by another worker or group of workers is a wage differential.
Consumption	In Keynesian economics consumption refers to personal consumption expenditure, i.e., the purchase of currently produced goods and services out of income, out of savings (net worth), or from borrowed funds. It refers to that part of disposable income that does not go to saving.
Wage	The payment for the service of a unit of labor, per unit time. In trade theory, it is the only payment to labor, usually unskilled labor. In empirical work, wage data may exclude other compenzation, which must be added to get the total cost of employment.
Profit	Profit refers to the return to the resource entrepreneurial ability; total revenue minus total cost.
Air France	Air France took over the Dutch company KLM in May 2004, resulting in the creation of Air France -KLM. Air France -KLM is the largest airline company in the world in terms of operating revenues, and the third-largest in the world in terms of passengers-kilometers.
Subsidy	Subsidy refers to government financial assistance to a domestic producer.
Bearer	A person in possession of a negotiable instrument that is payable to him, his order, or to whoever is in possession of the instrument is referred to as bearer.
Competitiveness	Competitiveness usually refers to characteristics that permit a firm to compete effectively with other firms due to low cost or superior technology, perhaps internationally.
Consumerism	Consumerism is a term used to describe the effects of equating personal happiness with purchasing material possessions and consumption.
Import penetration	Import penetration refers to a measure of the importance of imports in the domestic economy, either by sector or overall, usually defined as the value of imports divided by the value of apparent consumption.
Economic policy	Economic policy refers to the actions that governments take in the economic field. It covers the systems for setting interest rates and government deficit as well as the labor market, national ownership, and many other areas of government.
Policy	Similar to a script in that a policy can be a less than completely rational decision-making method. Involves the use of a pre-existing set of decision steps for any problem that presents itself.
Economic development	Increase in the economic standard of living of a country's population, normally accomplished by increasing its stocks of physical and human capital and improving its technology is an economic development.
Investment	Investment refers to spending for the production and accumulation of capital and additions to

Go to **Cram101.com** for the Practice Tests for this Chapter.

inventories. In a financial sense, buying an asset with the expectation of making a return.

Relatively efficient market
One in which few impediments to international trade and investment exist is a relatively efficient market.

Bargaining power
Bargaining power refers to the ability to influence the setting of prices or wages, usually arising from some sort of monopoly or monopsony position

Efficient market
Efficient market refers to a market in which, at a minimum, current price changes are independent of past price changes, or, more strongly, price reflects all available information.

Market system
All the product and resource markets of a market economy and the relationships among them are called a market system.

Antiglobaliz-tion
Antiglobalization is a term most commonly ascribed to the political stance of people and groups who oppose certain aspects of globalization in its current form, often including the domination of current global trade agreements and trade-governing bodies such as the World Trade Organization by powerful corporations.

Expense
In accounting, an expense represents an event in which an asset is used up or a liability is incurred. In terms of the accounting equation, expenses reduce owners' equity.

Localization
As an element of wireless marketing strategy, transmitting messages that are relevant to the user's current geographical location are referred to as localization.

Frequency
Frequency refers to the speed of the up and down movements of a fluctuating economic variable; that is, the number of times per unit of time that the variable completes a cycle of up and down movement.

Product design
Product Design is defined as the idea generation, concept development, testing and manufacturing or implementation of a physical object or service. It is possibly the evolution of former discipline name - Industrial Design.

Leadership
Management merely consists of leadership applied to business situations; or in other words: management forms a sub-set of the broader process of leadership.

Discount
The difference between the face value of a bond and its selling price, when a bond is sold for less than its face value it's referred to as a discount.

Receiver
A person that is appointed as a custodian of other people's property by a court of law or a creditor of the owner, pending a lawsuit or reorganization is called a receiver.

Browser
A program that allows a user to connect to the World Wide Web by simply typing in a URL is a browser.

Information system
An information system is a system whether automated or manual, that comprises people, machines, and/or methods organized to collect, process, transmit, and disseminate data that represent user information.

Flexible manufacturing
Flexible manufacturing refers to designing machines to do multiple tasks so that they can produce a variety of products.

Flexible manufacturing technologies
Manufacturing technologies designed to improve job scheduling, reduce setup time, and improve quality control are called flexible manufacturing technologies.

Firm
An organization that employs resources to produce a good or service for profit and owns and operates one or more plants is referred to as a firm.

Amortize
To provide for the payment of a debt by creating a sinking fund or paying in installments is

to amortize.

Diffusion	Diffusion is the process by which a new idea or new product is accepted by the market. The rate of diffusion is the speed that the new idea spreads from one consumer to the next.
Competitive advantage	A business is said to have a competitive advantage when its unique strengths, often based on cost, quality, time, and innovation, offer consumers a greater percieved value and there by diffetiating it from its competitors.
Gain	In finance, gain is a profit or an increase in value of an investment such as a stock or bond. Gain is calculated by fair market value or the proceeds from the sale of the investment minus the sum of the purchase price and all costs associated with it.
Incentive	An incentive is any factor (financial or non-financial) that provides a motive for a particular course of action, or counts as a reason for preferring one choice to the alternatives.
Economic forces	Forces that affect the availability, production, and distribution of a society's resources among competing users are referred to as economic forces.
Closing	The finalization of a real estate sales transaction that passes title to the property from the seller to the buyer is referred to as a closing. Closing is a sales term which refers to the process of making a sale. It refers to reaching the final step, which may be an exchange of money or acquiring a signature.
Manufacturing costs	Costs incurred in a manufacturing process, which consist of direct material, direct labor, and manufacturing overhead are referred to as manufacturing costs.
Subsidiary	A company that is controlled by another company or corporation is a subsidiary.
Leverage	Leverage is using given resources in such a way that the potential positive or negative outcome is magnified. In finance, this generally refers to borrowing.
Brand	A name, symbol, or design that identifies the goods or services of one seller or group of sellers and distinguishes them from the goods and services of competitors is a brand.
Advertising	Advertising refers to paid, nonpersonal communication through various media by organizations and individuals who are in some way identified in the advertising message.
Differentiated product	A firm's product that is not identical to products of other firms in the same industry is a differentiated product.
Market position	Market position is a measure of the position of a company or product on a market.
Coalition	An informal alliance among managers who support a specific goal is called coalition.
Forming	The first stage of team development, where the team is formed and the objectives for the team are set is referred to as forming.
Exchange rate	Exchange rate refers to the price at which one country's currency trades for another, typically on the exchange market.
Regulation	Regulation refers to restrictions state and federal laws place on business with regard to the conduct of its activities.
Exchange	The trade of things of value between buyer and seller so that each is better off after the trade is called the exchange.
Complexity	The technical sophistication of the product and hence the amount of understanding required to use it is referred to as complexity. It is the opposite of simplicity.
Centralized system	An organizational system whereby advertising along with other marketing activities such as sales, marketing research, and planning are divided along functional lines and are run from

one central marketing department is called centralized system.

Category killer

Category killer is a term used in marketing and strategic management to describe a product, service, brand, or company that has such a distinct sustainable competitive advantage that competing firms find it almost impossible to operate profitably in that industry. The existence of a category killer will eliminate almost all market entity, whether real or virtual.

Nintendo

Nintendo has the reputation of historically being both the oldest intact company in the video game console market and one of the most influential and well-known console manufacturers, as well as being the most dominant entity in the handheld console market.

Distribution

Distribution in economics, the manner in which total output and income is distributed among individuals or factors.

Reuters

Reuters is best known as a news service that provides reports from around the world to newspapers and broadcasters. Its main focus is on supplying the financial markets with information and trading products.

Business opportunity

A business opportunity involves the sale or lease of any product, service, equipment, etc. that will enable the purchaser-licensee to begin a business

Productivity

Productivity refers to the total output of goods and services in a given period of time divided by work hours.

Advertising campaign

A comprehensive advertising plan that consists of a series of messages in a variety of media that center on a single theme or idea is referred to as an advertising campaign.

Warehouse

Warehouse refers to a location, often decentralized, that a firm uses to store, consolidate, age, or mix stock; house product-recall programs; or ease tax burdens.

Inventory

Tangible property held for sale in the normal course of business or used in producing goods or services for sale is an inventory.

Retailing

All activities involved in selling, renting, and providing goods and services to ultimate consumers for personal, family, or household use is referred to as retailing.

Accounting

A system that collects and processes financial information about an organization and reports that information to decision makers is referred to as accounting.

International division

Division responsible for a firm's international activities is an international division.

Journal

Book of original entry, in which transactions are recorded in a general ledger system, is referred to as a journal.

Retail sale

The sale of goods and services to consumers for their own use is a retail sale.

Beneficiary

The person for whose benefit an insurance policy, trust, will, or contract is established is a beneficiary. In the case of a contract, the beneficiary is called a third-party beneficiary.

Appeal

Appeal refers to the act of asking an appellate court to overturn a decision after the trial court's final judgment has been entered.

Fragmentation

Fragmentation refers to the splitting of production processes into separate parts that can be done in different locations, including in different countries.

Wholesale

According to the United Nations Statistics Division Wholesale is the resale of new and used goods to retailers, to industrial, commercial, institutional or professional users, or to other wholesalers, or involves acting as an agent or broker in buying merchandise for, or selling merchandise, to such persons or companies.

Buying power	The dollar amount available to purchase securities on margin is buying power. The amount is calculated by adding the cash held in the brokerage accounts and the amount that could be spent if securities were fully margined to their limit. If an investor uses their buying power, they are purchasing securities on credit.
Per capita	Per capita refers to per person. Usually used to indicate the average per person of any given statistic, commonly income.
Merchant	Under the Uniform Commercial Code, one who regularly deals in goods of the kind sold in the contract at issue, or holds himself out as having special knowledge or skill relevant to such goods, or who makes the sale through an agent who regularly deals in such goods or claims such knowledge or skill is referred to as merchant.
Security	Security refers to a claim on the borrower future income that is sold by the borrower to the lender. A security is a type of transferable interest representing financial value.
Political economy	Early name for the discipline of economics. A field within economics encompassing several alternatives to neoclassical economics, including Marxist economics. Also called radical political economy.
Enterprise	Enterprise refers to another name for a business organization. Other similar terms are business firm, sometimes simply business, sometimes simply firm, as well as company, and entity.
Pension	A pension is a steady income given to a person (usually after retirement). Pensions are typically payments made in the form of a guaranteed annuity to a retired or disabled employee.
Privilege	Generally, a legal right to engage in conduct that would otherwise result in legal liability is a privilege. Privileges are commonly classified as absolute or conditional. Occasionally, privilege is also used to denote a legal right to refrain from particular behavior.
Conglomerate	A conglomerate is a large company that consists of divisions of often seemingly unrelated businesses.
Keiretsu	Keiretsu is a set of companies with interlocking business relationships and shareholdings. It is a type of business group.
Toshiba	Toshiba is a Japanese high technology electrical and electronics manufacturing firm, headquartered in Tokyo, Japan. It is the 7th largest integrated manufacturer of electric and electronic equipment in the world.
Loyalty	Marketers tend to define customer loyalty as making repeat purchases. Some argue that it should be defined attitudinally as a strongly positive feeling about the brand.
Affiliates	Local television stations that are associated with a major network are called affiliates. Affiliates agree to preempt time during specified hours for programming provided by the network and carry the advertising contained in the program.
Wholesaling	Wholesaling consists of the sale of goods/merchandise to retailers, to industrial, commercial, institutional, or other professional business users or to other wholesalers and related subordinated services.
Screening	Screening in economics refers to a strategy of combating adverse selection, one of the potential decision-making complications in cases of asymmetric information.
Objection	In the trial of a case the formal remonstrance made by counsel to something that has been said or done, in order to obtain the court's ruling thereon is an objection.
Core	A core is the set of feasible allocations in an economy that cannot be improved upon by subset of the set of the economy's consumers (a coalition). In construction, when the force

in an element is within a certain center section, the core, the element will only be under compression.

Information technology
Information technology refers to technology that helps companies change business by allowing them to use new methods.

Inventory control
Inventory control, in the field of loss prevention, are systems designed to introduce technical barriers to shoplifting.

Comprehensive
A comprehensive refers to a layout accurate in size, color, scheme, and other necessary details to show how a final ad will look. For presentation only, never for reproduction.

Adoption
In corporation law, a corporation's acceptance of a pre-incorporation contract by action of its board of directors, by which the corporation becomes liable on the contract, is referred to as adoption.

Point of Sale
Point of sale can mean a retail shop, a checkout counter in a shop, or a variable location where a transaction occurs.

Demographic
A demographic is a term used in marketing and broadcasting, to describe a demographic grouping or a market segment.

Rationalization
Rationalization in economics is an attempt to change a pre-existing ad-hoc workflow into one that is based on a set of published rules.

Distribution channel
A distribution channel is a chain of intermediaries, each passing a product down the chain to the next organization, before it finally reaches the consumer or end-user.

Customs
Customs is an authority or agency in a country responsible for collecting customs duties and for controlling the flow of people, animals and goods (including personal effects and hazardous items) in and out of the country.

Channel
Channel, in communications (sometimes called communications channel), refers to the medium used to convey information from a sender (or transmitter) to a receiver.

Gap
In December of 1995, Gap became the first major North American retailer to accept independent monitoring of the working conditions in a contract factory producing its garments. Gap is the largest specialty retailer in the United States.

Direct investment
Direct investment refers to a domestic firm actually investing in and owning a foreign subsidiary or division.

Structural impediments initiative
A 1990 agreement between the United States and Japan to decrease nontariff barriers restricting imports into Japan is referred to as the structural impediments initiative.

Trade barrier
An artificial disincentive to export and/or import, such as a tariff, quota, or other NTB is called a trade barrier.

Negotiation
Negotiation is the process whereby interested parties resolve disputes, agree upon courses of action, bargain for individual or collective advantage, and/or attempt to craft outcomes which serve their mutual interests.

Foreign direct investment
Foreign direct investment refers to the buying of permanent property and businesses in foreign nations.

Rationing
Rationing is the controlled distribution of resources and scarce goods or services: it restricts how much people are allowed to buy or consume.

Estate
An estate is the totality of the legal rights, interests, entitlements and obligations attaching to property. In the context of wills and probate, it refers to the totality of the property which the deceased owned or in which some interest was held.

Go to **Cram101.com** for the Practice Tests for this Chapter.

Publicity	Publicity refers to any information about an individual, product, or organization that's distributed to the public through the media and that's not paid for or controlled by the seller.
Target market	One or more specific groups of potential consumers toward which an organization directs its marketing program are a target market.
Hearing	A hearing is a proceeding before a court or other decision-making body or officer. A hearing is generally distinguished from a trial in that it is usually shorter and often less formal.
Joint venture	Joint venture refers to an undertaking by two parties for a specific purpose and duration, taking any of several legal forms.
Revenue	Revenue is a U.S. business term for the amount of money that a company receives from its activities, mostly from sales of products and/or services to customers.
Mission statement	Mission statement refers to an outline of the fundamental purposes of an organization.
Foundation	A Foundation is a type of philanthropic organization set up by either individuals or institutions as a legal entity (either as a corporation or trust) with the purpose of distributing grants to support causes in line with the goals of the foundation.
Market share	That fraction of an industry's output accounted for by an individual firm or group of firms is called market share.
Auction	A preexisting business model that operates successfully on the Internet by announcing an item for sale and permitting multiple purchasers to bid on them under specified rules and condition is an auction.
Yield	The interest rate that equates a future value or an annuity to a given present value is a yield.
Holding	The holding is a court's determination of a matter of law based on the issue presented in the particular case. In other words: under this law, with these facts, this result.
Heir	In common law jurisdictions an heir is a person who is entitled to receive a share of the decedent's property via the rules of inheritance in the jurisdiction where the decedent died or owned property at the time of his death.
Specialist	A specialist is a trader who makes a market in one or several stocks and holds the limit order book for those stocks.
Cooperative	A business owned and controlled by the people who use it, producers, consumers, or workers with similar needs who pool their resources for mutual gain is called cooperative.
Mass production	The process of making a large number of a limited variety of products at very low cost is referred to as mass production.
Committee	A long-lasting, sometimes permanent team in the organization structure created to deal with tasks that recur regularly is the committee.
Hierarchy	A system of grouping people in an organization according to rank from the top down in which all subordinate managers must report to one person is called a hierarchy.
Stock	In financial terminology, stock is the capital raized by a corporation, through the issuance and sale of shares.
Context	The effect of the background under which a message often takes on more and richer meaning is a context. Context is especially important in cross-cultural interactions because some cultures are said to be high context or low context.

Targeting	In advertizing, targeting is to select a demographic or other group of people to advertise to, and create advertisements appropriately.
Pillsbury	Pillsbury the company was the first in the United States to use steam rollers for processing grain. The finished product required transportation, so the Pillsburys assisted in funding railroad development in Minnesota.
Nestle	Nestle is the world's biggest food and beverage company. In the 1860s, a pharmacist, developed a food for babies who were unable to be breastfed. His first success was a premature infant who could not tolerate his own mother's milk nor any of the usual substitutes. The value of the new product was quickly recognized when his new formula saved the child's life.
Value chain	The sequence of business functions in which usefulness is added to the products or services of a company is a value chain.
Competitive disadvantage	A situation in which a firm is not implementing using strategies that are being used by competing organizations is competitive disadvantage.
Margin	A deposit by a buyer in stocks with a seller or a stockbroker, as security to cover fluctuations in the market in reference to stocks that the buyer has purchased but for which he has not paid is a margin. Commodities are also traded on margin.
Premium	Premium refers to the fee charged by an insurance company for an insurance policy. The rate of losses must be relatively predictable: In order to set the premium (prices) insurers must be able to estimate them accurately.
Increase in demand	Increase in demand refers to an increase in the quantity demanded of a good or service at every price; a shift of the demand curve to the right.
Option	A contract that gives the purchaser the option to buy or sell the underlying financial instrument at a specified price, called the exercise price or strike price, within a specific period of time.
Agent	A person who makes economic decisions for another economic actor. A hired manager operates as an agent for a firm's owner.
Intermediaries	Intermediaries specialize in information either to bring together two parties to a transaction or to buy in order to sell again.
Marketing Plan	Marketing plan refers to a road map for the marketing activities of an organization for a specified future period of time, such as one year or five years.
Marketing strategy	Marketing strategy refers to the means by which a marketing goal is to be achieved, usually characterized by a specified target market and a marketing program to reach it.
Controlling	A management function that involves determining whether or not an organization is progressing toward its goals and objectives, and taking corrective action if it is not is called controlling.
Perceived quality	A dimension of quality identified by David Garvin that refers to a subjective assessment of a product's quality based on criteria defined by the observer is a perceived quality.
Cost advantage	Possession of a lower cost of production or operation than a competing firm or country is cost advantage.
Markup	Markup is a term used in marketing to indicate how much the price of a product is above the cost of producing and distributing the product.
Promotion	Promotion refers to all the techniques sellers use to motivate people to buy products or services. An attempt by marketers to inform people about products and to persuade them to

Go to **Cram101.com** for the Practice Tests for this Chapter.

Go to **Cram101.com** for the Practice Tests for this Chapter.
And, **NEVER** highlight a book again!

participate in an exchange.

Aid	Assistance provided by countries and by international institutions such as the World Bank to developing countries in the form of monetary grants, loans at low interest rates, in kind, or a combination of these is called aid. Aid can also refer to assistance of any type rendered to benefit some group or individual.
Market segments	Market segments refer to the groups that result from the process of market segmentation; these groups ideally have common needs and will respond similarly to a marketing action.
Controller	Controller refers to the financial executive primarily responsible for management accounting and financial accounting. Also called chief accounting officer.
Evaluation	The consumer's appraisal of the product or brand on important attributes is called evaluation.
Nike	Because Nike creates goods for a wide range of sports, they have competition from every sports and sports fashion brand there is. Nike has no direct competitors because there is no single brand which can compete directly with their range of sports and non-sports oriented gear, except for Reebok.
Boycott	To protest by refusing to purchase from someone, or otherwise do business with them. In international trade, a boycott most often takes the form of refusal to import a country's goods.
Balance	In banking and accountancy, the outstanding balance is the amount of money owned, (or due), that remains in a deposit account (or a loan account) at a given date, after all past remittances, payments and withdrawal have been accounted for. It can be positive (then, in the balance sheet of a firm, it is an asset) or negative (a liability).
Adidas	Adidas is a German sports apparel manufacturer, part of the Adidas Group. The company was named after its founder, Adolf Dassler, who started producing shoes in the 1920s in Herzogenaurach near Nuremberg with the help of his brother Rudolf Dassler who later formed rival shoe company PUMA AG.
Logo	Logo refers to device or other brand name that cannot be spoken.
Contract	A contract is a "promise" or an "agreement" that is enforced or recognized by the law. In the civil law, a contract is considered to be part of the general law of obligations.
Activism	Activism, in a general sense, can be described as intentional action to bring about social or political change. This action is in support of, or opposition to, one side of an often controversial argument.
Union	A worker association that bargains with employers over wages and working conditions is called a union.
Minimum wage	The lowest wage employers may legally pay for an hour of work is the minimum wage.
Strike	The withholding of labor services by an organized group of workers is referred to as a strike.
Compliance	A type of influence process where a receiver accepts the position advocated by a source to obtain favorable outcomes or to avoid punishment is the compliance.
Quota	A government-imposed restriction on quantity, or sometimes on total value, used to restrict the import of something to a specific quantity is called a quota.
Corruption	The unauthorized use of public office for private gain. The most common forms of corruption are bribery, extortion, and the misuse of inside information.
Labor law	Labor law is the body of laws, administrative rulings, and precedents which addresses the

Go to **Cram101.com** for the Practice Tests for this Chapter.

legal rights of, and restrictions on, workers and their organizations.

Independent contractor

Independent contractor refers to a self-employed person as distinguished from one who is employed as an employee.

Public relations

Public relations refers to the management function that evaluates public attitudes, changes policies and procedures in response to the public's requests, and executes a program of action and information to earn public understanding and acceptance.

Draft

A signed, written order by which one party instructs another party to pay a specified sum to a third party, at sight or at a specific date is a draft.

Insurance

Insurance refers to a system by which individuals can reduce their exposure to risk of large losses by spreading the risks among a large number of persons.

Audit

An examination of the financial reports to ensure that they represent what they claim and conform with generally accepted accounting principles is referred to as audit.

Allegation

An allegation is a statement of a fact by a party in a pleading, which the party claims it will prove. Allegations remain assertions without proof, only claims until they are proved.

Child labor

Originally, the employment of children in a manner detrimental to their health and social development. Now that the law contains strong child labor prohibitions, the term refers to the employment of children below the legal age limit.

Business Week

Business Week is a business magazine published by McGraw-Hill. It was first published in 1929 under the direction of Malcolm Muir, who was serving as president of the McGraw-Hill Publishing company at the time. It is considered to be the standard both in industry and among students.

Press release

A written public news announcement normally distributed to major news services is referred to as press release.

Task force

A temporary team or committee formed to solve a specific short-term problem involving several departments is the task force.

Collaboration

Collaboration occurs when the interaction between groups is very important to goal attainment and the goals are compatible. Wherein people work together —applying both to the work of individuals as well as larger collectives and societies.

Partnership

In the common law, a partnership is a type of business entity in which partners share with each other the profits or losses of the business undertaking in which they have all invested.

Sweatshop

A sweatshop is a factory or workshop that has attributes in common with the workplaces of the pejoratively-named sweating system of the 1840s. Sweatshops arose at a time when workers did not have the protections afforded by trade unions or labor laws, and sweatshops are synonymous with working conditions that violate human rights sensibilities and sometimes public policies. .

Social responsibility

Social responsibility is a doctrine that claims that an entity whether it is state, government, corporation, organization or individual has a responsibility to society.

Protectionism

Protectionism refers to advocacy of protection. The word has a negative connotation, and few advocates of protection in particular situations will acknowledge being protectionists.

Developing country

Developing country refers to a country whose per capita income is low by world standards. Same as LDC. As usually used, it does not necessarily connote that the country's income is rising.

Fiscal year

A fiscal year is a 12-month period used for calculating annual ("yearly") financial reports in businesses and other organizations. In many jurisdictions, regulatory laws regarding

accounting require such reports once per twelve months, but do not require that the twelve months constitute a calendar year (i.e. January to December).

Futures
Futures refer to contracts for the sale and future delivery of stocks or commodities, wherein either party may waive delivery, and receive or pay, as the case may be, the difference in market price at the time set for delivery.

Stockholder
A stockholder is an individual or company (including a corporation) that legally owns one or more shares of stock in a joined stock company. The shareholders are the owners of a corporation. Companies listed at the stock market strive to enhance shareholder value.

Currency crisis
Occurs when a speculative attack on the exchange value of a currency results in a sharp depreciation in the value of the currency or forces authorities to expend large volumes of international currency reserves and sharply increase interest rates to defend the prevailing exchange rate are referred to as currency crisis.

Oversupply
Oversupply refers to a stock or supply of a given product or service that is greater than that which can be cleared under prevailing prices levels and market conditions.

Layoff
A layoff is the termination of an employee or (more commonly) a group of employees for business reasons, such as the decision that certain positions are no longer necessary.

Downturn
A decline in a stock market or economic cycle is a downturn.

Analyst
Analyst refers to a person or tool with a primary function of information analysis, generally with a more limited, practical and short term set of goals than a researcher.

Microsoft
Microsoft is a multinational computer technology corporation with 2004 global annual sales of US$39.79 billion and 71,553 employees in 102 countries and regions as of July 2006. It develops, manufactures, licenses, and supports a wide range of software products for computing devices.

Budget
Budget refers to an account, usually for a year, of the planned expenditures and the expected receipts of an entity. For a government, the receipts are tax revenues.

Annual report
An annual report is prepared by corporate management that presents financial information including financial statements, footnotes, and the management discussion and analysis.

Shareholder
A shareholder is an individual or company (including a corporation) that legally owns one or more shares of stock in a joined stock company.

Equity
Equity is the name given to the set of legal principles, in countries following the English common law tradition, which supplement strict rules of law where their application would operate harshly, so as to achieve what is sometimes referred to as "natural justice."

Merchandising
Merchandising refers to the business of acquiring finished goods for resale, either in a wholesale or a retail operation.

Overtime
Overtime is the amount of time someone works beyond normal working hours.

Administrator
Administrator refers to the personal representative appointed by a probate court to settle the estate of a deceased person who died.

Supervisor
A Supervisor is an employee of an organization with some of the powers and responsibilities of management, occupying a role between true manager and a regular employee. A Supervisor position is typically the first step towards being promoted into a management role.

World Bank
The World Bank is a group of five international organizations responsible for providing finance and advice to countries for the purposes of economic development and poverty reduction, and for encouraging and safeguarding international investment.

Concession
A concession is a business operated under a contract or license associated with a degree of

exclusivity in exploiting a business within a certain geographical area. For example, sports arenas or public parks may have concession stands; and public services such as water supply may be operated as concessions.

Pledge	In law a pledge (also pawn) is a bailment of personal property as a security for some debt or engagement.
Convergence	The blending of various facets of marketing functions and communication technology to create more efficient and expanded synergies is a convergence.
Administrative model	A set of decision-making principles that recognize that a completely rational analysis of information and choice options is often not feasible in realistic decision-making is referred to as administrative model.
Scientific management	Studying workers to find the most efficient ways of doing things and then teaching people those techniques is scientific management.
Henri Fayol	Henri Fayol (1841-1925) was a French management theorist whose theories concerning scientific organization of labor were widely influential in the beginning of 20th century. He was the first to identify the four functions of management: planning, organizing, directing, and controlling, although his version was a bit different: plan, organize, command, coordinate, and control.
Bureaucracy	Bureaucracy refers to an organization with many layers of managers who set rules and regulations and oversee all decisions.
Capitalism	Capitalism refers to an economic system in which capital is mostly owned by private individuals and corporations. Contrasts with communism.
Weber	Weber was a German political economist and sociologist who is considered one of the founders of the modern study of sociology and public administration. His major works deal with rationalization in sociology of religion and government, but he also wrote much in the field of economics. His most popular work is his essay The Protestant Ethic and the Spirit of Capitalism.
Organizational structure	Organizational structure is the way in which the interrelated groups of an organization are constructed. From a managerial point of view the main concerns are ensuring effective communication and coordination.
Organizational Behavior	The study of human behavior in organizational settings, the interface between human behavior and the organization, and the organization itself is called organizational behavior.
Human relations approach	Human relations approach refers the idea that the best way to improve production was to respect workers and show concern for their needs. Became popular in the 1920s and remained influential through the 1950s.
Human resources	Human resources refers to the individuals within the firm, and to the portion of the firm's organization that deals with hiring, firing, training, and other personnel issues.
Authority	Authority in agency law, refers to an agent's ability to affect his principal's legal relations with third parties. Also used to refer to an actor's legal power or ability to do something. In addition, sometimes used to refer to a statute, case, or other legal source that justifies a particular result.
Acquisition	A company's purchase of the property and obligations of another company is an acquisition.
Commercial bank	A firm that engages in the business of banking is a commercial bank.
Entrepreneur	The owner/operator. The person who organizes, manages, and assumes the risks of a firm, taking a new idea or a new product and turning it into a successful business is an entrepreneur.

Go to **Cram101.com** for the Practice Tests for this Chapter.

Organization structure	The system of task, reporting, and authority relationships within which the organization does its work is referred to as the organization structure.
Organization design	The structuring of workers so that they can best accomplish the firm's goals is referred to as organization design.
Administration	Administration refers to the management and direction of the affairs of governments and institutions; a collective term for all policymaking officials of a government; the execution and implementation of public policy.
Consultant	A professional that provides expert advice in a particular field or area in which customers occassionaly require this type of knowledge is a consultant.
Performance management	The means through which managers ensure that employees' activities and outputs are congruent with the organization's goals is referred to as performance management.
Devise	In a will, a gift of real property is called a devise.
Informal communication channel	A communication channel that exists outside formally authorized channels without regard for the organization's hierarchy of authority is an informal communication channel.
Communication channel	The pathways through which messages are communicated are called a communication channel.
Human resource management	The process of evaluating human resource needs, finding people to fill those needs, and getting the best work from each employee by providing the right incentives and job environment, all with the goal of meeting the needs of the firm are called human resource management.
Resource management	Resource management is the efficient and effective deployment of an organization's resources when they are needed. Such resources may include financial resources, inventory, human skills, production resources, or information technology.
Personnel	A collective term for all of the employees of an organization. Personnel is also commonly used to refer to the personnel management function or the organizational unit responsible for administering personnel programs.
Trust	An arrangement in which shareholders of independent firms agree to give up their stock in exchange for trust certificates that entitle them to a share of the trust's common profits.
Compromise	Compromise occurs when the interaction is moderately important to meeting goals and the goals are neither completely compatible nor completely incompatible.
Organization chart	Organization chart refers to a visual device, which shows the relationship and divides the organization's work; it shows who is accountable for the completion of specific work and who reports to whom.
Mistake	In contract law a mistake is incorrect understanding by one or more parties to a contract and may be used as grounds to invalidate the agreement. Common law has identified three different types of mistake in contract: unilateral mistake, mutual mistake, and common mistake.
Writ	Writ refers to a commandment of a court given for the purpose of compelling certain action from the defendant, and usually executed by a sheriff or other judicial officer.
Control system	A control system is a device or set of devices that manage the behavior of other devices. Some devices or systems are not controllable.A control system is an interconnection of components connected or related in such a manner as to command, direct, or regulate itself or another system.
Harvard	Harvard Business Review is a research-based magazine written for business practitioners, it

Business Review	claims a high ranking business readership and enjoys the reverence of academics, executives, and management consultants. It has been the frequent publishing home for well known scholars and management thinkers.
Theory Y	Theory Y refers to concept described by Douglas McGregor reflecting an approach to management that takes a positive and optimistic perspective on workers.
Theory X	Theory X refers to concept described by Douglas McGregor indicating an approach to management that takes a negative and pessimistic view of workers.
Apprenticeship	A work-study training method with both on-the-job and classroom training is an apprenticeship.Most of their training is on the job, working for an employer who helps the apprentices learn their trade, art or craft. Less formal, theoretical education is involved.
Financial control	A process in which a firm periodically compares its actual revenues, costs, and expenses with its projected ones is called financial control.
Interest	In finance and economics, interest is the price paid by a borrower for the use of a lender's money. In other words, interest is the amount of paid to "rent" money for a period of time.
Transparency	Transparency refers to a concept that describes a company being so open to other companies working with it that the once-solid barriers between them become see-through and electronic information is shared as if the companies were one.
Labor union	A group of workers organized to advance the interests of the group is called a labor union.
Acquirer	An acquirer is a company offering debit and credit card acceptance services for merchants. Often the company is partially or wholly owned by a bank, sometimes a bank itself offers acquiring services.
Zanussi	Zanussi is a leading brand for domestic kitchen appliances in Europe. Exported from Italy since 1946, Zanussi is widely recognized for its innovative products and distinctive modern design.
Partition	Partition refers to proceeding the object of which is to enable those who own property as joint tenants or tenants in common to put an end to the tenancy so as to vest in each a sole estate in specific property or an allotment of the lands and tenements. If a division of the estate is impracticable, the estate ought to be sold and the proceeds divided.
Layout	Layout refers to the physical arrangement of the various parts of an advertisement including the headline, subheads, illustrations, body copy, and any identifying marks.
Euro	The common currency of a subset of the countries of the EU, adopted January 1, 1999 is called euro.
Siemens	Siemens is the world's largest conglomerate company. Worldwide, Siemens and its subsidiaries employs 461,000 people (2005) in 190 countries and reported global sales of €75.4 billion in fiscal year 2005.
Wall Street Journal	Dow Jones & Company was founded in 1882 by reporters Charles Dow, Edward Jones and Charles Bergstresser. Jones converted the small Customers' Afternoon Letter into The Wall Street Journal, first published in 1889, and began delivery of the Dow Jones News Service via telegraph. The Journal featured the Jones 'Average', the first of several indexes of stock and bond prices on the New York Stock Exchange.
Collectivism	Collectivism is a term used to describe that things should be owned by the group and used for the benefit of all rather than being owned by individuals.
Welfare	Welfare refers to the economic well being of an individual, group, or economy. For individuals, it is conceptualized by a utility function. For groups, including countries and the world, it is a tricky philosophical concept, since individuals fare differently.

Go to **Cram101.com** for the Practice Tests for this Chapter.

Go to **Cram101.com** for the Practice Tests for this Chapter.
And, **NEVER** highlight a book again!

Quality circle	A quality circle is a volunteer group composed of workers who meet together to discuss workplace improvement, and make presentations to management with their ideas.
Welfare state	A concept of the mixed economy arising in Europe in the late nineteenth century and introduced in the United States in the 1930s is called welfare state.
Integration	Economic integration refers to reducing barriers among countries to transactions and to movements of goods, capital, and labor, including harmonization of laws, regulations, and standards. Integrated markets theoretically function as a unified market.
Petition	A petition is a request to an authority, most commonly a government official or public entity. In the colloquial sense, a petition is a document addressed to some official and signed by numerous individuals.
Consideration	Consideration in contract law, a basic requirement for an enforceable agreement under traditional contract principles, defined in this text as legal value, bargained for and given in exchange for an act or promise. In corporation law, cash or property contributed to a corporation in exchange for shares, or a promise to contribute such cash or property.
Standing	Standing refers to the legal requirement that anyone seeking to challenge a particular action in court must demonstrate that such action substantially affects his legitimate interests before he will be entitled to bring suit.
Cray	Cray Inc. is a supercomputer manufacturer based in Seattle, Washington. The company's predecessor, Cray Research, Inc., was founded in 1972 by computer designer Seymour Cray. Already a legend in his field by this time, Cray put his company on the map in 1976 with the release of the Cray-1 vector computer.
Empowerment	Giving employees the authority and responsibility to respond quickly to customer requests is called empowerment.
Distributive bargaining	Distributive bargaining is the approach to bargaining or negotiation that is used when the parties are trying to divide something up--distribute something.
Best practice	Best practice is a management idea which asserts that there is a technique, method, process, activity, incentive or reward that is more effective at delivering a particular outcome than any other technique, method, process, etc.
Matrix management	Matrix management combines the aspects of a functional organization with those of a projectized organization. Project team members in a matrix organization report to both a functional manager and a project manager.
Matrix structure	An organizational structure which typically crosses a functional approach with a product or service-based design, often resulting in employees having two bosses is the matrix structure.
Juran	Juran is known as a business and industrial quality "guru," while making significant contributions to management theory, human resource management and consulting as well. He wrote several books, and is known worldwide as one of the most important 20th century thinkers in quality management.
Not invented here	Not Invented Here (NIH) is a pejorative term used to describe a persistent corporate or institutional culture that either intentionally or unintentionally avoids using previously performed research or knowledge because the research and developed knowledge was not originally executed in-house.
Continuity	A media scheduling strategy where a continuous pattern of advertising is used over the time span of the advertising campaign is continuity.
Participative management	Participative management or participatory management is the practice of empowering employees to participate in organizational decision making.

Paradox	As used in economics, paradox means something unexpected, rather than the more extreme normal meaning of something seemingly impossible. Some paradoxes are just theoretical results that go against what one thinks of as normal.
Comparative advantage	The ability to produce a good at lower cost, relative to other goods, compared to another country is a comparative advantage.
Endowment	Endowment refers to the amount of something that a person or country simply has, rather than their having somehow to acquire it.
Inputs	The inputs used by a firm or an economy are the labor, raw materials, electricity and other resources it uses to produce its outputs.
Complementary products	Products that use similar technologies and can coexist in a family of products are called complementary products. They tend to be purchased jointly and whose demands therefore are related.
Complement	A good that is used in conjunction with another good is a complement. For example, cameras and film would complement eachother.
Synergy	Corporate synergy occurs when corporations interact congruently. A corporate synergy refers to a financial benefit that a corporation expects to realize when it merges with or acquires another corporation.
Red tape	Red tape is a derisive term for excessive regulations or rigid conformity to formal rules that are considered redundant or bureaucratic and hinders or prevents action or decision-making.
Corporate tax	Corporate tax refers to a direct tax levied by various jurisdictions on the profits made by companies or associations. As a general principle, this varies substantially between jurisdictions.
Legal system	Legal system refers to system of rules that regulate behavior and the processes by which the laws of a country are enforced and through which redress of grievances is obtained.
Transaction cost	A transaction cost is a cost incurred in making an economic exchange. For example, most people, when buying or selling a stock, must pay a commission to their broker; that commission is a transaction cost of doing the stock deal.
Ancillary	An ancillary receiver is a receiver who has been appointed in aid of, and in subordination to, the primary receiver.
Outsourcing	Outsourcing refers to a production activity that was previously done inside a firm or plant that is now conducted outside that firm or plant.
Vertical integration	Vertical integration refers to production of different stages of processing of a product within the same firm.
Enabling	Enabling refers to giving workers the education and tools they need to assume their new decision-making powers.
Vendor	A person who sells property to a vendee is a vendor. The words vendor and vendee are more commonly applied to the seller and purchaser of real estate, and the words seller and buyer are more commonly applied to the seller and purchaser of personal property.
Buyer	A buyer refers to a role in the buying center with formal authority and responsibility to select the supplier and negotiate the terms of the contract.
Delegation	Delegation is the handing of a task over to another person, usually a subordinate. It is the assignment of authority and responsibility to another person to carry out specific activities.

Go to **Cram101.com** for the Practice Tests for this Chapter.

Public good	A good that is provided for users collectively where use by one does not preclude use of the same units of the good by others is referred to as public good. Police protection is an example of a public good.
Market access	The ability of firms from one country to sell in another is market access.
Asset	An item of property, such as land, capital, money, a share in ownership, or a claim on others for future payment, such as a bond or a bank deposit is an asset.
Market opportunities	Market opportunities refer to areas where a company believes there are favorable demand trends, needs, and/or wants that are not being satisfied, and where it can compete effectively.
Spot market	Spot market refers to a market in which commodities are bought and sold for cash and immediate delivery.
Barriers to entry	In economics and especially in the theory of competition, barriers to entry are obstacles in the path of a firm which wants to enter a given market.
Financial institution	A financial institution acts as an agent that provides financial services for its clients. Financial institutions generally fall under financial regulation from a government authority.
Risk premium	In finance, the risk premium can be the expected rate of return above the risk-free interest rate.
Perceived risk	The anxieties felt because the consumer cannot anticipate the outcomes of a purchase but believes that there may be negative consequences is called a perceived risk.
Feedback loop	Feedback loop consists of a response and feedback. It is a system where outputs are fed back into the system as inputs, increasing or decreasing effects.
Scarcity	Scarcity is defined as not having sufficient resources to produce enough to fulfill unlimited subjective wants. Alternatively, scarcity implies that not all of society's goals can be attained at the same time, so that trade-offs one good against others are made.
Case study	A case study is a particular method of qualitative research. Rather than using large samples and following a rigid protocol to examine a limited number of variables, case study methods involve an in-depth, longitudinal examination of a single instance or event: a case. They provide a systematic way of looking at events, collecting data, analyzing information, and reporting the results.
Household	An economic unit that provides the economy with resources and uses the income received to purchase goods and services that satisfy economic wants is called household.
Cartel	Cartel refers to a group of firms that seeks to raise the price of a good by restricting its supply. The term is usually used for international groups, especially involving state-owned firms and/or governments.
Attachment	Attachment in general, the process of taking a person's property under an appropriate judicial order by an appropriate officer of the court. Used for a variety of purposes, including the acquisition of jurisdiction over the property seized and the securing of property that may be used to satisfy a debt.
Groupthink	Groupthink is a situation in which pressures for cohesion and togetherness are so strong as to produce narrowly considered and bad decisions; this can be especially true via conformity pressures in groups.
Radical innovation	Radical innovation refers to a new product, service, or technology, that changes or creates whole industries.
Product	In business and engineering, new product development is the complete process of bringing a

Go to **Cram101.com** for the Practice Tests for this Chapter.

development	new product to market. There are two parallel aspects to this process : one involves product engineering ; the other marketing analysis. Marketers see new product development as the first stage in product life cycle management, engineers as part of Product Lifecycle Management.
Administrative cost	An administrative cost is all executive, organizational, and clerical costs associated with the general management of an organization rather than with manufacturing, marketing, or selling
Instrument	Instrument refers to an economic variable that is controlled by policy makers and can be used to influence other variables, called targets. Examples are monetary and fiscal policies used to achieve external and internal balance.
Global competition	Global competition exists when competitive conditions across national markets are linked strongly enough to form a true international market and when leading competitors compete head to head in many different countries.
Advertising agency	A firm that specializes in the creation, production, and placement of advertising messages and may provide other services that facilitate the marketing communications process is an advertising agency.
Realization	Realization is the sale of assets when an entity is being liquidated.
Venture capital firm	A financial intermediary that pools the resources of its partners and uses the funds to help entrepreneurs start up new businesses is referred to as a venture capital firm.
Venture capital	Venture capital is capital provided by outside investors for financing of new, growing or struggling businesses. Venture capital investments generally are high risk investments but offer the potential for above average returns.
Genzyme	Genzyme Corporation is a biotechnology company based in Cambridge, Massachusetts. Genzyme specializes in developing and commercializing orphan drugs. Many of its drugs are replacement enzymes which treat lysosomal storage disorders. Genzyme is known for charging extraordinary prices in order to recoup expenses from small patient populations.
Labor force	In economics the labor force is the group of people who have a potential for being employed.
Private sector	The households and business firms of the economy are referred to as private sector.
Trade association	An industry trade group or trade association is generally a public relations organization founded and funded by corporations that operate in a specific industry. Its purpose is generally to promote that industry through PR activities such as advertizing, education, political donations, political pressure, publishing, and astroturfing.
Purchasing	Purchasing refers to the function in a firm that searches for quality material resources, finds the best suppliers, and negotiates the best price for goods and services.
Consortia	B2B marketplaces sponsored by a group of otherwise competitive enterprises in a specific industry like automobile manufacturing or airline operations are called a consortia.
Applied research	Applied research is conducted to solve particular problems or answer specific questions.
Federal government	Federal government refers to the government of the United States, as distinct from the state and local governments.
Food and Drug Administration	The Food and Drug Administration is an agency of the United States Department of Health and Human Services and is responsible for regulating food (human and animal), dietary supplements, drugs (human and animal), cosmetics, medical devices (human and animal) and radiation emitting devices (including non-medical devices), biologics, and blood products in the United States.

Industrial policy	Industrial policy refers to government policy to influence which industries expand and, perhaps implicitly, which contract, via subsidies, tax breaks, and other aids for favored industries.
Collective responsibility	Cabinet collective responsibility is constitutional convention in the states that use the Westminster System. It means that members of the Cabinet must publicly support all governmental decisions made in Cabinet, even if they do not privately agree with them.
Multinational corporations	Firms that own production facilities in two or more countries and produce and sell their products globally are referred to as multinational corporations.
Multinational corporation	An organization that manufactures and markets products in many different countries and has multinational stock ownership and multinational management is referred to as multinational corporation.
Emerging markets	The term emerging markets is commonly used to describe business and market activity in industrializing or emerging regions of the world. It is sometimes loosely used as a replacement for emerging economies, but really signifies a business phenomenon that is not fully described by or constrained to geography or economic strength; such countries are considered to be in a transitional phase between developing and developed status.
Emerging market	The term emerging market is commonly used to describe business and market activity in industrializing or emerging regions of the world.
Imperialism	Imperialism is a policy of extending control or authority over foreign entities as a means of acquisition and/or maintenance of empires. This is either through direct territorial conquest or settlement, or through indirect methods of exerting control on the politics and/or economy of these other entities. The term is often used to describe the policy of a nation's dominance over distant lands, regardless of whether the nation considers itself part of the empire.
Corporate Strategy	Corporate strategy is concerned with the firm's choice of business, markets and activities and thus it defines the overall scope and direction of the business.
Business model	A business model is the instrument by which a business intends to generate revenue and profits. It is a summary of how a company means to serve its employees and customers, and involves both strategy (what an business intends to do) as well as an implementation.
Open market	In economics, the open market is the term used to refer to the environment in which bonds are bought and sold.
Middle class	Colloquially, the term is often applied to people who have a degree of economic independence, but not a great deal of social influence or power in their society. The term often encompasses merchants and professionals, bureaucrats, and some farmers and skilled workers[citation needed]. While most Americans identify themselves as middle class, only 20% live the lifestyle indicative of the American middle class.
Consumer market	All the individuals or households that want goods and services for personal consumption or use are a consumer market.
Purchasing power	The amount of goods that money will buy, usually measured by the CPI is referred to as purchasing power.
Ford	Ford is an American company that manufactures and sells automobiles worldwide. Ford introduced methods for large-scale manufacturing of cars, and large-scale management of an industrial workforce, especially elaborately engineered manufacturing sequences typified by the moving assembly lines.
Marginal cost	Marginal cost refers to the increase in cost that accompanies a unit increase in output; the partial derivative of the cost function with respect to output.

Brand management	Brand management is the application of marketing techniques to a specific product, product line, or brand. It seeks to increase the product's perceived value to the customer and thereby increase brand franchise and brand equity.
Senior executive	Senior executive means a chief executive officer, chief operating officer, chief financial officer and anyone in charge of a principal business unit or function.
Repositioning	Changing the position an offering occupies in a consumer's mind relative to competitive offerings and so expanding or otherwise altering its potential market is called repositioning.
Motorola	The Six Sigma quality system was developed at Motorola even though it became most well known because of its use by General Electric. It was created by engineer Bill Smith, under the direction of Bob Galvin (son of founder Paul Galvin) when he was running the company.
Working capital	The dollar difference between total current assets and total current liabilities is called working capital.
Dealer	People who link buyers with sellers by buying and selling securities at stated prices are referred to as a dealer.
Fixed capital	Fixed capital is a concept in economics and accounting, first theoretically analysed in some depth by the economist David Ricardo. It refers to any kind of real or physical capital that is not used up in the production of a product. It is contrasted with circulating capital.
Supply chain	Supply chain refers to the flow of goods, services, and information from the initial sources of materials and services to the delivery of products to consumers.
Supply chain management	Supply chain management deals with the planning and execution issues involved in managing a supply chain. Supply chain management spans all movement and storage of raw materials, work-in-process inventory, and finished goods from point-of-origin to point-of-consumption.
Consolidation	The combination of two or more firms, generally of equal size and market power, to form an entirely new entity is a consolidation.
Expatriate	Employee sent by his or her company to live and manage operations in a different country is called an expatriate.
Market development	Selling existing products to new markets is called market development.
Credibility	The extent to which a source is perceived as having knowledge, skill, or experience relevant to a communication topic and can be trusted to give an unbiased opinion or present objective information on the issue is called credibility.
Expatriate manager	A national of one country appointed to a management position in another country is an expatriate manager.
Corporate culture	The whole collection of beliefs, values, and behaviors of a firm that send messages to those within and outside the company about how business is done is the corporate culture.
Assignment	A transfer of property or some right or interest is referred to as assignment.
Parent company	Parent company refers to the entity that has a controlling influence over another company. It may have its own operations, or it may have been set up solely for the purpose of owning the Subject Company.
Business unit	The lowest level of the company which contains the set of functions that carry a product through its life span from concept through manufacture, distribution, sales and service is a business unit.
Cost structure	The relative proportion of an organization's fixed, variable, and mixed costs is referred to

Go to **Cram101.com** for the Practice Tests for this Chapter.
And, **NEVER** highlight a book again!

	as cost structure.
Current cost	Asset measure based on the cost of purchasing an asset today identical to the one currently held, or the cost of purchasing an asset that provides services like the one currently held, if an identical one cannot be purchased is a current cost.
Technological change	The introduction of new methods of production or new products intended to increase the productivity of existing inputs or to raise marginal products is a technological change.
Business development	Business development emcompasses a number of techniques designed to grow an economic enterprise. Such techniques include, but are not limited to, assessments of marketing opportunities and target markets, intelligence gathering on customers and competitors, generating leads for possible sales, followup sales activity, and formal proposal writing.
Downsizing	The process of eliminating managerial and non-managerial positions are called downsizing.
Gillette	On October 1, 2005, Gillette finalized its purchase by Procter & Gamble. As a result of this merger, the Gillette Company no longer exists. Its last day of market trading - symbol G on the New York Stock Exchange - was September 30, 2005. The merger created the world's largest personal care and household products company.
Boeing	Boeing is the world's largest aircraft manufacturer by revenue. Headquartered in Chicago, Illinois, Boeing is the second-largest defense contractor in the world. In 2005, the company was the world's largest civil aircraft manufacturer in terms of value.
Senior management	Senior management is generally a team of individuals at the highest level of organizational management who have the day-to-day responsibilities of managing a corporation.
Company culture	Company culture is the term given to the values and practices shared by the employees of a firm.
Market economy	A market economy is an economic system in which the production and distribution of goods and services takes place through the mechanism of free markets guided by a free price system rather than by the state in a planned economy.

Standardization	Standardization, in the context related to technologies and industries, is the process of establishing a technical standard among competing entities in a market, where this will bring benefits without hurting competition.
Global strategy	Global strategy refers to strategy focusing on increasing profitability by reaping cost reductions from experience curve and location economies.
Standardized product	Standardized product refers to a product whose buyers are indifferent to the seller from whom they purchase it, as long as the price charged by all sellers is the same; a product all units of which are identical and thus are perfect substitutes.
Core	A core is the set of feasible allocations in an economy that cannot be improved upon by subset of the set of the economy's consumers (a coalition). In construction, when the force in an element is within a certain center section, the core, the element will only be under compression.
Michael Porter	Michael Porter is a leading contributor to strategic management theory, Porter's main academic objectives focus on how a firm or a region, can build a competitive advantage and develop competitive strategy. Porter's strategic system consists primarily of 5 forces analysis, strategic groups, the value chain, and market positioning stratagies.
Harvard Business Review	Harvard Business Review is a research-based magazine written for business practitioners, it claims a high ranking business readership and enjoys the reverence of academics, executives, and management consultants. It has been the frequent publishing home for well known scholars and management thinkers.
Competitive advantage	A business is said to have a competitive advantage when its unique strengths, often based on cost, quality, time, and innovation, offer consumers a greater percieved value and there by differtiating it from its competitors.
Economy	The income, expenditures, and resources that affect the cost of running a business and household are called an economy.
Scope	Scope of a project is the sum total of all projects products and their requirements or features.
Competitiveness	Competitiveness usually refers to characteristics that permit a firm to compete effectively with other firms due to low cost or superior technology, perhaps internationally.
Inputs	The inputs used by a firm or an economy are the labor, raw materials, electricity and other resources it uses to produce its outputs.
Integration	Economic integration refers to reducing barriers among countries to transactions and to movements of goods, capital, and labor, including harmonization of laws, regulations, and standards. Integrated markets theoretically function as a unified market.
Industry	A group of firms that produce identical or similar products is an industry. It is also used specifically to refer to an area of economic production focused on manufacturing which involves large amounts of capital investment before any profit can be realized, also called "heavy industry".
Joint venture	Joint venture refers to an undertaking by two parties for a specific purpose and duration, taking any of several legal forms.
Partnership	In the common law, a partnership is a type of business entity in which partners share with each other the profits or losses of the business undertaking in which they have all invested.
Manufacturing	Production of goods primarily by the application of labor and capital to raw materials and other intermediate inputs, in contrast to agriculture, mining, forestry, fishing, and services a manufacturing.

87

Toyota	Toyota is a Japanese multinational corporation that manufactures automobiles, trucks and buses. Toyota is the world's second largest automaker by sales. Toyota also provides financial services through its subsidiary, Toyota Financial Services, and participates in other lines of business.
Strategic choice	Strategic choice refers to an organization's strategy; the ways an organization will attempt to fulfill its mission and achieve its long-term goals.
Firm	An organization that employs resources to produce a good or service for profit and owns and operates one or more plants is referred to as a firm.
Volatility	Volatility refers to the extent to which an economic variable, such as a price or an exchange rate, moves up and down over time.
Management	Management characterizes the process of leading and directing all or part of an organization, often a business, through the deployment and manipulation of resources. Early twentieth-century management writer Mary Parker Follett defined management as "the art of getting things done through people."
Context	The effect of the background under which a message often takes on more and richer meaning is a context. Context is especially important in cross-cultural interactions because some cultures are said to be high context or low context.
Instrument	Instrument refers to an economic variable that is controlled by policy makers and can be used to influence other variables, called targets. Examples are monetary and fiscal policies used to achieve external and internal balance.
Revenue	Revenue is a U.S. business term for the amount of money that a company receives from its activities, mostly from sales of products and/or services to customers.
Brand	A name, symbol, or design that identifies the goods or services of one seller or group of sellers and distinguishes them from the goods and services of competitors is a brand.
Technology	The body of knowledge and techniques that can be used to combine economic resources to produce goods and services is called technology.
Profit	Profit refers to the return to the resource entrepreneurial ability; total revenue minus total cost.
Economies of scale	In economics, returns to scale and economies of scale are related terms that describe what happens as the scale of production increases. They are different terms and not to be used interchangeably.
Economies of scope	The ability to use one resource to provide many different products and services is referred to as economies of scope.
Market potential	Market potential refers to maximum total sales of a product by all firms to a segment during a specified time period under specified environmental conditions and marketing efforts of the firms.
Market	A market is, as defined in economics, a social arrangement that allows buyers and sellers to discover information and carry out a voluntary exchange of goods or services.
Factor endowments	A country's endowment with resources such as land, labor, and capital are referred to as factor endowments.
Efficient market	Efficient market refers to a market in which, at a minimum, current price changes are independent of past price changes, or, more strongly, price reflects all available information.
Factor endowment	Factor endowment refers to the quantity of a primary factor present in a country.

Factor cost	Factor cost is a measure of National Income or output based on the cost of factors of production, instead of market prices. This allows the effect of any subsidy or indirect tax to be removed from the final measure.
Endowment	Endowment refers to the amount of something that a person or country simply has, rather than their having somehow to acquire it.
Labor	People's physical and mental talents and efforts that are used to help produce goods and services are called labor.
Cost advantage	Possession of a lower cost of production or operation than a competing firm or country is cost advantage.
Value chain	The sequence of business functions in which usefulness is added to the products or services of a company is a value chain.
Production	The creation of finished goods and services using the factors of production: land, labor, capital, entrepreneurship, and knowledge.
Marketing	Promoting and selling products or services to customers, or prospective customers, is referred to as marketing.
Gain	In finance, gain is a profit or an increase in value of an investment such as a stock or bond. Gain is calculated by fair market value or the proceeds from the sale of the investment minus the sum of the purchase price and all costs associated with it.
Learning curve	Learning curve is a function that measures how labor-hours per unit decline as units of production increase because workers are learning and becoming better at their jobs.
Distribution	Distribution in economics, the manner in which total output and income is distributed among individuals or factors.
Transnational strategy	Plan to exploit experience-based cost and location economies, transfer core competencies with the firm, and pay attention to local responsiveness is called transnational strategy.
Transnational	Transnational focuses on the heightened interconnectivity between people all around the world and the loosening of boundaries between countries.
Operation	A standardized method or technique that is performed repetitively, often on different materials resulting in different finished goods is called an operation.
Regulation	Regulation refers to restrictions state and federal laws place on business with regard to the conduct of its activities.
Preference	The act of a debtor in paying or securing one or more of his creditors in a manner more favorable to them than to other creditors or to the exclusion of such other creditors is a preference. In the absence of statute, a preference is perfectly good, but to be legal it must be bona fide, and not a mere subterfuge of the debtor to secure a future benefit to himself or to prevent the application of his property to his debts.
Service	Service refers to a "non tangible product" that is not embodied in a physical good and that typically effects some change in another product, person, or institution. Contrasts with good.
Nestle	Nestle is the world's biggest food and beverage company. In the 1860s, a pharmacist, developed a food for babies who were unable to be breastfed. His first success was a premature infant who could not tolerate his own mother's milk nor any of the usual substitutes. The value of the new product was quickly recognized when his new formula saved the child's life.
Subsidiary	A company that is controlled by another company or corporation is a subsidiary.

Asset	An item of property, such as land, capital, money, a share in ownership, or a claim on others for future payment, such as a bond or a bank deposit is an asset.
International strategy	Trying to create value by transferring core competencies to foreign markets where indigenous competitors lack those competencies is called international strategy.
Innovation	Innovation refers to the first commercially successful introduction of a new product, the use of a new method of production, or the creation of a new form of business organization.
Compromise	Compromise occurs when the interaction is moderately important to meeting goals and the goals are neither completely compatible nor completely incompatible.
Configuration	An organization's shape, which reflects the division of labor and the means of coordinating the divided tasks is configuration.
Core competency	A company's core competency are things that a firm can (alsosns) do well and that meet the following three conditions. 1. It provides customer benefits, 2. It is hard for competitors to imitate, and 3. it can be leveraged widely to many products and market. A core competency can take various forms, including technical/subject matter knowhow, a reliable process, and/or close relationships with customers and suppliers. It may also include product development or culture such as employee dedication. Modern business theories suggest that most activities that are not part of a company's core competency should be outsourced.
Basic research	Involves discovering new knowledge rather than solving specific problems is called basic research.
Security	Security refers to a claim on the borrower future income that is sold by the borrower to the lender. A security is a type of transferable interest representing financial value.
Decentralization	Decentralization is the process of redistributing decision-making closer to the point of service or action. This gives freedom to managers at lower levels of the organization to make decisions.
Exchange rate	Exchange rate refers to the price at which one country's currency trades for another, typically on the exchange market.
Exchange	The trade of things of value between buyer and seller so that each is better off after the trade is called the exchange.
Strike	The withholding of labor services by an organized group of workers is referred to as a strike.
Supply	Supply is the aggregate amount of any material good that can be called into being at a certain price point; it comprises one half of the equation of supply and demand. In classical economic theory, a curve representing supply is one of the factors that produce price.
Leadership	Management merely consists of leadership applied to business situations; or in other words: management forms a sub-set of the broader process of leadership.
Competitor	Other organizations in the same industry or type of business that provide a good or service to the same set of customers is referred to as a competitor.
Restructuring	Restructuring is the corporate management term for the act of partially dismantling and reorganizing a company for the purpose of making it more efficient and therefore more profitable.
Flexible manufacturing technologies	Manufacturing technologies designed to improve job scheduling, reduce setup time, and improve quality control are called flexible manufacturing technologies.
Flexible	Flexible manufacturing refers to designing machines to do multiple tasks so that they can

manufacturing	produce a variety of products.
Acquisition	A company's purchase of the property and obligations of another company is an acquisition.
Investment	Investment refers to spending for the production and accumulation of capital and additions to inventories. In a financial sense, buying an asset with the expectation of making a return.
Cemex	Although it is not a monopoly, Cemex, along with Holcim-Apasco, controls the Mexican cement market. This has given rise to allegations that because of the oligopolistic structure in the Mexican cement market (as in many other markets in Mexico) consumers pay a higher price for cement than in other countries. However given the peculiarities of the Mexican cement market, the fact that it is sold mostly in bags, and the fact that cement is not an easily transported commodity make this accuzation difficult, if not impossible to prove.
Niche	In industry, a niche is a situation or an activity perfectly suited to a person. A niche can imply a working position or an area suited to a person who occupies it. Basically, a job where a person is able to succeed and thrive.
Retaliation	The use of an increased trade barrier in response to another country increasing its trade barrier, either as a way of undoing the adverse effects of the latter's action or of punishing it is retaliation.
Cost efficiency	Cost efficiency refers to the amount of output associated with an additional dollar spent on input; the MPP of an input divided by its price. Also refers to is a ratio of the excess return over a fund's benchmark, divided by management expenses. It calculates the value added (i.e. the excess over index returns) contributed by each percentage point of management expenses.
Portfolio	In finance, a portfolio is a collection of investments held by an institution or a private individual. Holding but not always a portfolio is part of an investment and risk-limiting strategy called diversification. By owning several assets, certain types of risk (in particular specific risk) can be reduced.
Marketing strategy	Marketing strategy refers to the means by which a marketing goal is to be achieved, usually characterized by a specified target market and a marketing program to reach it.
Channel	Channel, in communications (sometimes called communications channel), refers to the medium used to convey information from a sender (or transmitter) to a receiver.
Domestic	From or in one's own country. A domestic producer is one that produces inside the home country. A domestic price is the price inside the home country. Opposite of 'foreign' or 'world.'.
Globalization	The increasing world-wide integration of markets for goods, services and capital that attracted special attention in the late 1990s is called globalization.
Option	A contract that gives the purchaser the option to buy or sell the underlying financial instrument at a specified price, called the exercise price or strike price, within a specific period of time.
Tariff	A tax imposed by a nation on an imported good is called a tariff.
Sponsorship	When the advertiser assumes responsibility for the production and usually the content of a television program as well as the advertising that appears within it, we have sponsorship.
Capital	Capital generally refers to financial wealth, especially that used to start or maintain a business. In classical economics, capital is one of four factors of production, the others being land and labor and entrepreneurship.
Export	In economics, an export is any good or commodity, shipped or otherwise transported out of a country, province, town to another part of the world in a legitimate fashion, typically for

Go to **Cram101.com** for the Practice Tests for this Chapter.

use in trade or sale.

Airbus	In 2003, for the first time in its 33-year history, Airbus delivered more jet-powered airliners than Boeing. Boeing states that the Boeing 777 has outsold its Airbus counterparts, which include the A340 family as well as the A330-300. The smaller A330-200 competes with the 767, outselling its Boeing counterpart.
Boeing	Boeing is the world's largest aircraft manufacturer by revenue. Headquartered in Chicago, Illinois, Boeing is the second-largest defense contractor in the world. In 2005, the company was the world's largest civil aircraft manufacturer in terms of value.
Shares	Shares refer to an equity security, representing a shareholder's ownership of a corporation. Shares are one of a finite number of equal portions in the capital of a company, entitling the owner to a proportion of distributed, non-reinvested profits known as dividends and to a portion of the value of the company in case of liquidation.
Market access	The ability of firms from one country to sell in another is market access.
Caterpillar	Caterpillar is a United States based corporation headquartered in Peoria, Illinois. Caterpillar is "the world's largest manufacturer of construction and mining equipment, diesel and natural gas engines, and industrial gas turbines."
Competitive Strategy	An outline of how a business intends to compete with other firms in the same industry is called competitive strategy.
Chief executive officer	A chief executive officer is the highest-ranking corporate officer or executive officer of a corporation, or agency. In closely held corporations, it is general business culture that the office chief executive officer is also the chairman of the board.
Attachment	Attachment in general, the process of taking a person's property under an appropriate judicial order by an appropriate officer of the court. Used for a variety of purposes, including the acquisition of jurisdiction over the property seized and the securing of property that may be used to satisfy a debt.
Profit margin	Profit margin is a measure of profitability. It is calculated using a formula and written as a percentage or a number. Profit margin = Net income before tax and interest / Revenue.
Margin	A deposit by a buyer in stocks with a seller or a stockbroker, as security to cover fluctuations in the market in reference to stocks that the buyer has purchased but for which he has not paid is a margin. Commodities are also traded on margin.
Balance	In banking and accountancy, the outstanding balance is the amount of money owned, (or due), that remains in a deposit account (or a loan account) at a given date, after all past remittances, payments and withdrawal have been accounted for. It can be positive (then, in the balance sheet of a firm, it is an asset) or negative (a liability).
Users	Users refer to people in the organization who actually use the product or service purchased by the buying center.
Downturn	A decline in a stock market or economic cycle is a downturn.
Trend	Trend refers to the long-term movement of an economic variable, such as its average rate of increase or decrease over enough years to encompass several business cycles.
Developed country	A developed country is one that enjoys a relatively high standard of living derived through an industrialized, diversified economy. Countries with a very high Human Development Index are generally considered developed countries.
Developing country	Developing country refers to a country whose per capita income is low by world standards. Same as LDC. As usually used, it does not necessarily connote that the country's income is rising.

Contract	A contract is a "promise" or an "agreement" that is enforced or recognized by the law. In the civil law, a contract is considered to be part of the general law of obligations.
Foreign Corrupt Practices Act	The Foreign Corrupt Practices Act of 1977 is a United States federal law requiring any company that has publicly-traded stock to maintain records that accurately and fairly represent the company's transactions; additionally, requires any publicly-traded company to have an adequate system of internal accounting controls.
Bribery	When one person gives another person money, property, favors, or anything else of value for a favor in return, we have bribery. Often referred to as a payoff or 'kickback.'
Bid	A bid price is a price offered by a buyer when he/she buys a good. In the context of stock trading on a stock exchange, the bid price is the highest price a buyer of a stock is willing to pay for a share of that given stock.
Fund	Independent accounting entity with a self-balancing set of accounts segregated for the purposes of carrying on specific activities is referred to as a fund.
Personnel	A collective term for all of the employees of an organization. Personnel is also commonly used to refer to the personnel management function or the organizational unit responsible for administering personnel programs.
Committee	A long-lasting, sometimes permanent team in the organization structure created to deal with tasks that recur regularly is the committee.
Dealer	People who link buyers with sellers by buying and selling securities at stated prices are referred to as a dealer.
Enterprise	Enterprise refers to another name for a business organization. Other similar terms are business firm, sometimes simply business, sometimes simply firm, as well as company, and entity.
Buyer	A buyer refers to a role in the buying center with formal authority and responsibility to select the supplier and negotiate the terms of the contract.
Expropriation	Expropriation is the act of removing from control the owner of an item of property. The term is used to both refer to acts by a government or by any group of people.
Franchise	A contractual right to sell certain products or services, use certain trademarks, or perform activities in a geographical region is called a franchise.
Inventory	Tangible property held for sale in the normal course of business or used in producing goods or services for sale is an inventory.
Purchasing	Purchasing refers to the function in a firm that searches for quality material resources, finds the best suppliers, and negotiates the best price for goods and services.
Derivative	A derivative is a generic term for specific types of investments from which payoffs over time are derived from the performance of assets (such as commodities, shares or bonds), interest rates, exchange rates, or indices (such as a stock market index, consumer price index (CPI) or an index of weather conditions).
Product cost	Product cost refers to sum of the costs assigned to a product for a specific purpose. A concept used in applying the cost plus approach to product pricing in which only the costs of manufacturing the product are included in the cost amount to which the markup is added.
Optimum	Optimum refers to the best. Usually refers to a most preferred choice by consumers subject to a budget constraint or a profit maximizing choice by firms or industry subject to a technological constraint.
Specialist	A specialist is a trader who makes a market in one or several stocks and holds the limit

order book for those stocks.

Distribution channel	A distribution channel is a chain of intermediaries, each passing a product down the chain to the next organization, before it finally reaches the consumer or end-user.
Product strategy	Decisions on the management of products or services based on the conditions of a given market is product strategy. Two general strategies that are well known in the marketing discipline are marketing mix and relational marketing.
Interest	In finance and economics, interest is the price paid by a borrower for the use of a lender's money. In other words, interest is the amount of paid to "rent" money for a period of time.
John Deere	John Deere (February 7, 1804 - May 17, 1886) was an American blacksmith and manufacturer who founded one of the largest agricultural and construction equipment manufacturers in the world.
Manufacturing costs	Costs incurred in a manufacturing process, which consist of direct material, direct labor, and manufacturing overhead are referred to as manufacturing costs.
Market share	That fraction of an industry's output accounted for by an individual firm or group of firms is called market share.
Mitsubishi	In a statement, the Mitsubishi says that forced labor is inconsistent with the company's values, and that the various lawsuits targeting Mitsubishi are misdirected. Instead, a spokesman says the Mitsubishi of World War II is not the same Mitsubishi of today. The conglomerate also rejected a Chinese slave labor lawsuit demand by saying it bore no responsibility since it was national policy to employ Chinese laborers."
Licensing agreement	Detailed and comprehensive written agreement between the licensor and licensee that sets forth the express terms of their agreement is called a licensing agreement.
Licensing	Licensing is a form of strategic alliance which involves the sale of a right to use certain proprietary knowledge (so called intellectual property) in a defined way.
International Harvester	International Harvester was an American corporation based in Chicago that produced a multitude of agricultural machinery and vehicles. In 1924, International Harvester introduced the Farmall tractor, a smaller general-purpose tractor, to fend off competition from the Ford Motor Company's Fordson tractors. The Farmall was the first tractor in the United States to incorporate a tricycle-like design (or row-crop front axle), which could be used on tall crops such as cotton and corn.
Holding company	A corporation whose purpose or function is to own or otherwise hold the shares of other corporations either for investment or control is called holding company.
Holding	The holding is a court's determination of a matter of law based on the issue presented in the particular case. In other words: under this law, with these facts, this result.
Entrepreneur	The owner/operator. The person who organizes, manages, and assumes the risks of a firm, taking a new idea or a new product and turning it into a successful business is an entrepreneur.
Corporation	A legal entity chartered by a state or the Federal government that is distinct and separate from the individuals who own it is a corporation. This separation gives the corporation unique powers which other legal entities lack.
Principal	In agency law, one under whose direction an agent acts and for whose benefit that agent acts is a principal.
Business cycle	Business cycle refers to the pattern followed by macroeconommic variables, such as GDP and unemployment that rise and fall irregularly over time, relative to trend.

Go to **Cram101.com** for the Practice Tests for this Chapter.

Product line	A group of products that are physically similar or are intended for a similar market are called the product line.
Total revenue	Total revenue refers to the total number of dollars received by a firm from the sale of a product; equal to the total expenditures for the product produced by the firm; equal to the quantity sold multiplied by the price at which it is sold.
Contribution	In business organization law, the cash or property contributed to a business by its owners is referred to as contribution.
Foundation	A Foundation is a type of philanthropic organization set up by either individuals or institutions as a legal entity (either as a corporation or trust) with the purpose of distributing grants to support causes in line with the goals of the foundation.
Depression	Depression refers to a prolonged period characterized by high unemployment, low output and investment, depressed business confidence, falling prices, and widespread business failures. A milder form of business downturn is a recession.
Senior executive	Senior executive means a chief executive officer, chief operating officer, chief financial officer and anyone in charge of a principal business unit or function.
Production line	A production line is a set of sequential operations established in a factory whereby materials are put through a refining process to produce an end-product that is suitable for onward consumption; or components are assembled to make a finished article.
Family business	A family business is a company owned, controlled, and operated by members of one or several families. Many companies that are now publicly held were founded as family businesses. Many family businesses have non-family members as employees, but, particularly in smaller companies, the top positions are often allocated to family members.
Agent	A person who makes economic decisions for another economic actor. A hired manager operates as an agent for a firm's owner.
Net worth	Net worth is the total assets minus total liabilities of an individual or company
Advertisement	Advertisement is the promotion of goods, services, companies and ideas, usually by an identified sponsor. Marketers see advertising as part of an overall promotional strategy.
Incorporation	Incorporation is the forming of a new corporation. The corporation may be a business, a non-profit organization or even a government of a new city or town.
Wholly owned subsidiary	A subsidiary in which the firm owns 100 percent of the stock is a wholly owned subsidiary.
Senior management	Senior management is generally a team of individuals at the highest level of organizational management who have the day-to-day responsibilities of managing a corporation.
Flexible manufacturing system	A series of manufacturing machines, controlled and integrated by a computer, which is designed to perform a series of manufacturing operations automatically are referred to as a flexible manufacturing system.
Quality control	The measurement of products and services against set standards is referred to as quality control.
Quality circle	A quality circle is a volunteer group composed of workers who meet together to discuss workplace improvement, and make presentations to management with their ideas.
Assembly line	An assembly line is a manufacturing process in which interchangeable parts are added to a product in a sequential manner to create a finished product.
Productivity	Productivity refers to the total output of goods and services in a given period of time divided by work hours.

Go to **Cram101.com** for the Practice Tests for this Chapter.

Automation	Automation allows machines to do work previously accomplished by people.
Union	A worker association that bargains with employers over wages and working conditions is called a union.
Labor relations	The field of labor relations looks at the relationship between management and workers, particularly groups of workers represented by a labor union.
Press release	A written public news announcement normally distributed to major news services is referred to as press release.
Value added	The value of output minus the value of all intermediate inputs, representing therefore the contribution of, and payments to, primary factors of production a value added.
Ministry of International Trade and Industry	The Ministry of International Trade and Industry was the single most powerful agency in the Japanese government. At the height of its influence, it ran Japan as a centrally-managed economy, funding research and directing investment. in 2001, its role was taken over by the newly created Ministry of Economy, Trade, and Industry.
International trade	The export of goods and services from a country and the import of goods and services into a country is referred to as the international trade.
License	A license in the sphere of Intellectual Property Rights (IPR) is a document, contract or agreement giving permission or the 'right' to a legally-definable entity to do something (such as manufacture a product or to use a service), or to apply something (such as a trademark), with the objective of achieving commercial gain.
Policy	Similar to a script in that a policy can be a less than completely rational decision-making method. Involves the use of a pre-existing set of decision steps for any problem that presents itself.
Expatriate	Employee sent by his or her company to live and manage operations in a different country is called an expatriate.
Analyst	Analyst refers to a person or tool with a primary function of information analysis, generally with a more limited, practical and short term set of goals than a researcher.
Operating margin	In business, operating margin is the ratio of operating income divided by net sales.
Product development	In business and engineering, new product development is the complete process of bringing a new product to market. There are two parallel aspects to this process : one involves product engineering ; the other marketing analysis. Marketers see new product development as the first stage in product life cycle management, engineers as part of Product Lifecycle Management.
Applied research	Applied research is conducted to solve particular problems or answer specific questions.
Research and development	The use of resources for the deliberate discovery of new information and ways of doing things, together with the application of that information in inventing new products or processes is referred to as research and development.
Market segments	Market segments refer to the groups that result from the process of market segmentation; these groups ideally have common needs and will respond similarly to a marketing action.
Premium	Premium refers to the fee charged by an insurance company for an insurance policy. The rate of losses must be relatively predictable: In order to set the premium (prices) insurers must be able to estimate them accurately.
Diversification	Investing in a collection of assets whose returns do not always move together, with the result that overall risk is lower than for individual assets is referred to as diversification.

Go to **Cram101.com** for the Practice Tests for this Chapter.

Real terms	A wage expressed in real terms is just the real wage.
Ford	Ford is an American company that manufactures and sells automobiles worldwide. Ford introduced methods for large-scale manufacturing of cars, and large-scale management of an industrial workforce, especially elaborately engineered manufacturing sequences typified by the moving assembly lines.
Dividend payout ratio	A measure of the percentage of earnings paid out in dividends; found by dividing cash dividends by the net income available to each class of stock is the dividend payout ratio.
Retained earnings	Cumulative earnings of a company that are not distributed to the owners and are reinvested in the business are called retained earnings.
Payout ratio	A measure of the percentage of earnings distributed in the form of cash dividends to common stockholders is referred to as the payout ratio. More specifically, the firm's cash dividend divided by the firm's earnings in the same reporting period.
Dividend	Amount of corporate profits paid out for each share of stock is referred to as dividend.
Valuation	In finance, valuation is the process of estimating the market value of a financial asset or liability. They can be done on assets (for example, investments in marketable securities such as stocks, options, business enterprises, or intangible assets such as patents and trademarks) or on liabilities (e.g., Bonds issued by a company).
Expense	In accounting, an expense represents an event in which an asset is used up or a liability is incurred. In terms of the accounting equation, expenses reduce owners' equity.
Balance sheet	A statement of the assets, liabilities, and net worth of a firm or individual at some given time often at the end of its "fiscal year," is referred to as a balance sheet.
Safety stock	Safety stock is additional inventory planned to buffer against the variability in supply and demand plans, that could otherwise result in inventory shortages.
Stock	In financial terminology, stock is the capital raized by a corporation, through the issuance and sale of shares.
Inventory control	Inventory control, in the field of loss prevention, are systems designed to introduce technical barriers to shoplifting.
Control system	A control system is a device or set of devices that manage the behavior of other devices. Some devices or systems are not controllable.A control system is an interconnection of components connected or related in such a manner as to command, direct, or regulate itself or another system.
Apprenticeship	A work-study training method with both on-the-job and classroom training is an apprenticeship.Most of their training is on the job, working for an employer who helps the apprentices learn their trade, art or craft. Less formal, theoretical education is involved.
Management development	The process of training and educating employees to become good managers and then monitoring the progress of their managerial skills over time is management development.
Wage	The payment for the service of a unit of labor, per unit time. In trade theory, it is the only payment to labor, usually unskilled labor. In empirical work, wage data may exclude other compenzation, which must be added to get the total cost of employment.
Distribution center	Designed to facilitate the timely movement of goods and represent a very important part of a supply chain is a distribution center.
Peak	Peak refers to the point in the business cycle when an economic expansion reaches its highest point before turning down. Contrasts with trough.
Management	A management system is the framework of processes and procedures used to ensure that an

Go to **Cram101.com** for the Practice Tests for this Chapter.

system	organization can fulfill all tasks required to achieve its objectives.
Value system	A value system refers to how an individual or a group of individuals organize their ethical or ideological values. A well-defined value system is a moral code.
Cooperative	A business owned and controlled by the people who use it, producers, consumers, or workers with similar needs who pool their resources for mutual gain is called cooperative.
Public relations	Public relations refers to the management function that evaluates public attitudes, changes policies and procedures in response to the public's requests, and executes a program of action and information to earn public understanding and acceptance.
Multinational enterprise	Multinational enterprise refers to a firm, usually a corporation, that operates in two or more countries.
Marketing channel	Individuals and firms involved in the process of making a product or service available for use or consumption by consumers or industrial users is a marketing channel.
Economic environment	The economic environment represents the external conditions under which people are engaged in, and benefit from, economic activity. It includes aspects of economic status, paid employment, and finances.
Federal Reserve	The Federal Reserve System was created via the Federal Reserve Act of December 23rd, 1913. All national banks were required to join the system and other banks could join. The Reserve Banks opened for business on November 16th, 1914. Federal Reserve Notes were created as part of the legislation, to provide an elastic supply of currency.
Interest rate	The rate of return on bonds, loans, or deposits. When one speaks of 'the' interest rate, it is usually in a model where there is only one.
Tight money	A term to indicate time periods in which financing may be difficult to find and interest rates may be quite high by normal standards is called tight money.
Recession	A significant decline in economic activity. In the U.S., recession is approximately defined as two successive quarters of falling GDP, as judged by NBER.
Depreciation	Depreciation is an accounting and finance term for the method of attributing the cost of an asset across the useful life of the asset. Depreciation is a reduction in the value of a currency in floating exchange rate.
Liquidity	Liquidity refers to the capacity to turn assets into cash, or the amount of assets in a portfolio that have that capacity.
Commodity	Could refer to any good, but in trade a commodity is usually a raw material or primary product that enters into international trade, such as metals or basic agricultural products.
Aid	Assistance provided by countries and by international institutions such as the World Bank to developing countries in the form of monetary grants, loans at low interest rates, in kind, or a combination of these is called aid. Aid can also refer to assistance of any type rendered to benefit some group or individual.
Capacity utilization rate	In economics, the capacity utilization rate is the percentage of a company, industry, or country's production capacity that is actually or currently used. It is sometimes called the operating rate.
Capacity utilization	Capacity utilization is a concept in Economics which refers to the extent to which an enterprise or a nation actually uses its installed productive capacity. Thus, it refers to the relationship between actual output produced and potential output that could be produced with installed equipment, if capacity was fully used.
Closing	The finalization of a real estate sales transaction that passes title to the property from

the seller to the buyer is referred to as a closing. Closing is a sales term which refers to the process of making a sale. It refers to reaching the final step, which may be an exchange of money or acquiring a signature.

Realization	Realization is the sale of assets when an entity is being liquidated.
Negotiation	Negotiation is the process whereby interested parties resolve disputes, agree upon courses of action, bargain for individual or collective advantage, and/or attempt to craft outcomes which serve their mutual interests.
Consideration	Consideration in contract law, a basic requirement for an enforceable agreement under traditional contract principles, defined in this text as legal value, bargained for and given in exchange for an act or promise. In corporation law, cash or property contributed to a corporation in exchange for shares, or a promise to contribute such cash or property.
Political instability	Events such as riots, revolutions, or government upheavals that affect the operations of an international company is called political instability.
Bankruptcy	Bankruptcy is a legally declared inability or impairment of ability of an individual or organization to pay their creditors.
Exporter	A firm that sells its product in another country is an exporter.
Treasurer	In many governments, a treasurer is the person responsible for running the treasury. Treasurers are also employed by organizations to look after funds.
A share	In finance the term A share has two distinct meanings, both relating to securities. The first is a designation for a 'class' of common or preferred stock. A share of common or preferred stock typically has enhanced voting rights or other benefits compared to the other forms of shares that may have been created. The equity structure, or how many types of shares are offered, is determined by the corporate charter.
Recovery	Characterized by rizing output, falling unemployment, rizing profits, and increasing economic activity following a decline is a recovery.
Price competition	Price competition is where a company tries to distinguish its product or service from competing products on the basis of low price.
Inflation	An increase in the overall price level of an economy, usually as measured by the CPI or by the implicit price deflator is called inflation.
Adjusted for inflation	Adjusted for inflation refers to correcting for price changes to yield an equivalent real rate, or real non-inflationary number. The adjustment divides nominal amounts for different years by price indices for those years -- eg the CPI or the implicit price deflator -- and multiplies by 100. This converts to real values, ie valued at the prices of the base year for the price index.
Warehouse	Warehouse refers to a location, often decentralized, that a firm uses to store, consolidate, age, or mix stock; house product-recall programs; or ease tax burdens.
Consolidation	The combination of two or more firms, generally of equal size and market power, to form an entirely new entity is a consolidation.
Collaboration	Collaboration occurs when the interaction between groups is very important to goal attainment and the goals are compatible. Wherein people work together —applying both to the work of individuals as well as larger collectives and societies.
Licensee	A person lawfully on land in possession of another for purposes unconnected with the business interests of the possessor is referred to as the licensee.
Total quality	A product-quality program in which the objective is complete elimination of product defects

Go to **Cram101.com** for the Practice Tests for this Chapter.

control	is called total quality control.
Extension	Extension refers to an out-of-court settlement in which creditors agree to allow the firm more time to meet its financial obligations. A new repayment schedule will be developed, subject to the acceptance of creditors.
Deming prize	Japanese quality award for individuals and groups that have contributed to the field of quality control is called the deming prize.
Deming	Deming is widely credited with improving production in the United States during World War II, although he is perhaps best known for his work in Japan. There, from 1950 onward he taught top management how to improve design (and thus service), product quality, testing and sales (the latter through global markets).
Warranty	An obligation of a company to replace defective goods or correct any deficiencies in performance or quality of a product is called a warranty.
Quality improvement	Quality is inversely proportional to variability thus quality Improvement is the reduction of variability in products and processes.
Maturity	Maturity refers to the final payment date of a loan or other financial instrument, after which point no further interest or principal need be paid.
Target market	One or more specific groups of potential consumers toward which an organization directs its marketing program are a target market.
Countertrade	Countertrade is exchanging goods or services that are paid for, in whole or part, with other goods or services.
Cost structure	The relative proportion of an organization's fixed, variable, and mixed costs is referred to as cost structure.
Fair trade	The Fair Trade movement promotes international labor, environmental and social standards for the production of labelled and unlabelled goods ranging from handcrafts to agricultural commodities. The movement focuses in particular on exports from developing countries to developed countries.
Restrictive business practice	Restrictive business practice refers to action by a firm or group of firms to restrict entry by other firms, that is, to prevent other firms from selling their product or in their market. Considered a restraint of competition.
Direct sale	A direct sale is a sale to customers through distributors or self-employed sales people rather than through shops. Includes both personal contact with consumers in their homes (and other nonstore locations such as offices) and phone solicitations initiated by a retailer.
Liaison	An individual who serves as a bridge between groups, tying groups together and facilitating the communication flow needed to integrate group activities is a liaison.
Advertising campaign	A comprehensive advertising plan that consists of a series of messages in a variety of media that center on a single theme or idea is referred to as an advertising campaign.
Advertising	Advertising refers to paid, nonpersonal communication through various media by organizations and individuals who are in some way identified in the advertising message.
Production efficiency	A situation in which the economy cannot produce more of one good without producing less of some other good is referred to as production efficiency.
Complaint	The pleading in a civil case in which the plaintiff states his claim and requests relief is called complaint. In the common law, it is a formal legal document that sets out the basic facts and legal reasons that the filing party (the plaintiffs) believes are sufficient to support a claim against another person, persons, entity or entities (the defendants) that

Go to **Cram101.com** for the Practice Tests for this Chapter.

entitles the plaintiff(s) to a remedy (either money damages or injunctive relief).

Raw material	Raw material refers to a good that has not been transformed by production; a primary product.
Industrial robot	An industrial robot is officially defined by ISO as an automatically controlled, reprogrammable, multipurpose manipulator programmable in three or more axes.
Estate	An estate is the totality of the legal rights, interests, entitlements and obligations attaching to property. In the context of wills and probate, it refers to the totality of the property which the deceased owned or in which some interest was held.
Gap	In December of 1995, Gap became the first major North American retailer to accept independent monitoring of the working conditions in a contract factory producing its garments. Gap is the largest specialty retailer in the United States.
Sales promotion	Sales promotion refers to the promotional tool that stimulates consumer purchasing and dealer interest by means of short-term activities.
Promotion	Promotion refers to all the techniques sellers use to motivate people to buy products or services. An attempt by marketers to inform people about products and to persuade them to participate in an exchange.
Differentiated product	A firm's product that is not identical to products of other firms in the same industry is a differentiated product.
Dumping	Dumping refers to a practice of charging a very low price in a foreign market for such economic purposes as putting rival suppliers out of business.
Protectionism	Protectionism refers to advocacy of protection. The word has a negative connotation, and few advocates of protection in particular situations will acknowledge being protectionists.
Vertical integration	Vertical integration refers to production of different stages of processing of a product within the same firm.
Management philosophy	Management philosophy refers to a philosophy that links key goal-related issues with key collaboration issues to come up with general ways by which the firm will manage its affairs.
Management team	A management team is directly responsible for managing the day-to-day operations (and profitability) of a company.
Management control	That aspect of management concerned with the comparison of actual versus planned performance as well as the development and implementation of procedures to correct substandard performance is called management control.
Employee development	Employee development is the strategic investment, by an organization, in the training of its members.
Tangible	Having a physical existence is referred to as the tangible. Personal property other than real estate, such as cars, boats, stocks, or other assets.
Labor productivity	In labor economics labor productivity is a measure of the efficiency of the labor force. It is usually measured as output per hour of all people. When comparing labor productivity one mostly looks at the change over time.
Capital expenditure	A substantial expenditure that is used by a company to acquire or upgrade physical assets such as equipment, property, industrial buildings, including those which improve the quality and life of an asset is referred to as a capital expenditure.
Labor force	In economics the labor force is the group of people who have a potential for being employed.
Bureaucracy	Bureaucracy refers to an organization with many layers of managers who set rules and regulations and oversee all decisions.

Go to **Cram101.com** for the Practice Tests for this Chapter.

Fortune magazine	Fortune magazine is America's longest-running business magazine. Currently owned by media conglomerate Time Warner, it was founded in 1930 by Henry Luce. It is known for its regular features ranking companies by revenue.
Guardian	A person to whom the law has entrusted the custody and control of the person, or estate, or both, of an incompetent person is a guardian.
Narrowcasting	The reaching of a very specialized market through programming aimed at particular target audiences is narrowcasting. Cable television networks offer excellent opportunities for narrowcasting.
Monopoly	A monopoly is defined as a persistent market situation where there is only one provider of a kind of product or service.
Regulatory agency	Regulatory agency refers to an agency, commission, or board established by the Federal government or a state government to regulates businesses in the public interest.
Conglomerate	A conglomerate is a large company that consists of divisions of often seemingly unrelated businesses.
Authority	Authority in agency law, refers to an agent's ability to affect his principal's legal relations with third parties. Also used to refer to an actor's legal power or ability to do something. In addition, sometimes used to refer to a statute, case, or other legal source that justifies a particular result.
Household	An economic unit that provides the economy with resources and uses the income received to purchase goods and services that satisfy economic wants is called household.
Budget	Budget refers to an account, usually for a year, of the planned expenditures and the expected receipts of an entity. For a government, the receipts are tax revenues.
Applicant	In many tribunal and administrative law suits, the person who initiates the claim is called the applicant.
Lease	A contract for the possession and use of land or other property, including goods, on one side, and a recompense of rent or other income on the other is the lease.
Jurisdiction	The power of a court to hear and decide a case is called jurisdiction. It is the practical authority granted to a formally constituted body or to a person to deal with and make pronouncements on legal matters and, by implication, to administer justice within a defined area of responsibility.
Business Week	Business Week is a business magazine published by McGraw-Hill. It was first published in 1929 under the direction of Malcolm Muir, who was serving as president of the McGraw-Hill Publishing company at the time. It is considered to be the standard both in industry and among students.
Business plan	A detailed written statement that describes the nature of the business, the target market, the advantages the business will have in relation to competition, and the resources and qualifications of the owner is referred to as a business plan.
Direct marketing	Promotional element that uses direct communication with consumers to generate a response in the form of an order, a request for further information, or a visit to a retail outlet is direct marketing.
Receiver	A person that is appointed as a custodian of other people's property by a court of law or a creditor of the owner, pending a lawsuit or reorganization is called a receiver.
Remainder	A remainder in property law is a future interest created in a transferee that is capable of becoming possessory upon the natural termination of a prior estate created by the same instrument.

Covenant	A covenant is a signed written agreement between two or more parties. Also referred to as a contract.
Exempt	Employees who are not covered by the Fair Labor Standards Act are exempt. Exempt employees are not eligible for overtime pay.
Foreign ownership	Foreign ownership refers to the complete or majority ownership/control of businesses or resources in a country, by individuals who are not citizens of that country, or by companies whose headquarters are not in that country.
Tranche	In structured finance the word tranche refers to one of several related securitized bonds offered as part of the same deal. They are called tranches since each bond is a slice of the deal's risk. The legal documents usually refer to the tranches as "classes" of notes identified by letter (e.g. the Class A, Class B, Class C securities).
Controlling	A management function that involves determining whether or not an organization is progressing toward its goals and objectives, and taking corrective action if it is not is called controlling.
Formal contract	Formal contract refers to a contract that requires a special form or method of creation.
Merger	Merger refers to the combination of two firms into a single firm.
Managing director	Managing director is the term used for the chief executive of many limited companies in the United Kingdom, Commonwealth and some other English speaking countries. The title reflects their role as both a member of the Board of Directors but also as the senior manager.
Disney	Disney is one of the largest media and entertainment corporations in the world. Founded on October 16, 1923 by brothers Walt and Roy Disney as a small animation studio, today it is one of the largest Hollywood studios and also owns nine theme parks and several television networks, including the American Broadcasting Company (ABC).
Sony	Sony is a multinational corporation and one of the world's largest media conglomerates founded in Tokyo, Japan. One of its divisions Sony Electronics is one of the leading manufacturers of electronics, video, communications, and information technology products for the consumer and professional markets.
Wall Street Journal	Dow Jones & Company was founded in 1882 by reporters Charles Dow, Edward Jones and Charles Bergstresser. Jones converted the small Customers' Afternoon Letter into The Wall Street Journal, first published in 1889, and began delivery of the Dow Jones News Service via telegraph. The Journal featured the Jones 'Average', the first of several indexes of stock and bond prices on the New York Stock Exchange.
Journal	Book of original entry, in which transactions are recorded in a general ledger system, is referred to as a journal.
Complexity	The technical sophistication of the product and hence the amount of understanding required to use it is referred to as complexity. It is the opposite of simplicity.
Business strategy	Business strategy, which refers to the aggregated operational strategies of single business firm or that of an SBU in a diversified corporation refers to the way in which a firm competes in its chosen arenas.
Business model	A business model is the instrument by which a business intends to generate revenue and profits. It is a summary of how a company means to serve its employees and customers, and involves both strategy (what an business intends to do) as well as an implementation.
Exclusive license	A license that grants the licensee exclusive rights to use informational rights for a specified duration is referred to as an exclusive license.
Shareholder	A shareholder is an individual or company (including a corporation) that legally owns one or

more shares of stock in a joined stock company.

General manager	A manager who is responsible for several departments that perform different functions is called general manager.
Credit	Credit refers to a recording as positive in the balance of payments, any transaction that gives rise to a payment into the country, such as an export, the sale of an asset, or borrowing from abroad.
Customer service	The ability of logistics management to satisfy users in terms of time, dependability, communication, and convenience is called the customer service.
Smart card	A stored-value card that contains a computer chip that allows it to be loaded with digital cash from the owner's bank account whenever needed is called a smart card.
Proprietary	Proprietary indicates that a party, or proprietor, exercises private ownership, control or use over an item of property, usually to the exclusion of other parties. Where a party, holds or claims proprietary interests in relation to certain types of property (eg. a creative literary work, or software), that property may also be the subject of intellectual property law (eg. copyright or patents).
Digital Revolution	The Digital Revolution describes the effects of rapid drop in cost and ongoing improvement of digital devices such as computers replacing or emulating analog devices, enabling former unthinkable innovations like the World Wide Web (WWW). It includes changes in technology and society, and is often specifically used to refer to the controversies that occur as these technologies are widely adopted.
Media market	A media market is a region where the population can receive the same (or similar) television and radio station offerings, and may also include other types of media including newspapers or Internet content.
Frequency	Frequency refers to the speed of the up and down movements of a fluctuating economic variable; that is, the number of times per unit of time that the variable completes a cycle of up and down movement.
Digital technology	Technology characterized by use of the Internet and other digital processes to conduct or support business operations is referred to as digital technology.
Wholesale	According to the United Nations Statistics Division Wholesale is the resale of new and used goods to retailers, to industrial, commercial, institutional or professional users, or to other wholesalers, or involves acting as an agent or broker in buying merchandise for, or selling merchandise, to such persons or companies.
Impossibility	A doctrine under which a party to a contract is relieved of his or her duty to perform when that performance has become impossible because of the occurrence of an event unforeseen at the time of contracting is referred to as impossibility.
Operating profit	Operating profit is a measure of a company's earning power from ongoing operations, equal to earnings before the deduction of interest payments and income taxes.
Market value	Market value refers to the price of an asset agreed on between a willing buyer and a willing seller; the price an asset could demand if it is sold on the open market.
Heir	In common law jurisdictions an heir is a person who is entitled to receive a share of the decedent's property via the rules of inheritance in the jurisdiction where the decedent died or owned property at the time of his death.
General Electric Medical Systems	General Electric Medical Systems is a world leader in the field of medical diagnostic imaging technology, services and healthcare productivity and operates in more than 100 countries.

Go to **Cram101.com** for the Practice Tests for this Chapter.

General Electric	In 1876, Thomas Alva Edison opened a new laboratory in Menlo Park, New Jersey. Out of the laboratory was to come perhaps the most famous invention of all—a successful development of the incandescent electric lamp. By 1890, Edison had organized his various businesses into the Edison General Electric Company.
Weber	Weber was a German political economist and sociologist who is considered one of the founders of the modern study of sociology and public administration. His major works deal with rationalization in sociology of religion and government, but he also wrote much in the field of economics. His most popular work is his essay The Protestant Ethic and the Spirit of Capitalism.
Primary data	Facts and figures that are newly collected for the project are referred to as primary data.
Excess capacity	Excess capacity refers to plant resources that are underused when imperfectly competitive firms produce less output than that associated with purely competitive firms, who by definiation, are achieving minimum average total cost.
Balanced budget	From a Keynesian point of view, a balanced budget in the public sector is achieved when the government has enough fiscal discipline to be able to equate the revenues with expenditure over the business cycles. In other words, a government has a balanced budget if its income is equal to its expenditures.
Capital budget	A long-term budget that shows planned acquisition and disposal of capital assets, such as land, building, and equipment is a capital budget. Also a separate budget used by state governments for items such as new construction, major renovations, and acquisition of physical property.
Medicare	Medicare refers to federal program that is financed by payroll taxes and provides for compulsory hospital insurance for senior citizens and low-cost voluntary insurance to help older Americans pay physicians' fees.
Insurance	Insurance refers to a system by which individuals can reduce their exposure to risk of large losses by spreading the risks among a large number of persons.
Ambulatory care	Ambulatory care is any medical care delivered on an outpatient basis. Many medical conditions do not require hospital admission and can be managed without admission to a hospital. Many medical investigations can be performed on an ambulatory basis, including blood tests, X-rays, endoscopy and even biopsy procedures of superficial organs.
Health insurance	Health insurance is a type of insurance whereby the insurer pays the medical costs of the insured if the insured becomes sick due to covered causes, or due to accidents. The insurer may be a private organization or a government agency.
Failure rate	Failure rate is the frequency with an engineered system or component fails, expressed for example in failures per hour. Failure rate is usually time dependent. In the special case when the likelihood of failure remains constant as time passes, failure rate is simply the inverse of the mean time to failure, expressed for example in hours per failure.
Information technology	Information technology refers to technology that helps companies change business by allowing them to use new methods.
Siemens	Siemens is the world's largest conglomerate company. Worldwide, Siemens and its subsidiaries employs 461,000 people (2005) in 190 countries and reported global sales of €75.4 billion in fiscal year 2005.
Intervention	Intervention refers to an activity in which a government buys or sells its currency in the foreign exchange market in order to affect its currency's exchange rate.
Evaluation	The consumer's appraisal of the product or brand on important attributes is called evaluation.

Go to **Cram101.com** for the Practice Tests for this Chapter.

Accumulation	The acquisition of an increasing quantity of something. The accumulation of factors, especially capital, is a primary mechanism for economic growth.
Parent company	Parent company refers to the entity that has a controlling influence over another company. It may have its own operations, or it may have been set up solely for the purpose of owning the Subject Company.
Toshiba	Toshiba is a Japanese high technology electrical and electronics manufacturing firm, headquartered in Tokyo, Japan. It is the 7th largest integrated manufacturer of electric and electronic equipment in the world.
Service business	A business firm that provides services to consumers, such as accounting and legal services, is referred to as a service business.
Vendor	A person who sells property to a vendee is a vendor. The words vendor and vendee are more commonly applied to the seller and purchaser of real estate, and the words seller and buyer are more commonly applied to the seller and purchaser of personal property.
Electronic business	Electronic business is any business process that is empowered by an information system. Today, this is mostly done with Web-based technologies.
Business unit	The lowest level of the company which contains the set of functions that carry a product through its life span from concept through manufacture, distribution, sales and service is a business unit.
Training and development	All attempts to improve productivity by increasing an employee's ability to perform is training and development.
Hosting	Internet hosting service is a service that runs Internet servers, allowing organizations and individuals to serve content on the Internet.
Organization structure	The system of task, reporting, and authority relationships within which the organization does its work is referred to as the organization structure.
Supply chain	Supply chain refers to the flow of goods, services, and information from the initial sources of materials and services to the delivery of products to consumers.
Knowledge worker	Employees who own the means of producing a product or service are called a knowledge worker.
Concession	A concession is a business operated under a contract or license associated with a degree of exclusivity in exploiting a business within a certain geographical area. For example, sports arenas or public parks may have concession stands; and public services such as water supply may be operated as concessions.
Logistics	Those activities that focus on getting the right amount of the right products to the right place at the right time at the lowest possible cost is referred to as logistics.
Human resources	Human resources refers to the individuals within the firm, and to the portion of the firm's organization that deals with hiring, firing, training, and other personnel issues.
Coalition	An informal alliance among managers who support a specific goal is called coalition.
Knowledge base	Knowledge base refers to a database that includes decision rules for use of the data, which may be qualitative as well as quantitative.
Market development	Selling existing products to new markets is called market development.
Organic growth	Organic growth is the rate of business expansion through increasing output and sales as opposed to mergers, acquisitions and take-overs. Typically, the organic growth rate also excludes the impact of foreign exchange. Growth including foreign exchange, but excluding divestitures and acquistions is often referred to as, core growth.

Board of directors	The group of individuals elected by the stockholders of a corporation to oversee its operations is a board of directors.
Financial manager	Managers who make recommendations to top executives regarding strategies for improving the financial strength of a firm are referred to as a financial manager.
Free market	A free market is a market where price is determined by the unregulated interchange of supply and demand rather than set by artificial means.
Utility	Utility refers to the want-satisfying power of a good or service; the satisfaction or pleasure a consumer obtains from the consumption of a good or service.
Economics	The social science dealing with the use of scarce resources to obtain the maximum satisfaction of society's virtually unlimited economic wants is an economics.
Compliance	A type of influence process where a receiver accepts the position advocated by a source to obtain favorable outcomes or to avoid punishment is the compliance.
Level playing field	The objective of those who advocate protection on the grounds the foreign firms have an unfair advantage. A level playing field would remove such advantages, although it is not usually clear what sorts of advantage would be permitted to remain.
Staff position	A manager in a staff position has the authority and responsibility to advise people in the line positions but cannot issue direct orders to them.
Average cost	Average cost is equal to total cost divided by the number of goods produced (Quantity-Q). It is also equal to the sum of average variable costs (total variable costs divided by Q) plus average fixed costs (total fixed costs divided by Q).
Leverage	Leverage is using given resources in such a way that the potential positive or negative outcome is magnified. In finance, this generally refers to borrowing.
Information system	An information system is a system whether automated or manual, that comprises people, machines, and/or methods organized to collect, process, transmit, and disseminate data that represent user information.
Import quota	Import quota refers to a limit imposed by a nation on the quantity of a good that may be imported during some period of time.
Quota	A government-imposed restriction on quantity, or sometimes on total value, used to restrict the import of something to a specific quantity is called a quota.
Administration	Administration refers to the management and direction of the affairs of governments and institutions; a collective term for all policymaking officials of a government; the execution and implementation of public policy.
Broker	In commerce, a broker is a party that mediates between a buyer and a seller. A broker who also acts as a seller or as a buyer becomes a principal party to the deal.
Composition	An out-of-court settlement in which creditors agree to accept a fractional settlement on their original claim is referred to as composition.
Accounting	A system that collects and processes financial information about an organization and reports that information to decision makers is referred to as accounting.
Fixed cost	The cost that a firm bears if it does not produce at all and that is independent of its output. The presence of a fixed cost tends to imply increasing returns to scale. Contrasts with variable cost.
Variable cost	The portion of a firm or industry's cost that changes with output, in contrast to fixed cost is referred to as variable cost.

Variable	A variable is something measured by a number; it is used to analyze what happens to other things when the size of that number changes.
Lead market	Market where products are first introduced is a lead market.
Allocation of resources	Allocation of resources refers to the society's decisions on how to divide up its scarce input resources among the different outputs produced in the economy, and among the different firms or other organizations that produce those outputs.
Cabinet	The heads of the executive departments of a jurisdiction who report to and advise its chief executive; examples would include the president's cabinet, the governor's cabinet, and the mayor's cabinet.
Globalization of markets	Moving away from an economic system in which national markets are distinct entities, isolated by trade barriers and barriers of distance, time, and culture, and toward a system in which national markets are merging into one global market is globalization of markets.
World price	The price of a good on the 'world market,' meaning the price outside of any country's borders and therefore exclusive of any trade taxes or subsidies is the world price.
Multinational corporation	An organization that manufactures and markets products in many different countries and has multinational stock ownership and multinational management is referred to as multinational corporation.
Relative cost	Relative cost refers to the relationship between the price paid for advertising time or space and the size of the audience delivered; it is used to compare the prices of various media vehicles.
Volkswagen	Volkswagen or VW is an automobile manufacturer based in Wolfsburg, Germany in the state of Lower Saxony. It forms the core of this Group, one of the world's four largest car producers. Its German tagline is "Aus Liebe zum Automobil", which is translated as "For the love of the car" - or, For Love of the People's Cars,".
Attest	To bear witness to is called attest. To affirm, certify by oath or signature. It is an official act establishing authenticity.
Convergence	The blending of various facets of marketing functions and communication technology to create more efficient and expanded synergies is a convergence.
Commerce	Commerce is the exchange of something of value between two entities. It is the central mechanism from which capitalism is derived.
Corporate culture	The whole collection of beliefs, values, and behaviors of a firm that send messages to those within and outside the company about how business is done is the corporate culture.
Mistake	In contract law a mistake is incorrect understanding by one or more parties to a contract and may be used as grounds to invalidate the agreement. Common law has identified three different types of mistake in contract: unilateral mistake, mutual mistake, and common mistake.
Market research	Market research is the process of systematic gathering, recording and analyzing of data about customers, competitors and the market. Market research can help create a business plan, launch a new product or service, fine tune existing products and services, expand into new markets etc. It can be used to determine which portion of the population will purchase the product/service, based on variables like age, gender, location and income level. It can be found out what market characteristics your target market has.
Henry Ford	Henry Ford was the founder of the Ford Motor Company. His introduction of the Model T automobile revolutionized transportation and American industry.
Global competition	Global competition exists when competitive conditions across national markets are linked strongly enough to form a true international market and when leading competitors compete head

Go to Cram101.com for the Practice Tests for this Chapter.

	to head in many different countries.
Patronage	The power of elected and appointed officials to make partisan appointments to office or to confer contracts, honors, or other benefits on their political supporters. Patronage has always been one of the major tools by which political executives consolidate their power and attempt to control a bureaucracy.
Scarcity	Scarcity is defined as not having sufficient resources to produce enough to fulfill unlimited subjective wants. Alternatively, scarcity implies that not all of society's goals can be attained at the same time, so that trade-offs one good against others are made.
Multinational corporations	Firms that own production facilities in two or more countries and produce and sell their products globally are referred to as multinational corporations.
Accommodation	Accommodation is a term used to describe a delivery of nonconforming goods meant as a partial performance of a contract for the sale of goods, where a full performance is not possible.
Common law	The legal system that is based on the judgement and decree of courts rather than legislative action is called common law.
Common market	Common market refers to a group of countries that eliminate all barriers to movement of both goods and factors among themselves, and that also, on each product, agree to levy the same tariff on imports from outside the group.
Exporting	Selling products to another country is called exporting.
Shell	One of the original Seven Sisters, Royal Dutch/Shell is the world's third-largest oil company by revenue, and a major player in the petrochemical industry and the solar energy business. Shell has six core businesses: Exploration and Production, Gas and Power, Downstream, Chemicals, Renewables, and Trading/Shipping, and operates in more than 140 countries.
Marketing orientation	When an organization focuses its efforts on continuously collecting information about customers' needs and competitors' capabilities, sharing this information across departments, and using the information to create customer value, we have marketing orientation.
Suggested Retail Price	The Suggested Retail Price of a product is the price the manufacturer recommends that the retailer sell it for. This helps to standardize prices among locations.
Yield	The interest rate that equates a future value or an annuity to a given present value is a yield.
Brief	Brief refers to a statement of a party's case or legal arguments, usually prepared by an attorney. Also used to make legal arguments before appellate courts.
General Motors	General Motors is the world's largest automaker. Founded in 1908, today it employs about 327,000 people around the world. With global headquarters in Detroit, it manufactures its cars and trucks in 33 countries.
Boot	Boot is any type of personal property received in a real property transaction that is not like kind, such as cash, mortgage notes, a boat or stock. The exchanger pays taxes on the boot to the extent of recognized capital gain. In an exchange if any funds are not used in purchasing the replacement property, that also will be called boot.
Affirm	To confirm or uphold a former judgment or order of a court is to affirm. Appellate courts, for instance, may affirm the decisions of lower courts.
Dictum	Dictum refers to language in a judicial opinion that is not necessary for the decision of the case and that, while perhaps persuasive, does not bind subsequent courts.
Economic nationalism	Economic nationalism is a term used to describe policies which are guided by the idea of protecting domestic consumption, labor and capital formation, even if this requires the

Go to **Cram101.com** for the Practice Tests for this Chapter.

imposition of tariffs and other restrictions on the movement of labor, goods and capital. Economic nationalism may include such doctrines as protectionism and import substitution.

Customs	Customs is an authority or agency in a country responsible for collecting customs duties and for controlling the flow of people, animals and goods (including personal effects and hazardous items) in and out of the country.
Cosmopolitanism	Cosmopolitanism is the idea that all of humanity belongs to a single moral community. This is contrasted with ideologies of patriotism and nationalism. Cosmopolitanism may or may not entail some sort of world government or it may simply refer to more inclusive moral, economic, and/or political relationships between nations or individuals of different nations.
Property	Assets defined in the broadest legal sense. Property includes the unrealized receivables of a cash basis taxpayer, but not services rendered.
Complement	A good that is used in conjunction with another good is a complement. For example, cameras and film would complement eachother.
Management consulting	Management consulting refers to both the practice of helping companies to improve performance through analysis of existing business problems and development of future plans, as well as to the firms that specialize in this sort of consulting.
Nontariff barrier	Any policy that interferes with exports or imports other than a simple tariff, prominently including quotas and vers is referred to as nontariff barrier.
Amortize	To provide for the payment of a debt by creating a sinking fund or paying in installments is to amortize.
Sustainable competitive advantage	A strength, relative to competitors, in the markets served and the products offered is referred to as the sustainable competitive advantage.
Drawback	Drawback refers to rebate of import duties when the imported good is re-exported or used as input to the production of an exported good.
Multidomestic strategy	Emphasizing the need to be responsive to the unique conditions prevailing in different national markets is referred to as a multidomestic strategy.
Zanussi	Zanussi is a leading brand for domestic kitchen appliances in Europe. Exported from Italy since 1946, Zanussi is widely recognized for its innovative products and distinctive modern design.
Marketing mix	The marketing mix approach to marketing is a model of crafting and implementing marketing strategies. It stresses the "mixing" or blending of various factors in such a way that both organizational and consumer (target markets) objectives are attained.
Positioning	The art and science of fitting the product or service to one or more segments of the market in such a way as to set it meaningfully apart from competition is called positioning.
Corporate policy	Dimension of social responsibility that refers to the position a firm takes on social and political issues is referred to as corporate policy.
Global marketing	A strategy of using a common marketing plan and program for all countries in which a company operates, thus selling the product or services the same way everywhere in the world is called global marketing.
Dow Chemical	Dow Chemical is the world's largest producer of plastics, including polystyrene, polyurethanes, polyethylene, polypropylene, and synthetic rubbers. It is also a major producer of the chemicals calcium chloride, ethylene oxide, and various acrylates, surfactants, and cellulose resins. It produces many agricultural chemicals.

Bargaining power	Bargaining power refers to the ability to influence the setting of prices or wages, usually arising from some sort of monopoly or monopsony position
Labor union	A group of workers organized to advance the interests of the group is called a labor union.
Serviceability	A dimension of quality that refers to a product's ease of repair is referred to as serviceability.
Points	Loan origination fees that may be deductible as interest by a buyer of property. A seller of property who pays points reduces the selling price by the amount of the points paid for the buyer.
Nuisance	Nuisance refers to that which endangers life or health, gives offense to the senses, violates the laws of decency, or obstructs the reasonable and comfortable use of property.
Motorola	The Six Sigma quality system was developed at Motorola even though it became most well known because of its use by General Electric. It was created by engineer Bill Smith, under the direction of Bob Galvin (son of founder Paul Galvin) when he was running the company.
Currency risk	Currency risk is a form of risk that arises from the change in price of one currency against another. Whenever investors or companies have assets or business operations across national borders, they face currency risk if their positions are not hedged.
Hedge	Hedge refers to a process of offsetting risk. In the foreign exchange market, hedgers use the forward market to cover a transaction or open position and thereby reduce exchange risk. The term applies most commonly to trade.
Homogeneous	In the context of procurement/purchasing, homogeneous is used to describe goods that do not vary in their essential characteristic irrespective of the source of supply.
World Health Organization	The World Health Organization is a specialized agency of the United Nations, acting as a coordinating authority on international public health, headquartered in Geneva, Switzerland. It's constitution states that its mission "is the attainment by all peoples of the highest possible level of health". Its major task is to combat disease, especially key infectious diseases, and to promote the general health of the peoples of the world.
Retailing	All activities involved in selling, renting, and providing goods and services to ultimate consumers for personal, family, or household use is referred to as retailing.
Cost driver	Cost driver refers to a factor related to an activity that changes the volume or characteristics of that activity, and in doing so changes its costs. An activity can have more than one cost driver.
Experience curve	Experience curve refers to function that measures the decline in cost per unit in various value-chain functions such as manufacturing, marketing, distribution, and so on, as units produced increases.
Rationalization	Rationalization in economics is an attempt to change a pre-existing ad-hoc workflow into one that is based on a set of published rules.
Ford Motor Company	Ford Motor Company introduced methods for large-scale manufacturing of cars, and large-scale management of an industrial workforce, especially elaborately engineered manufacturing sequences typified by the moving assembly lines. Henry Ford's combination of highly efficient factories, highly paid workers, and low prices revolutionized manufacturing and came to be known around the world as Fordism by 1914.
Local content requirement	A requirement that some specific fraction of a good be produced domestically is called local content requirement.
Export subsidies	Government payments to domestic producers to enable them to reduce the price of a good or service to foreign buyers are referred to as export subsidies.

Go to **Cram101.com** for the Practice Tests for this Chapter.

Capital flow	International capital movement is referred to as capital flow.
Subsidy	Subsidy refers to government financial assistance to a domestic producer.
Honda	With more than 14 million internal combustion engines built each year, Honda is the largest engine-maker in the world. In 2004, the company began to produce diesel motors, which were both very quiet whilst not requiring particulate filters to pass pollution standards. It is arguable, however, that the foundation of their success is the motorcycle division.
Publicity	Publicity refers to any information about an individual, product, or organization that's distributed to the public through the media and that's not paid for or controlled by the seller.
Financial institution	A financial institution acts as an agent that provides financial services for its clients. Financial institutions generally fall under financial regulation from a government authority.
Deutsche Bank	Deutsche Bank was founded in Germany on January 22, 1870 as a specialist bank for foreign trade. Major projects in its first decades included the Northern Pacific Railroad in the United States (1883) and the Baghdad Railway (1888). It also financed bond offerings of the steel concern Krupp (1885) and introduced the chemical company Bayer on the Berlin stock market.
Bank of America	In 2004, a California jury decided that Bank of America had illegally raided the Social Security benefits of a million customers. The jury awarded damages that could exceed $1 billion. Bank of America had been accused of withholding customers' direct deposit social security benefit payments to cover debts in cases where a debt is owed to the bank by the customer (e.g.: due to an overdrawn account, various service fees, etc.), this is in direct violation of California state law.
Public sector	Public sector refers to the part of the economy that contains all government entities; government.
Interdependence	The extent to which departments depend on each other for resources or materials to accomplish their tasks is referred to as interdependence.
Takeover	A takeover in business refers to one company (the acquirer) purchasing another (the target). Such events resemble mergers, but without the formation of a new company.
Centralization	A structural policy in which decision-making authority is concentrated at the top of the organizational hierarchy is referred to as centralization.
Chrysler	The Chrysler Corporation was an American automobile manufacturer that existed independently from 1925–1998. The company was formed by Walter Percy Chrysler on June 6, 1925, with the remaining assets of Maxwell Motor Company.
Foreign subsidiary	A company owned in a foreign country by another company is referred to as foreign subsidiary.
International firm	International firm refers to those firms who have responded to stiff competition domestically by expanding their sales abroad. They may start a production facility overseas and send some of their managers, who report to a global division, to that country.
Product cycle	Product cycle refers to the life cycle of a new product, which first can be produced only in the country where it was developed, then as it becomes standardized and more familiar, can be produced in other countries and exported back to where it started.
Consumer finance	Consumer finance in the most basic sense of the word refers to any kind of lending to consumers. However, in the United States financial services industry, the term "consumer finance" often refers to a particular type of business, sub prime branch lending (that is lending to people with bad credit).

Geocentrism	Geocentrism in marketing is a global orientation with marketing strategies adapted to local country conditions.
Human resource management	The process of evaluating human resource needs, finding people to fill those needs, and getting the best work from each employee by providing the right incentives and job environment, all with the goal of meeting the needs of the firm are called human resource management.
Resource management	Resource management is the efficient and effective deployment of an organization's resources when they are needed. Such resources may include financial resources, inventory, human skills, production resources, or information technology.
Procurement	Procurement is the acquisition of goods or services at the best possible total cost of ownership, in the right quantity, at the right time, in the right place for the direct benefit or use of the governments, corporations, or individuals generally via, but not limited to a contract.
Ancillary	An ancillary receiver is a receiver who has been appointed in aid of, and in subordination to, the primary receiver.
Transaction cost	A transaction cost is a cost incurred in making an economic exchange. For example, most people, when buying or selling a stock, must pay a commission to their broker; that commission is a transaction cost of doing the stock deal.
Xerox	Xerox was founded in 1906 as "The Haloid Company" manufacturing photographic paper and equipment. The company came to prominence in 1959 with the introduction of the first plain paper photocopier using the process of xerography (electrophotography) developed by Chester Carlson, the Xerox 914.
Political risk	Refers to the many different actions of people, subgroups, and whole countries that have the potential to affect the financial status of a firm is called political risk.
Comparative advantage	The ability to produce a good at lower cost, relative to other goods, compared to another country is a comparative advantage.
Cash flow	In finance, cash flow refers to the amounts of cash being received and spent by a business during a defined period of time, sometimes tied to a specific project. Most of the time they are being used to determine gaps in the liquid position of a company.
Balance of trade	Balance of trade refers to the sum of the money gained by a given economy by selling exports, minus the cost of buying imports. They form part of the balance of payments, which also includes other transactions such as the international investment position.
Transport cost	Transport cost refers to the cost of transporting a good, especially in international trade.
Barriers to entry	In economics and especially in the theory of competition, barriers to entry are obstacles in the path of a firm which wants to enter a given market.
Castrol	Castrol was founded on March 19th 1899 by Charles "Cheers" Wakefield in England. It was originally named the Wakefield Oil Company. In 1909, the company began production of a new automotive lubricant named Castrol. The company developed specific oil applications for various applications of the new internal combustion engine, including automobiles, motorcycles, and aircraft.
Product positioning	Product positioning refers to the place an offering occupies in consumers' minds on important attributes relative to competitive offerings.
Tradeoff	The sacrifice of some or all of one economic goal, good, or service to achieve some other goal, good, or service is a tradeoff.
Strategic	Strategic Innovation is the creation of growth strategies, new product categories, services

Go to **Cram101.com** for the Practice Tests for this Chapter.

Innovation	or business models that change the game and generate significant new value for consumers, customers and the corporation.
Possession	Possession refers to respecting real property, exclusive dominion and control such as owners of like property usually exercise over it. Manual control of personal property either as owner or as one having a qualified right in it.
Structural change	Changes in the relative importance of different areas of an economy over time, usually measured in terms of their share of output, employment, or total spending is structural change.
Product design	Product Design is defined as the idea generation, concept development, testing and manufacturing or implementation of a physical object or service. It is possibly the evolution of former discipline name - Industrial Design.
Nissan	Nissan is Japan's second largest car company after Toyota. Nissan is among the top three Asian rivals of the "big three" in the US.
Argument	The discussion by counsel for the respective parties of their contentions on the law and the facts of the case being tried in order to aid the jury in arriving at a correct and just conclusion is called argument.
Theory of comparative advantage	Ricardo's theory that specialization and free trade will benefit all trading partners, even those that may be absolutely less efficient producers are theory of comparative advantage.
Global platform	Global refers to the home country conditions and competitive advantages from a global strategy that transcend the domicile country. A country is a desirable global platform in an industry if it provides an environment yielding firms domiciled in that country an advantage in competing globally in that particular industry.
Unskilled labor	Unskilled labor refers to labor with a low level of skill or human capital. Identified empirically as labor earning a low wage, with a low level of education, or in an occupational category associated with these.
Manufactured good	A manufactured good refers to goods that have been processed in any way.
Direct labor	The earnings of employees who work directly on the products being manufactured are direct labor.
Factors of production	Economic resources: land, capital, labor, and entrepreneurial ability are called factors of production.
Consumption	In Keynesian economics consumption refers to personal consumption expenditure, i.e., the purchase of currently produced goods and services out of income, out of savings (net worth), or from borrowed funds. It refers to that part of disposable income that does not go to saving.
Per capita	Per capita refers to per person. Usually used to indicate the average per person of any given statistic, commonly income.
Technological change	The introduction of new methods of production or new products intended to increase the productivity of existing inputs or to raise marginal products is a technological change.
Product differentiation	A strategy in which one firm's product is distinguished from competing products by means of its design, related services, quality, location, or other attributes is called product differentiation.
Traded good	A good that is exported or imported or -- sometimes -- a good that could be exported or imported if it weren't tariffs, or quotas, is referred to as traded good.

Trade theory	The body of economic thought that seeks to explain why and how countries engage in international trade and the welfare implication of that trade, encompassing especially the Ricardian Model, the Heckscher-Ohlin Model, and the New Trade Theory.
Trade barrier	An artificial disincentive to export and/or import, such as a tariff, quota, or other NTB is called a trade barrier.
National Cash Register	In 1884 John Henry Patterson and his brother Frank Jefferson Patterson bought the National Manufacturing Company which they renamed the National Cash Register Company. They turned the firm into one of the first modern American companies, introducing new, aggressive sales methods and business techniques. They established the first sales training school in 1893, and introduced a comprehensive social welfare program for factory workers.
Gillette	On October 1, 2005, Gillette finalized its purchase by Procter & Gamble. As a result of this merger, the Gillette Company no longer exists. Its last day of market trading - symbol G on the New York Stock Exchange - was September 30, 2005. The merger created the world's largest personal care and household products company.
Cartel	Cartel refers to a group of firms that seeks to raise the price of a good by restricting its supply. The term is usually used for international groups, especially involving state-owned firms and/or governments.
Efficient scale	The quantity of output that minimizes average total cost is referred to as efficient scale.
Minimum efficient scale	The smallest output of a firm consistent with minimum average cost. In small countries, in some industries the level of demand in autarky is not sufficient to support minimum efficient scale.
Incentive	An incentive is any factor (financial or non-financial) that provides a motive for a particular course of action, or counts as a reason for preferring one choice to the alternatives.
Market segmentation	The process of dividing the total market into several groups whose members have similar characteristics is market segmentation.
Segmentation Strategy	Segmentation strategy is a pricing strategy of focusing your marketing efforts to one or two narrow market segments and tailoring your marketing mix to these specialized markets, you can better meet the needs of that target market.
Patent	The legal right to the proceeds from and control over the use of an invented product or process, granted for a fixed period of time, usually 20 years. Patent is one form of intellectual property that is subject of the TRIPS agreement.
Pact	Pact refers to a set of principles endorsed by 21 of the largest U.S. ad agencies aimed at improving the research used in preparing and testing ads, providing a better creative product for clients, and controlling the cost of TV commercials.
Global advertising	Global advertising refers to the use of the same basic advertising message in all international markets.
International Business	International business refers to any firm that engages in international trade or investment.
Host country	The country in which the parent-country organization seeks to locate or has already located a facility is a host country.
Market position	Market position is a measure of the position of a company or product on a market.
Foreign direct investment	Foreign direct investment refers to the buying of permanent property and businesses in foreign nations.

Go to **Cram101.com** for the Practice Tests for this Chapter.

Direct investment	Direct investment refers to a domestic firm actually investing in and owning a foreign subsidiary or division.
Rebalancing	Rebalancing is the action of bringing a portfolio of investments that has deviated away from one's target asset allocation back into line. Under-weighted securities can be purchased with newly saved money; alternatively, over-weighted securities can be sold to purchase under-weighted securities.
International division	Division responsible for a firm's international activities is an international division.
Economic analysis	The process of deriving economic principles from relevant economic facts are called economic analysis. It is the comparison, with money as the index, of those costs and benefits to the wider economy that can be reasonably quantified, including all social costs and benefits of a project.
Case study	A case study is a particular method of qualitative research. Rather than using large samples and following a rigid protocol to examine a limited number of variables, case study methods involve an in-depth, longitudinal examination of a single instance or event: a case. They provide a systematic way of looking at events, collecting data, analyzing information, and reporting the results.
Big Business	Big business is usually used as a pejorative reference to the significant economic and political power which large and powerful corporations (especially multinational corporations), are capable of wielding.
Political economy	Early name for the discipline of economics. A field within economics encompassing several alternatives to neoclassical economics, including Marxist economics. Also called radical political economy.
Market failure	Any departure from the ideal benchmark of perfect competition, especially the complete absence of a market due to incomplete or asymmetric information is called market failure.
Market power	The ability of a single economic actor to have a substantial influence on market prices is market power.
Assessment	Collecting information and providing feedback to employees about their behavior, communication style, or skills is an assessment.
Transnational corporation	A firm that tries to simultaneously realize gains from experience curve economies, location economies, and global learning, while remaining locally responsive is called transnational corporation.
United Nations	An international organization created by multilateral treaty in 1945 to promote social and economic cooperation among nations and to protect human rights is the United Nations.
Hierarchy	A system of grouping people in an organization according to rank from the top down in which all subordinate managers must report to one person is called a hierarchy.

Go to **Cram101.com** for the Practice Tests for this Chapter.

Complexity	The technical sophistication of the product and hence the amount of understanding required to use it is referred to as complexity. It is the opposite of simplicity.
Business unit	The lowest level of the company which contains the set of functions that carry a product through its life span from concept through manufacture, distribution, sales and service is a business unit.
Management	Management characterizes the process of leading and directing all or part of an organization, often a business, through the deployment and manipulation of resources. Early twentieth-century management writer Mary Parker Follett defined management as "the art of getting things done through people."
Balance	In banking and accountancy, the outstanding balance is the amount of money owned, (or due), that remains in a deposit account (or a loan account) at a given date, after all past remittances, payments and withdrawal have been accounted for. It can be positive (then, in the balance sheet of a firm, it is an asset) or negative (a liability).
Organizational structure	Organizational structure is the way in which the interrelated groups of an organization are constructed. From a managerial point of view the main concerns are ensuring effective communication and coordination.
Organization structure	The system of task, reporting, and authority relationships within which the organization does its work is referred to as the organization structure.
Structural change	Changes in the relative importance of different areas of an economy over time, usually measured in terms of their share of output, employment, or total spending is structural change.
Corporation	A legal entity chartered by a state or the Federal government that is distinct and separate from the individuals who own it is a corporation. This separation gives the corporation unique powers which other legal entities lack.
Variable	A variable is something measured by a number; it is used to analyze what happens to other things when the size of that number changes.
Global matrix	Global Matrix is the largest and oldest non-GDS-affiliated software service provider in the North American retail travel industry. In business for over 35 years, the company's travel agency support and business management system is used by independent travel agencies in Canada, U.S., and Australia, and forms a unique foundation for the delivery of complete front-, mid-, and back-office functionality.
Consultant	A professional that provides expert advice in a particular field or area in which customers occassionaly require this type of knowledge is a consultant.
Channel	Channel, in communications (sometimes called communications channel), refers to the medium used to convey information from a sender (or transmitter) to a receiver.
Matrix structure	An organizational structure which typically crosses a functional approach with a product or service-based design, often resulting in employees having two bosses is the matrix structure.
Global matrix structure	Horizontal differentiation proceeds along two dimensions: product divisions and areas is called the global matrix structure.
Matrix organization	Matrix organization refers to an organization in which specialists from different parts of the organization are brought together to work on specific projects but still remain part of a traditional line-and-staff structure.
Dow Chemical	Dow Chemical is the world's largest producer of plastics, including polystyrene, polyurethanes, polyethylene, polypropylene, and synthetic rubbers. It is also a major producer of the chemicals calcium chloride, ethylene oxide, and various acrylates,

Go to **Cram101.com** for the Practice Tests for this Chapter.

surfactants, and cellulose resins. It produces many agricultural chemicals.

Interest	In finance and economics, interest is the price paid by a borrower for the use of a lender's money. In other words, interest is the amount of paid to "rent" money for a period of time.
Instrument	Instrument refers to an economic variable that is controlled by policy makers and can be used to influence other variables, called targets. Examples are monetary and fiscal policies used to achieve external and internal balance.
Core	A core is the set of feasible allocations in an economy that cannot be improved upon by subset of the set of the economy's consumers (a coalition). In construction, when the force in an element is within a certain center section, the core, the element will only be under compression.
Market opportunities	Market opportunities refer to areas where a company believes there are favorable demand trends, needs, and/or wants that are not being satisfied, and where it can compete effectively.
Configuration	An organization's shape, which reflects the division of labor and the means of coordinating the divided tasks is configuration.
Distribution	Distribution in economics, the manner in which total output and income is distributed among individuals or factors.
Industry	A group of firms that produce identical or similar products is an industry. It is also used specifically to refer to an area of economic production focused on manufacturing which involves large amounts of capital investment before any profit can be realized, also called "heavy industry".
Market	A market is, as defined in economics, a social arrangement that allows buyers and sellers to discover information and carry out a voluntary exchange of goods or services.
Asset	An item of property, such as land, capital, money, a share in ownership, or a claim on others for future payment, such as a bond or a bank deposit is an asset.
Liability	A liability is a present obligation of the enterprise arizing from past events, the settlement of which is expected to result in an outflow from the enterprise of resources embodying economic benefits.
Strategic plan	The formal document that presents the ways and means by which a strategic goal will be achieved is a strategic plan. A long-term flexible plan that does not regulate activities but rather outlines the means to achieve certain results, and provides the means to alter the course of action should the desired ends change.
Competitor	Other organizations in the same industry or type of business that provide a good or service to the same set of customers is referred to as a competitor.
Production	The creation of finished goods and services using the factors of production: land, labor, capital, entrepreneurship, and knowledge.
Tariff	A tax imposed by a nation on an imported good is called a tariff.
Subsidiary	A company that is controlled by another company or corporation is a subsidiary.
Marketing	Promoting and selling products or services to customers, or prospective customers, is referred to as marketing.
Product cycle	Product cycle refers to the life cycle of a new product, which first can be produced only in the country where it was developed, then as it becomes standardized and more familiar, can be produced in other countries and exported back to where it started.
Management	A management system is the framework of processes and procedures used to ensure that an

148

Go to **Cram101.com** for the Practice Tests for this Chapter.

Go to **Cram101.com** for the Practice Tests for this Chapter.
And, **NEVER** highlight a book again!

system	organization can fulfill all tasks required to achieve its objectives.
Specialist	A specialist is a trader who makes a market in one or several stocks and holds the limit order book for those stocks.
Operation	A standardized method or technique that is performed repetitively, often on different materials resulting in different finished goods is called an operation.
Principal	In agency law, one under whose direction an agent acts and for whose benefit that agent acts is a principal.
Leverage	Leverage is using given resources in such a way that the potential positive or negative outcome is magnified. In finance, this generally refers to borrowing.
Competitive advantage	A business is said to have a competitive advantage when its unique strengths, often based on cost, quality, time, and innovation, offer consumers a greater percieved value and there by differtiating it from its competitors.
Incentive	An incentive is any factor (financial or non-financial) that provides a motive for a particular course of action, or counts as a reason for preferring one choice to the alternatives.
Competitive Strategy	An outline of how a business intends to compete with other firms in the same industry is called competitive strategy.
Product development	In business and engineering, new product development is the complete process of bringing a new product to market. There are two parallel aspects to this process : one involves product engineering ; the other marketing analysis. Marketers see new product development as the first stage in product life cycle management, engineers as part of Product Lifecycle Management.
Quality assurance	Those activities associated with assuring the quality of a product or service is called quality assurance.
Manufacturing	Production of goods primarily by the application of labor and capital to raw materials and other intermediate inputs, in contrast to agriculture, mining, forestry, fishing, and services a manufacturing.
Procurement	Procurement is the acquisition of goods or services at the best possible total cost of ownership, in the right quantity, at the right time, in the right place for the direct benefit or use of the governments, corporations, or individuals generally via, but not limited to a contract.
Internationa-ization	Internationalization refers to another term for fragmentation. Used by Grossman and Helpman.
Export	In economics, an export is any good or commodity, shipped or otherwise transported out of a country, province, town to another part of the world in a legitimate fashion, typically for use in trade or sale.
Foundation	A Foundation is a type of philanthropic organization set up by either individuals or institutions as a legal entity (either as a corporation or trust) with the purpose of distributing grants to support causes in line with the goals of the foundation.
Exporting	Selling products to another country is called exporting.
Transnational	Transnational focuses on the heightened interconnectivity between people all around the world and the loosening of boundaries between countries.
Economy	The income, expenditures, and resources that affect the cost of running a business and household are called an economy.

Go to **Cram101.com** for the Practice Tests for this Chapter.
And, **NEVER** highlight a book again!

Fragmentation	Fragmentation refers to the splitting of production processes into separate parts that can be done in different locations, including in different countries.
Parent company	Parent company refers to the entity that has a controlling influence over another company. It may have its own operations, or it may have been set up solely for the purpose of owning the Subject Company.
Physical asset	A physical asset is an item of economic value that has a tangible or material existence. A physical asset usually refers to cash, equipment, inventory and properties owned by a business.
Credibility	The extent to which a source is perceived as having knowledge, skill, or experience relevant to a communication topic and can be trusted to give an unbiased opinion or present objective information on the issue is called credibility.
Interdependence	The extent to which departments depend on each other for resources or materials to accomplish their tasks is referred to as interdependence.
Transnational corporation	A firm that tries to simultaneously realize gains from experience curve economies, location economies, and global learning, while remaining locally responsive is called transnational corporation.
Marketing strategy	Marketing strategy refers to the means by which a marketing goal is to be achieved, usually characterized by a specified target market and a marketing program to reach it.
Service	Service refers to a "non tangible product" that is not embodied in a physical good and that typically effects some change in another product, person, or institution. Contrasts with good.
Line authority	A form of authority in which individuals in management positions have the formal power to direct and control immediate subordinates is referred to as line authority.
Authority	Authority in agency law, refers to an agent's ability to affect his principal's legal relations with third parties. Also used to refer to an actor's legal power or ability to do something. In addition, sometimes used to refer to a statute, case, or other legal source that justifies a particular result.
Line organization	An organization that has direct two-way lines of responsibility, authority, and communication running from the top to the bottom of the organization, with all people reporting to only one supervisor is referred to as line organization.
Task force	A temporary team or committee formed to solve a specific short-term problem involving several departments is the task force.
Committee	A long-lasting, sometimes permanent team in the organization structure created to deal with tasks that recur regularly is the committee.
Ad hoc	Ad hoc is a Latin phrase which means "for this purpose." It generally signifies a solution that has been tailored to a specific purpose and is makeshift and non-general, such as a handcrafted network protocol or a specific-purpose equation, as opposed to general solutions.
Analogy	Analogy is either the cognitive process of transferring information from a particular subject to another particular subject (the target), or a linguistic expression corresponding to such a process. In a narrower sense, analogy is an inference or an argument from a particular to another particular, as opposed to deduction, induction, and abduction, where at least one of the premises or the conclusion is general.
Assignment	A transfer of property or some right or interest is referred to as assignment.
Frequency	Frequency refers to the speed of the up and down movements of a fluctuating economic variable; that is, the number of times per unit of time that the variable completes a cycle

153

	of up and down movement.
Sony	Sony is a multinational corporation and one of the world's largest media conglomerates founded in Tokyo, Japan. One of its divisions Sony Electronics is one of the leading manufacturers of electronics, video, communications, and information technology products for the consumer and professional markets.
Personnel	A collective term for all of the employees of an organization. Personnel is also commonly used to refer to the personnel management function or the organizational unit responsible for administering personnel programs.
Eli Lilly	Eli Lilly is a global pharmaceutical company and one of the world's largest corporations. Eli Lilly was the first distributor of methadone, an analgesic used frequently in the treatment of heroin, opium and other opioid and narcotic drug addictions.
Interpersonal skills	Interpersonal skills are used to communicate with, understand, and motivate individuals and groups.
Promotion	Promotion refers to all the techniques sellers use to motivate people to buy products or services. An attempt by marketers to inform people about products and to persuade them to participate in an exchange.
Policy	Similar to a script in that a policy can be a less than completely rational decision-making method. Involves the use of a pre-existing set of decision steps for any problem that presents itself.
Restructuring	Restructuring is the corporate management term for the act of partially dismantling and reorganizing a company for the purpose of making it more efficient and therefore more profitable.
Trend	Trend refers to the long-term movement of an economic variable, such as its average rate of increase or decrease over enough years to encompass several business cycles.
Product management	Product management is a function within a company dealing with the day-to-day management and welfare of a product or family of products at all stages of the product lifecycle. The product management function is responsible for defining the products in the marketing mix.
Supply	Supply is the aggregate amount of any material good that can be called into being at a certain price point; it comprises one half of the equation of supply and demand. In classical economic theory, a curve representing supply is one of the factors that produce price.
Functional manager	A manager who is responsible for a department that performs a single functional task and has employees with similar training and skills is referred to as a functional manager.
Human resources	Human resources refers to the individuals within the firm, and to the portion of the firm's organization that deals with hiring, firing, training, and other personnel issues.
Logistics	Those activities that focus on getting the right amount of the right products to the right place at the right time at the lowest possible cost is referred to as logistics.
Financial market	In economics, a financial market is a mechanism which allows people to trade money for securities or commodities such as gold or other precious metals. In general, any commodity market might be considered to be a financial market, if the usual purpose of traders is not the immediate consumption of the commodity, but rather as a means of delaying or accelerating consumption over time.
Cost of capital	Cost of capital refers to the percentage cost of funds used for acquiring resources for an organization, typically a weighted average of the firms cost of equity and cost of debt.
Globalization	The increasing world-wide integration of markets for goods, services and capital that attracted special attention in the late 1990s is called globalization.

Go to **Cram101.com** for the Practice Tests for this Chapter.

Capital	Capital generally refers to financial wealth, especially that used to start or maintain a business. In classical economics, capital is one of four factors of production, the others being land and labor and entrepreneurship.
Competitiveness	Competitiveness usually refers to characteristics that permit a firm to compete effectively with other firms due to low cost or superior technology, perhaps internationally.
Profit	Profit refers to the return to the resource entrepreneurial ability; total revenue minus total cost.
Technology	The body of knowledge and techniques that can be used to combine economic resources to produce goods and services is called technology.
Cartel	Cartel refers to a group of firms that seeks to raise the price of a good by restricting its supply. The term is usually used for international groups, especially involving state-owned firms and/or governments.
Joint venture	Joint venture refers to an undertaking by two parties for a specific purpose and duration, taking any of several legal forms.
Domestic	From or in one's own country. A domestic producer is one that produces inside the home country. A domestic price is the price inside the home country. Opposite of 'foreign' or 'world.'.
Gain	In finance, gain is a profit or an increase in value of an investment such as a stock or bond. Gain is calculated by fair market value or the proceeds from the sale of the investment minus the sum of the purchase price and all costs associated with it.
General Electric	In 1876, Thomas Alva Edison opened a new laboratory in Menlo Park, New Jersey. Out of the laboratory was to come perhaps the most famous invention of all—a successful development of the incandescent electric lamp. By 1890, Edison had organized his various businesses into the Edison General Electric Company.
Patent	The legal right to the proceeds from and control over the use of an invented product or process, granted for a fixed period of time, usually 20 years. Patent is one form of intellectual property that is subject of the TRIPS agreement.
Product line	A group of products that are physically similar or are intended for a similar market are called the product line.
Market share	That fraction of an industry's output accounted for by an individual firm or group of firms is called market share.
Great Depression	The period of severe economic contraction and high unemployment that began in 1929 and continued throughout the 1930s is referred to as the Great Depression.
Trade barrier	An artificial disincentive to export and/or import, such as a tariff, quota, or other NTB is called a trade barrier.
Depression	Depression refers to a prolonged period characterized by high unemployment, low output and investment, depressed business confidence, falling prices, and widespread business failures. A milder form of business downturn is a recession.
Organizational development	The application of behavioral science knowledge in a longrange effort to improve an organization's ability to cope with change in its external environment and increase its problem-solving capabilities is referred to as organizational development.
Leadership	Management merely consists of leadership applied to business situations; or in other words: management forms a sub-set of the broader process of leadership.
Anticipation	In finance, anticipation is where debts are paid off early, generally in order to pay less

Go to **Cram101.com** for the Practice Tests for this Chapter.

Go to **Cram101.com** for the Practice Tests for this Chapter.
And, **NEVER** highlight a book again!

interest.

Trust	An arrangement in which shareholders of independent firms agree to give up their stock in exchange for trust certificates that entitle them to a share of the trust's common profits.
Prejudice	Prejudice is, as the name implies, the process of "pre-judging" something. It implies coming to a judgment on a subject before learning where the preponderance of evidence actually lies, or forming a judgment without direct experience.
Regular meeting	A meeting held by the board of directors that is held at regular intervals at the time and place established in the bylaws is called a regular meeting.
Management team	A management team is directly responsible for managing the day-to-day operations (and profitability) of a company.
Hierarchy	A system of grouping people in an organization according to rank from the top down in which all subordinate managers must report to one person is called a hierarchy.
Appeal	Appeal refers to the act of asking an appellate court to overturn a decision after the trial court's final judgment has been entered.
Reorganization	Reorganization occurs, among other instances, when one corporation acquires another in a merger or acquisition, a single corporation divides into two or more entities, or a corporation makes a substantial change in its capital structure.
Common market	Common market refers to a group of countries that eliminate all barriers to movement of both goods and factors among themselves, and that also, on each product, agree to levy the same tariff on imports from outside the group.
Innovation	Innovation refers to the first commercially successful introduction of a new product, the use of a new method of production, or the creation of a new form of business organization.
Enterprise	Enterprise refers to another name for a business organization. Other similar terms are business firm, sometimes simply business, sometimes simply firm, as well as company, and entity.
Rebalancing	Rebalancing is the action of bringing a portfolio of investments that has deviated away from one's target asset allocation back into line. Under-weighted securities can be purchased with newly saved money; alternatively, over-weighted securities can be sold to purchase under-weighted securities.
Closing	The finalization of a real estate sales transaction that passes title to the property from the seller to the buyer is referred to as a closing. Closing is a sales term which refers to the process of making a sale. It refers to reaching the final step, which may be an exchange of money or acquiring a signature.
Global strategy	Global strategy refers to strategy focusing on increasing profitability by reaping cost reductions from experience curve and location economies.
Cost advantage	Possession of a lower cost of production or operation than a competing firm or country is cost advantage.
General manager	A manager who is responsible for several departments that perform different functions is called general manager.
Bureaucracy	Bureaucracy refers to an organization with many layers of managers who set rules and regulations and oversee all decisions.
Competitive market	A market in which no buyer or seller has market power is called a competitive market.
Equity	Equity is the name given to the set of legal principles, in countries following the English

Go to **Cram101.com** for the Practice Tests for this Chapter.

common law tradition, which supplement strict rules of law where their application would operate harshly, so as to achieve what is sometimes referred to as "natural justice."

Stockholder	A stockholder is an individual or company (including a corporation) that legally owns one or more shares of stock in a joined stock company. The shareholders are the owners of a corporation. Companies listed at the stock market strive to enhance shareholder value.
Shares	Shares refer to an equity security, representing a shareholder's ownership of a corporation. Shares are one of a finite number of equal portions in the capital of a company, entitling the owner to a proportion of distributed, non-reinvested profits known as dividends and to a portion of the value of the company in case of liquidation.
Layoff	A layoff is the termination of an employee or (more commonly) a group of employees for business reasons, such as the decision that certain positions are no longer necessary.
Contract	A contract is a "promise" or an "agreement" that is enforced or recognized by the law. In the civil law, a contract is considered to be part of the general law of obligations.
Value added	The value of output minus the value of all intermediate inputs, representing therefore the contribution of, and payments to, primary factors of production a value added.
Growth strategy	A strategy based on investing in companies and sectors which are growing faster than their peers is a growth strategy. The benefits are usually in the form of capital gains rather than dividends.
Revenue	Revenue is a U.S. business term for the amount of money that a company receives from its activities, mostly from sales of products and/or services to customers.
Middle management	Middle management refers to the level of management that includes general managers, division managers, and branch and plant managers who are responsible for tactical planning and controlling.
Firm	An organization that employs resources to produce a good or service for profit and owns and operates one or more plants is referred to as a firm.
Speculation	The purchase or sale of an asset in hopes that its price will rise or fall respectively, in order to make a profit is called speculation.
Brand	A name, symbol, or design that identifies the goods or services of one seller or group of sellers and distinguishes them from the goods and services of competitors is a brand.
Digital Revolution	The Digital Revolution describes the effects of rapid drop in cost and ongoing improvement of digital devices such as computers replacing or emulating analog devices, enabling former unthinkable innovations like the World Wide Web (WWW). It includes changes in technology and society, and is often specifically used to refer to the controversies that occur as these technologies are widely adopted.
Advertising	Advertising refers to paid, nonpersonal communication through various media by organizations and individuals who are in some way identified in the advertising message.
Points	Loan origination fees that may be deductible as interest by a buyer of property. A seller of property who pays points reduces the selling price by the amount of the points paid for the buyer.
Assembly line	An assembly line is a manufacturing process in which interchangeable parts are added to a product in a sequential manner to create a finished product.
Tactic	A short-term immediate decision that, in its totality, leads to the achievement of strategic goals is called a tactic.
Divisional	A divisional structure is found in diversified organizations, they contain separate divisions

structure	that are based around individual product lines or on the geographic areas of the markets being served.
Small business	Small business refers to a business that is independently owned and operated, is not dominant in its field of operation, and meets certain standards of size in terms of employees or annual receipts.
Capital requirement	The capital requirement is a bank regulation, which sets a framework on how banks and depository institutions must handle their capital. The categorization of assets and capital is highly standardized so that it can be risk weighted.
Retained earnings	Cumulative earnings of a company that are not distributed to the owners and are reinvested in the business are called retained earnings.
Working capital	The dollar difference between total current assets and total current liabilities is called working capital.
Fund	Independent accounting entity with a self-balancing set of accounts segregated for the purposes of carrying on specific activities is referred to as a fund.
Operating profit	Operating profit is a measure of a company's earning power from ongoing operations, equal to earnings before the deduction of interest payments and income taxes.
Commercial bank	A firm that engages in the business of banking is a commercial bank.
Transfer price	Transfer price refers to the price one subunit charges for a product or service supplied to another subunit of the same organization.
Fixed asset	Fixed asset, also known as property, plant, and equipment (PP&E), is a term used in accountancy for assets and property which cannot easily be converted into cash. This can be compared with current assets such as cash or bank accounts, which are described as liquid assets. In most cases, only tangible assets are referred to as fixed.
Exchange	The trade of things of value between buyer and seller so that each is better off after the trade is called the exchange.
Licensing agreement	Detailed and comprehensive written agreement between the licensor and licensee that sets forth the express terms of their agreement is called a licensing agreement.
Licensing	Licensing is a form of strategic alliance which involves the sale of a right to use certain proprietary knowledge (so called intellectual property) in a defined way.
Trade liberalization	Reduction of tariffs and removal or relaxation of NTBs is referred to as trade liberalization.
Developing country	Developing country refers to a country whose per capita income is low by world standards. Same as LDC. As usually used, it does not necessarily connote that the country's income is rising.
Manufacturing costs	Costs incurred in a manufacturing process, which consist of direct material, direct labor, and manufacturing overhead are referred to as manufacturing costs.
Motorola	The Six Sigma quality system was developed at Motorola even though it became most well known because of its use by General Electric. It was created by engineer Bill Smith, under the direction of Bob Galvin (son of founder Paul Galvin) when he was running the company.
Zenith	Zenith is an American manufacturer of televisions headquartered in Lincolnshire, Illinois. It was the inventor of the modern remote control, and it introduced HDTV in North America.
Expatriate manager	A national of one country appointed to a management position in another country is an expatriate manager.

Go to **Cram101.com** for the Practice Tests for this Chapter.

Go to **Cram101.com** for the Practice Tests for this Chapter.
And, **NEVER** highlight a book again!

Expatriate	Employee sent by his or her company to live and manage operations in a different country is called an expatriate.
Foreign subsidiary	A company owned in a foreign country by another company is referred to as foreign subsidiary.
Accounting	A system that collects and processes financial information about an organization and reports that information to decision makers is referred to as accounting.
Merchandising	Merchandising refers to the business of acquiring finished goods for resale, either in a wholesale or a retail operation.
Host country	The country in which the parent-country organization seeks to locate or has already located a facility is a host country.
Localization	As an element of wireless marketing strategy, transmitting messages that are relevant to the user's current geographical location are referred to as localization.
Delegation	Delegation is the handing of a task over to another person, usually a subordinate. It is the assignment of authority and responsibility to another person to carry out specific activities.
Integration	Economic integration refers to reducing barriers among countries to transactions and to movements of goods, capital, and labor, including harmonization of laws, regulations, and standards. Integrated markets theoretically function as a unified market.
Return on sales	Return on sales refers to the percent of net income generated by each dollar of sales; computed by dividing net income before taxes by sales revenue.
Royalties	Remuneration paid to the owners of technology, patents, or trade names for the use of same name are called royalties.
Financial assets	Financial assets refer to monetary claims or obligations by one party against another party. Examples are bonds, mortgages, bank loans, and equities.
Bubble economy	Term for an economy in which the presence of one or more bubbles in its asset markets is a dominant feature of its performance. Japan was said to be a bubble economy in the late 1980s.
Stock market	An organized marketplace in which common stocks are traded. In the United States, the largest stock market is the New York Stock Exchange, on which are traded the stocks of the largest U.S. companies.
Market value	Market value refers to the price of an asset agreed on between a willing buyer and a willing seller; the price an asset could demand if it is sold on the open market.
Recession	A significant decline in economic activity. In the U.S., recession is approximately defined as two successive quarters of falling GDP, as judged by NBER.
Stock	In financial terminology, stock is the capital raized by a corporation, through the issuance and sale of shares.
Best efforts	Best efforts refer to a distribution in which the investment banker agrees to work for a commission rather than actually underwriting the issue for resale. It is a procedure that is used by smaller investment bankers with relatively unknown companies. The investment banker is not directly taking the risk for distribution.
Digital technology	Technology characterized by use of the Internet and other digital processes to conduct or support business operations is referred to as digital technology.
Profit margin	Profit margin is a measure of profitability. It is calculated using a formula and written as a percentage or a number. Profit margin = Net income before tax and interest / Revenue.

Go to **Cram101.com** for the Practice Tests for this Chapter.
And, **NEVER** highlight a book again!

Fiscal year	A fiscal year is a 12-month period used for calculating annual ("yearly") financial reports in businesses and other organizations. In many jurisdictions, regulatory laws regarding accounting require such reports once per twelve months, but do not require that the twelve months constitute a calendar year (i.e. January to December).
Portfolio	In finance, a portfolio is a collection of investments held by an institution or a private individual. Holding but not always a portfolio is part of an investment and risk-limiting strategy called diversification. By owning several assets, certain types of risk (in particular specific risk) can be reduced.
Margin	A deposit by a buyer in stocks with a seller or a stockbroker, as security to cover fluctuations in the market in reference to stocks that the buyer has purchased but for which he has not paid is a margin. Commodities are also traded on margin.
Negotiation	Negotiation is the process whereby interested parties resolve disputes, agree upon courses of action, bargain for individual or collective advantage, and/or attempt to craft outcomes which serve their mutual interests.
International Business	International business refers to any firm that engages in international trade or investment.
Context	The effect of the background under which a message often takes on more and richer meaning is a context. Context is especially important in cross-cultural interactions because some cultures are said to be high context or low context.
Administration	Administration refers to the management and direction of the affairs of governments and institutions; a collective term for all policymaking officials of a government; the execution and implementation of public policy.
Compliance	A type of influence process where a receiver accepts the position advocated by a source to obtain favorable outcomes or to avoid punishment is the compliance.
Regulation	Regulation refers to restrictions state and federal laws place on business with regard to the conduct of its activities.
Market development	Selling existing products to new markets is called market development.
Corporate goal	A strategic performance target that the entire organization must reach to pursue its vision is a corporate goal.
Evaluation	The consumer's appraisal of the product or brand on important attributes is called evaluation.
Senior executive	Senior executive means a chief executive officer, chief operating officer, chief financial officer and anyone in charge of a principal business unit or function.
Regulatory agency	Regulatory agency refers to an agency, commission, or board established by the Federal government or a state government to regulates businesses in the public interest.
Union	A worker association that bargains with employers over wages and working conditions is called a union.
Marketing Plan	Marketing plan refers to a road map for the marketing activities of an organization for a specified future period of time, such as one year or five years.
Investment	Investment refers to spending for the production and accumulation of capital and additions to inventories. In a financial sense, buying an asset with the expectation of making a return.
Senior management	Senior management is generally a team of individuals at the highest level of organizational management who have the day-to-day responsibilities of managing a corporation.

Go to **Cram101.com** for the Practice Tests for this Chapter.
And, **NEVER** highlight a book again!

Decentralization	Decentralization is the process of redistributing decision-making closer to the point of service or action. This gives freedom to managers at lower levels of the organization to make decisions.
Centralization	A structural policy in which decision-making authority is concentrated at the top of the organizational hierarchy is referred to as centralization.
Product strategy	Decisions on the management of products or services based on the conditions of a given market is product strategy. Two general strategies that are well known in the marketing discipline are marketing mix and relational marketing.
Communication channel	The pathways through which messages are communicated are called a communication channel.
Extension	Extension refers to an out-of-court settlement in which creditors agree to allow the firm more time to meet its financial obligations. A new repayment schedule will be developed, subject to the acceptance of creditors.
Niche	In industry, a niche is a situation or an activity perfectly suited to a person. A niche can imply a working position or an area suited to a person who occupies it. Basically, a job where a person is able to succeed and thrive.
Compromise	Compromise occurs when the interaction is moderately important to meeting goals and the goals are neither completely compatible nor completely incompatible.
Trial	An examination before a competent tribunal, according to the law of the land, of the facts or law put in issue in a cause, for the purpose of determining such issue is a trial. When the court hears and determines any issue of fact or law for the purpose of determining the rights of the parties, it may be considered a trial.
Corporate level	Corporate level refers to level at which top management directs overall strategy for the entire organization.
Users	Users refer to people in the organization who actually use the product or service purchased by the buying center.
Business strategy	Business strategy, which refers to the aggregated operational strategies of single business firm or that of an SBU in a diversified corporation refers to the way in which a firm competes in its chosen arenas.
Shelf life	Shelf life is the length of time that corresponds to a tolerable loss in quality of a processed food and other perishable items.
Composition	An out-of-court settlement in which creditors agree to accept a fractional settlement on their original claim is referred to as composition.
Supply chain	Supply chain refers to the flow of goods, services, and information from the initial sources of materials and services to the delivery of products to consumers.
Holding	The holding is a court's determination of a matter of law based on the issue presented in the particular case. In other words: under this law, with these facts, this result.
Liaison	An individual who serves as a bridge between groups, tying groups together and facilitating the communication flow needed to integrate group activities is a liaison.
Research and development	The use of resources for the deliberate discovery of new information and ways of doing things, together with the application of that information in inventing new products or processes is referred to as research and development.
Resource allocation	Resource allocation refers to the manner in which an economy distributes its resources among the potential uses so as to produce a particular set of final goods.

Go to **Cram101.com** for the Practice Tests for this Chapter.

Consideration	Consideration in contract law, a basic requirement for an enforceable agreement under traditional contract principles, defined in this text as legal value, bargained for and given in exchange for an act or promise. In corporation law, cash or property contributed to a corporation in exchange for shares, or a promise to contribute such cash or property.
Budget constraint	Budget constraint refers to the maximum quantity of goods that could be purchased for a given level of income and a given set of prices.
Budget	Budget refers to an account, usually for a year, of the planned expenditures and the expected receipts of an entity. For a government, the receipts are tax revenues.
Assessment	Collecting information and providing feedback to employees about their behavior, communication style, or skills is an assessment.
Holding company	A corporation whose purpose or function is to own or otherwise hold the shares of other corporations either for investment or control is called holding company.
Diversification	Investing in a collection of assets whose returns do not always move together, with the result that overall risk is lower than for individual assets is referred to as diversification.
Acquisition	A company's purchase of the property and obligations of another company is an acquisition.
Merger	Merger refers to the combination of two firms into a single firm.
Diversification strategy	Diversification strategy is a corporate strategy that takes the organization away from both its current markets and products, as opposed to either market or product development.
Shareholder	A shareholder is an individual or company (including a corporation) that legally owns one or more shares of stock in a joined stock company.
Synergy	Corporate synergy occurs when corporations interact congruently. A corporate synergy refers to a financial benefit that a corporation expects to realize when it merges with or acquires another corporation.
Household	An economic unit that provides the economy with resources and uses the income received to purchase goods and services that satisfy economic wants is called household.
Merchant	Under the Uniform Commercial Code, one who regularly deals in goods of the kind sold in the contract at issue, or holds himself out as having special knowledge or skill relevant to such goods, or who makes the sale through an agent who regularly deals in such goods or claims such knowledge or skill is referred to as merchant.
Business development	Business development emcompasses a number of techniques designed to grow an economic enterprise. Such techniques include, but are not limited to, assessments of marketing opportunities and target markets, intelligence gathering on customers and competitors, generating leads for possible sales, followup sales activity, and formal proposal writing.
Productivity	Productivity refers to the total output of goods and services in a given period of time divided by work hours.
Purchasing	Purchasing refers to the function in a firm that searches for quality material resources, finds the best suppliers, and negotiates the best price for goods and services.
Inventory	Tangible property held for sale in the normal course of business or used in producing goods or services for sale is an inventory.
Best of the best	Term used to refer to outstanding world class benchmark firms is referred to as best of the best.
Partnership	In the common law, a partnership is a type of business entity in which partners share with each other the profits or losses of the business undertaking in which they have all invested.

Go to **Cram101.com** for the Practice Tests for this Chapter.

Go to **Cram101.com** for the Practice Tests for this Chapter.
And, **NEVER** highlight a book again!

Forming	The first stage of team development, where the team is formed and the objectives for the team are set is referred to as forming.
Conversion	Conversion refers to any distinct act of dominion wrongfully exerted over another's personal property in denial of or inconsistent with his rights therein. That tort committed by a person who deals with chattels not belonging to him in a manner that is inconsistent with the ownership of the lawful owner.
Sales forecast	Sales forecast refers to the maximum total sales of a product that a firm expects to sell during a specified time period under specified environmental conditions and its own marketing efforts.
Quota	A government-imposed restriction on quantity, or sometimes on total value, used to restrict the import of something to a specific quantity is called a quota.
Parent corporation	Parent corporation refers to a corporation that owns a controlling interest of another corporation, called a subsidiary corporation.
Mentor	An experienced employee who supervises, coaches, and guides lower-level employees by introducing them to the right people and generally being their organizational sponsor is a mentor.
Empowerment	Giving employees the authority and responsibility to respond quickly to customer requests is called empowerment.
Communication network	A communication network refer to networks that form spontaneously and naturally as the interactions among workers continue over time.
Effective communication	When the intended meaning equals the perceived meaning it is called effective communication.
International management	International management refers to the management of business operations conducted in more than one country.
Mentoring	Mentoring refers to a developmental relationship between a more experienced mentor and a less experienced partner referred to as a mentee or protégé. Usually - but not necessarily - the mentor/protégé pair will be of the same sex.
Edict	Edict refers to a command or prohibition promulgated by a sovereign and having the effect of
Siemens	Siemens is the world's largest conglomerate company. Worldwide, Siemens and its subsidiaries employs 461,000 people (2005) in 190 countries and reported global sales of €75.4 billion in fiscal year 2005.
Entry barrier	An entry barrier or barrier to entry is an obstacle in the path of a potential firm which wants to enter a given market.
Consignment	Consignment refers to a bailment for sale. The consignee does not undertake the absolute obligation to sell or pay for the goods.
Rebate	Rebate refers to a sales promotion in which money is returned to the consumer based on proof of purchase.
Switching costs	Switching costs is a term used in microeconomics, strategic management, and marketing to describe any impediment to a customer's changing of suppliers. In many markets, consumers are forced to incur costs when switching from one supplier to another. These costs are called switching costs and can come in many different shapes.
Heir	In common law jurisdictions an heir is a person who is entitled to receive a share of the decedent's property via the rules of inheritance in the jurisdiction where the decedent died or owned property at the time of his death.

Sales engineer	A salesperson who specializes in identifying, analyzing, and solving customer problems and who brings know-how and technical expertise to the selling situations, but does not actually sell goods and services is a sales engineer.
Credit	Credit refers to a recording as positive in the balance of payments, any transaction that gives rise to a payment into the country, such as an export, the sale of an asset, or borrowing from abroad.
Large country	Large country refers to a country that is large enough for its international transactions to affect economic variables abroad, usually for its trade to matter for world prices.
Information system	An information system is a system whether automated or manual, that comprises people, machines, and/or methods organized to collect, process, transmit, and disseminate data that represent user information.
Virtual organization	A temporary alliance between two or more organizations that band together to undertake a specific venture is a virtual organization.
Utility	Utility refers to the want-satisfying power of a good or service; the satisfaction or pleasure a consumer obtains from the consumption of a good or service.
Cost structure	The relative proportion of an organization's fixed, variable, and mixed costs is referred to as cost structure.
Transparency	Transparency refers to a concept that describes a company being so open to other companies working with it that the once-solid barriers between them become see-through and electronic information is shared as if the companies were one.
Economics	The social science dealing with the use of scarce resources to obtain the maximum satisfaction of society's virtually unlimited economic wants is an economics.
Balance sheet	A statement of the assets, liabilities, and net worth of a firm or individual at some given time often at the end of its "fiscal year," is referred to as a balance sheet.
Profit center	Responsibility center where the manager is accountable for revenues and costs is referred to as a profit center.
Controller	Controller refers to the financial executive primarily responsible for management accounting and financial accounting. Also called chief accounting officer.
Value system	A value system refers to how an individual or a group of individuals organize their ethical or ideological values. A well-defined value system is a moral code.
Installations	Support goods, consisting of buildings and fixed equipment are called installations.
Turnkey	A turnkey is a project in which a separate entity is responsible for setting up a plant or equipment (e.g. trains/infrastructure) and putting it into operations.
Rationalization	Rationalization in economics is an attempt to change a pre-existing ad-hoc workflow into one that is based on a set of published rules.
Option	A contract that gives the purchaser the option to buy or sell the underlying financial instrument at a specified price, called the exercise price or strike price, within a specific period of time.
Markup	Markup is a term used in marketing to indicate how much the price of a product is above the cost of producing and distributing the product.
International division	Division responsible for a firm's international activities is an international division.
Management	The process of training and educating employees to become good managers and then monitoring

development	the progress of their managerial skills over time is management development.
Best practice	Best practice is a management idea which asserts that there is a technique, method, process, activity, incentive or reward that is more effective at delivering a particular outcome than any other technique, method, process, etc.
Management philosophy	Management philosophy refers to a philosophy that links key goal-related issues with key collaboration issues to come up with general ways by which the firm will manage its affairs.
Organization culture	The set of values that helps the organization's employees understand which actions are considered acceptable and which unacceptable is referred to as the organization culture.
Strategic planning	The process of determining the major goals of the organization and the policies and strategies for obtaining and using resources to achieve those goals is called strategic planning.
Gap	In December of 1995, Gap became the first major North American retailer to accept independent monitoring of the working conditions in a contract factory producing its garments. Gap is the largest specialty retailer in the United States.
Gross margin	Gross margin is an ambiguous phrase that expresses the relationship between gross profit and sales revenue as Gross Margin = Revenue - costs of good sold.
Net income	Net income is equal to the income that a firm has after subtracting costs and expenses from the total revenue. Expenses will typically include tax expense.
Expense	In accounting, an expense represents an event in which an asset is used up or a liability is incurred. In terms of the accounting equation, expenses reduce owners' equity.
Hearing	A hearing is a proceeding before a court or other decision-making body or officer. A hearing is generally distinguished from a trial in that it is usually shorter and often less formal.
Tangible	Having a physical existence is referred to as the tangible. Personal property other than real estate, such as cars, boats, stocks, or other assets.
Market position	Market position is a measure of the position of a company or product on a market.
Takeover	A takeover in business refers to one company (the acquirer) purchasing another (the target). Such events resemble mergers, but without the formation of a new company.
Harvard Business Review	Harvard Business Review is a research-based magazine written for business practitioners, it claims a high ranking business readership and enjoys the reverence of academics, executives, and management consultants. It has been the frequent publishing home for well known scholars and management thinkers.
Bottleneck	An operation where the work to be performed approaches or exceeds the capacity available to do it is a bottleneck.
United Nations	An international organization created by multilateral treaty in 1945 to promote social and economic cooperation among nations and to protect human rights is the United Nations.
Administrator	Administrator refers to the personal representative appointed by a probate court to settle the estate of a deceased person who died.
Strategy implementation	Strategy implementation refers to the process of devising structures and allocating resources to enact the strategy a company has chosen.
Brand manager	A manager who has direct responsibility for one brand or one product line is called a brand manager.
Market testing	Market testing refers to exposing actual products to prospective consumers under realistic purchase conditions to see if they will buy.

Go to **Cram101.com** for the Practice Tests for this Chapter.

Go to **Cram101.com** for the Practice Tests for this Chapter.
And, **NEVER** highlight a book again!

Homogeneous	In the context of procurement/purchasing, homogeneous is used to describe goods that do not vary in their essential characteristic irrespective of the source of supply.
Market potential	Market potential refers to maximum total sales of a product by all firms to a segment during a specified time period under specified environmental conditions and marketing efforts of the firms.
Economies of scale	In economics, returns to scale and economies of scale are related terms that describe what happens as the scale of production increases. They are different terms and not to be used interchangeably.
Scope	Scope of a project is the sum total of all projects products and their requirements or features.
Distribution channel	A distribution channel is a chain of intermediaries, each passing a product down the chain to the next organization, before it finally reaches the consumer or end-user.
Bid	A bid price is a price offered by a buyer when he/she buys a good. In the context of stock trading on a stock exchange, the bid price is the highest price a buyer of a stock is willing to pay for a share of that given stock.
Strategic alliance	Strategic alliance refers to a long-term partnership between two or more companies established to help each company build competitive market advantages.
Organization model	The Stages of Organization Model provides a system-level language for understanding the evolutionary development of organizations. The model describes seven types of dynamic equilibrium, each of which can provide a coherent basis for action. They represent the increasing complexity possible when people learn the lessons of early stages of activity and incorporate this learning while tackling more advanced challenges.
Entrepreneurship	The assembling of resources to produce new or improved products and technologies is referred to as entrepreneurship.
Human resource management	The process of evaluating human resource needs, finding people to fill those needs, and getting the best work from each employee by providing the right incentives and job environment, all with the goal of meeting the needs of the firm are called human resource management.
Resource management	Resource management is the efficient and effective deployment of an organization's resources when they are needed. Such resources may include financial resources, inventory, human skills, production resources, or information technology.
Loyalty	Marketers tend to define customer loyalty as making repeat purchases. Some argue that it should be defined attitudinally as a strongly positive feeling about the brand.
Preference	The act of a debtor in paying or securing one or more of his creditors in a manner more favorable to them than to other creditors or to the exclusion of such other creditors is a preference. In the absence of statute, a preference is perfectly good, but to be legal it must be bona fide, and not a mere subterfuge of the debtor to secure a future benefit to himself or to prevent the application of his property to his debts.
Cooperative	A business owned and controlled by the people who use it, producers, consumers, or workers with similar needs who pool their resources for mutual gain is called cooperative.
Strategic management	A philosophy of management that links strategic planning with dayto-day decision making. Strategic management seeks a fit between an organization's external and internal environments.
Journal	Book of original entry, in which transactions are recorded in a general ledger system, is referred to as a journal.

Go to **Cram101.com** for the Practice Tests for this Chapter.

Go to **Cram101.com** for the Practice Tests for this Chapter.
And, **NEVER** highlight a book again!

Strategy execution	The managerial exercise of supervizing the ongoing pursuit of strategy, implementing it, improving the efficiency with which it is executed, and showing measurable progress in achieving the targeted results is strategy execution.
Due process	Due process of law is a legal concept that ensures the government will respect all of a person's legal rights instead of just some or most of those legal rights when the government deprives a person of life, liberty, or property.
Multinational corporation	An organization that manufactures and markets products in many different countries and has multinational stock ownership and multinational management is referred to as multinational corporation.
Procedural justice	The extent to which the dynamics of an organization's decision-making processes are judged to be fair by those most affected by them is called the procedural justice.
Value judgment	Value judgment refers to an opinion of what is desirable or undesirable; belief regarding what ought or ought not to be.
Allocation of resources	Allocation of resources refers to the society's decisions on how to divide up its scarce input resources among the different outputs produced in the economy, and among the different firms or other organizations that produce those outputs.
Level playing field	The objective of those who advocate protection on the grounds the foreign firms have an unfair advantage. A level playing field would remove such advantages, although it is not usually clear what sorts of advantage would be permitted to remain.
Globalization of markets	Moving away from an economic system in which national markets are distinct entities, isolated by trade barriers and barriers of distance, time, and culture, and toward a system in which national markets are merging into one global market is globalization of markets.
Organizational commitment	A person's identification with and attachment to an organization is called organizational commitment.
Formal organization	Formal organization refers to the structure that details lines of responsibility, authority, and position; that is, the structure shown on organization charts.
Attachment	Attachment in general, the process of taking a person's property under an appropriate judicial order by an appropriate officer of the court. Used for a variety of purposes, including the acquisition of jurisdiction over the property seized and the securing of property that may be used to satisfy a debt.
Allocate	Allocate refers to the assignment of income for various tax purposes. A multistate corporation's nonbusiness income usually is distributed to the state where the nonbusiness assets are located; it is not apportioned with the rest of the entity's income.
Corporate culture	The whole collection of beliefs, values, and behaviors of a firm that send messages to those within and outside the company about how business is done is the corporate culture.
Multinational corporations	Firms that own production facilities in two or more countries and produce and sell their products globally are referred to as multinational corporations.
Diffusion	Diffusion is the process by which a new idea or new product is accepted by the market. The rate of diffusion is the speed that the new idea spreads from one consumer to the next.
Adoption	In corporation law, a corporation's acceptance of a pre-incorporation contract by action of its board of directors, by which the corporation becomes liable on the contract, is referred to as adoption.
Diffusion of innovation	Diffusion of innovation is a concept suggesting that customers first enter a market at different times, depending on their attitude to innovation and new products, and their willingness to take risks. Customers can thus be classified as innovators, early adopters,

Go to **Cram101.com** for the Practice Tests for this Chapter.

early majority, late majority and laggards.

Intangible asset	An intangible assets is defined as an asset that is not physical in nature. The most common types are trade secrets (e.g., customer lists and know-how), copyrights, patents, trademarks, and goodwill.
Joint Economic Committee	The Joint Economic Committee is one of only four joint committees of the U.S. Congress. The committee was established as a part of the Employment Act of 1946, which deemed the committee responsible for reporting the current economic condition of the United States and for making suggestions for improvement to the economy.
Contribution	In business organization law, the cash or property contributed to a business by its owners is referred to as contribution.
Task environment	Task environment includes specific organizations, groups, and individuals that influence the organization.
Accumulation	The acquisition of an increasing quantity of something. The accumulation of factors, especially capital, is a primary mechanism for economic growth.
Confirmed	When the seller's bank agrees to assume liability on the letter of credit issued by the buyer's bank the transaction is confirmed. The term means that the credit is not only backed up by the issuing foreign bank, but that payment is also guaranteed by the notifying American bank.
Slope coefficient	Coefficient term in a cost estimation model that indicates the amount by which total cost changes when a one-unit change occurs in the level of activity within the relevant range is referred to as the slope coefficient.
Slope	The slope of a line in the plane containing the x and y axes is generally represented by the letter m, and is defined as the change in the y coordinate divided by the corresponding change in the x coordinate, between two distinct points on the line.
Inflating	Inflating refers to determining real gross domestic product by increasing the dollar value of the nominal gross domestic product produced in a year in which prices are lower than those in a base year.
Accord	An agreement whereby the parties agree to accept something different in satisfaction of the original contract is an accord.
Capacity utilization rate	In economics, the capacity utilization rate is the percentage of a company, industry, or country's production capacity that is actually or currently used. It is sometimes called the operating rate.
Capacity utilization	Capacity utilization is a concept in Economics which refers to the extent to which an enterprise or a nation actually uses its installed productive capacity. Thus, it refers to the relationship between actual output produced and potential output that could be produced with installed equipment, if capacity was fully used.
Global competition	Global competition exists when competitive conditions across national markets are linked strongly enough to form a true international market and when leading competitors compete head to head in many different countries.
Alpha	Alpha is a risk-adjusted measure of the so-called "excess return" on an investment. It is a common measure of assessing active manager's performance as it is the return in excess of a benchmark index or "risk-free" investment.
Respondent	Respondent refers to a term often used to describe the party charged in an administrative proceeding. The party adverse to the appellant in a case appealed to a higher court.
Vendor	A person who sells property to a vendee is a vendor. The words vendor and vendee are more

Go to **Cram101.com** for the Practice Tests for this Chapter.
And, **NEVER** highlight a book again!

commonly applied to the seller and purchaser of real estate, and the words seller and buyer are more commonly applied to the seller and purchaser of personal property.

Categorizing	The act of placing strengths and weaknesses into categories in generic internal assessment is called categorizing.
Discount	The difference between the face value of a bond and its selling price, when a bond is sold for less than its face value it's referred to as a discount.
Buyer	A buyer refers to a role in the buying center with formal authority and responsibility to select the supplier and negotiate the terms of the contract.
Marketing management	Marketing management refers to the process of planning and executing the conception, pricing, promotion, and distribution of ideas, goods, and services to create mutually beneficial exchanges.
Relationship marketing	Marketing whose goal is to keep individual customers over time by offering them products that exactly meet their requirements is called relationship marketing.
Sales management	Planning the selling program and implementing and controlling the personal selling effort of the firm is called sales management.
Personal selling	Personal selling is interpersonal communication, often face to face, between a sales representative and an individual or group, usually with the objective of making a sale.
Advertising agency	A firm that specializes in the creation, production, and placement of advertising messages and may provide other services that facilitate the marketing communications process is an advertising agency.
Standardized product	Standardized product refers to a product whose buyers are indifferent to the seller from whom they purchase it, as long as the price charged by all sellers is the same; a product all units of which are identical and thus are perfect substitutes.
License	A license in the sphere of Intellectual Property Rights (IPR) is a document, contract or agreement giving permission or the 'right' to a legally-definable entity to do something (such as manufacture a product or to use a service), or to apply something (such as a trademark), with the objective of achieving commercial gain.
Shell	One of the original Seven Sisters, Royal Dutch/Shell is the world's third-largest oil company by revenue, and a major player in the petrochemical industry and the solar energy business. Shell has six core businesses: Exploration and Production, Gas and Power, Downstream, Chemicals, Renewables, and Trading/Shipping, and operates in more than 140 countries.
New product development	New product development is the complete process of bringing a new product to market. There are two parallel aspects to this process : one involves product engineering ; the other marketing analysis.
Global marketing	A strategy of using a common marketing plan and program for all countries in which a company operates, thus selling the product or services the same way everywhere in the world is called global marketing.
Marketing mix	The marketing mix approach to marketing is a model of crafting and implementing marketing strategies. It stresses the "mixing" or blending of various factors in such a way that both organizational and consumer (target markets) objectives are attained.
Collaboration	Collaboration occurs when the interaction between groups is very important to goal attainment and the goals are compatible. Wherein people work together —applying both to the work of individuals as well as larger collectives and societies.
Account executive	The individual who serves as the liaison between the advertising agency and the client is the account executive. The account executive is responsible for managing all of the services the

Go to **Cram101.com** for the Practice Tests for this Chapter.

agency provides to the client and representing the agency's point of view to the client.

Bargaining power	Bargaining power refers to the ability to influence the setting of prices or wages, usually arising from some sort of monopoly or monopsony position

Innovation	Innovation refers to the first commercially successful introduction of a new product, the use of a new method of production, or the creation of a new form of business organization.
Operation	A standardized method or technique that is performed repetitively, often on different materials resulting in different finished goods is called an operation.
Market	A market is, as defined in economics, a social arrangement that allows buyers and sellers to discover information and carry out a voluntary exchange of goods or services.
Labor	People's physical and mental talents and efforts that are used to help produce goods and services are called labor.
Subsidiary	A company that is controlled by another company or corporation is a subsidiary.
Trend	Trend refers to the long-term movement of an economic variable, such as its average rate of increase or decrease over enough years to encompass several business cycles.
Corporation	A legal entity chartered by a state or the Federal government that is distinct and separate from the individuals who own it is a corporation. This separation gives the corporation unique powers which other legal entities lack.
Transnational	Transnational focuses on the heightened interconnectivity between people all around the world and the loosening of boundaries between countries.
Knowledge management	Sharing, organizing and disseminating information in the simplest and most relevant way possible for the users of the information is a knowledge management.
Management	Management characterizes the process of leading and directing all or part of an organization, often a business, through the deployment and manipulation of resources. Early twentieth-century management writer Mary Parker Follett defined management as "the art of getting things done through people."
Competitive Strategy	An outline of how a business intends to compete with other firms in the same industry is called competitive strategy.
Core	A core is the set of feasible allocations in an economy that cannot be improved upon by subset of the set of the economy's consumers (a coalition). In construction, when the force in an element is within a certain center section, the core, the element will only be under compression.
Portfolio	In finance, a portfolio is a collection of investments held by an institution or a private individual. Holding but not always a portfolio is part of an investment and risk-limiting strategy called diversification. By owning several assets, certain types of risk (in particular specific risk) can be reduced.
Leadership	Management merely consists of leadership applied to business situations; or in other words: management forms a sub-set of the broader process of leadership.
Value chain	The sequence of business functions in which usefulness is added to the products or services of a company is a value chain.
Production	The creation of finished goods and services using the factors of production: land, labor, capital, entrepreneurship, and knowledge.
Marketing	Promoting and selling products or services to customers, or prospective customers, is referred to as marketing.
Manufacturing	Production of goods primarily by the application of labor and capital to raw materials and other intermediate inputs, in contrast to agriculture, mining, forestry, fishing, and services a manufacturing.
Negotiation	Negotiation is the process whereby interested parties resolve disputes, agree upon courses of

action, bargain for individual or collective advantage, and/or attempt to craft outcomes which serve their mutual interests.

Fund	Independent accounting entity with a self-balancing set of accounts segregated for the purposes of carrying on specific activities is referred to as a fund.
Integration	Economic integration refers to reducing barriers among countries to transactions and to movements of goods, capital, and labor, including harmonization of laws, regulations, and standards. Integrated markets theoretically function as a unified market.
Personnel	A collective term for all of the employees of an organization. Personnel is also commonly used to refer to the personnel management function or the organizational unit responsible for administering personnel programs.
Parent company	Parent company refers to the entity that has a controlling influence over another company. It may have its own operations, or it may have been set up solely for the purpose of owning the Subject Company.
Applied research	Applied research is conducted to solve particular problems or answer specific questions.
Research and development	The use of resources for the deliberate discovery of new information and ways of doing things, together with the application of that information in inventing new products or processes is referred to as research and development.
Delegation	Delegation is the handing of a task over to another person, usually a subordinate. It is the assignment of authority and responsibility to another person to carry out specific activities.
Authority	Authority in agency law, refers to an agent's ability to affect his principal's legal relations with third parties. Also used to refer to an actor's legal power or ability to do something. In addition, sometimes used to refer to a statute, case, or other legal source that justifies a particular result.
Asset	An item of property, such as land, capital, money, a share in ownership, or a claim on others for future payment, such as a bond or a bank deposit is an asset.
Domestic	From or in one's own country. A domestic producer is one that produces inside the home country. A domestic price is the price inside the home country. Opposite of 'foreign' or 'world.'.
Expatriate	Employee sent by his or her company to live and manage operations in a different country is called an expatriate.
Assignment	A transfer of property or some right or interest is referred to as assignment.
Subculture	A subgroups within the larger, or national, culture with unique values, ideas, and attitudes is a subculture.
Expatriate manager	A national of one country appointed to a management position in another country is an expatriate manager.
Bond	Bond refers to a debt instrument, issued by a borrower and promising a specified stream of payments to the purchaser, usually regular interest payments plus a final repayment of principal.
Budget	Budget refers to an account, usually for a year, of the planned expenditures and the expected receipts of an entity. For a government, the receipts are tax revenues.
Policy	Similar to a script in that a policy can be a less than completely rational decision-making method. Involves the use of a pre-existing set of decision steps for any problem that presents itself.

Go to **Cram101.com** for the Practice Tests for this Chapter.

Management team	A management team is directly responsible for managing the day-to-day operations (and profitability) of a company.
Conflict resolution	Conflict resolution is the process of resolving a dispute or a conflict. Successful conflict resolution occurs by providing each side's needs, and adequately addressing their interests so that they are each satisfied with the outcome. Conflict resolution aims to end conflicts before they start or lead to physical fighting.
Senior management	Senior management is generally a team of individuals at the highest level of organizational management who have the day-to-day responsibilities of managing a corporation.
Financial manager	Managers who make recommendations to top executives regarding strategies for improving the financial strength of a firm are referred to as a financial manager.
Committee	A long-lasting, sometimes permanent team in the organization structure created to deal with tasks that recur regularly is the committee.
Multinational corporation	An organization that manufactures and markets products in many different countries and has multinational stock ownership and multinational management is referred to as multinational corporation.
Complexity	The technical sophistication of the product and hence the amount of understanding required to use it is referred to as complexity. It is the opposite of simplicity.
Economy	The income, expenditures, and resources that affect the cost of running a business and household are called an economy.
Decentralization	Decentralization is the process of redistributing decision-making closer to the point of service or action. This gives freedom to managers at lower levels of the organization to make decisions.
Control system	A control system is a device or set of devices that manage the behavior of other devices. Some devices or systems are not controllable. A control system is an interconnection of components connected or related in such a manner as to command, direct, or regulate itself or another system.
Channel	Channel, in communications (sometimes called communications channel), refers to the medium used to convey information from a sender (or transmitter) to a receiver.
Competitive market	A market in which no buyer or seller has market power is called a competitive market.
Competitor	Other organizations in the same industry or type of business that provide a good or service to the same set of customers is referred to as a competitor.
Collaboration	Collaboration occurs when the interaction between groups is very important to goal attainment and the goals are compatible. Wherein people work together —applying both to the work of individuals as well as larger collectives and societies.
Cooperative	A business owned and controlled by the people who use it, producers, consumers, or workers with similar needs who pool their resources for mutual gain is called cooperative.
Compliance	A type of influence process where a receiver accepts the position advocated by a source to obtain favorable outcomes or to avoid punishment is the compliance.
Interest	In finance and economics, interest is the price paid by a borrower for the use of a lender's money. In other words, interest is the amount of paid to "rent" money for a period of time.
Financial control	A process in which a firm periodically compares its actual revenues, costs, and expenses with its projected ones is called financial control.
Interdependence	The extent to which departments depend on each other for resources or materials to accomplish

Go to **Cram101.com** for the Practice Tests for this Chapter.
And, **NEVER** highlight a book again!

	their tasks is referred to as interdependence.
Strategic choice	Strategic choice refers to an organization's strategy; the ways an organization will attempt to fulfill its mission and achieve its long-term goals.
Corporate level	Corporate level refers to level at which top management directs overall strategy for the entire organization.
Centralization	A structural policy in which decision-making authority is concentrated at the top of the organizational hierarchy is referred to as centralization.
Proprietary	Proprietary indicates that a party, or proprietor, exercises private ownership, control or use over an item of property, usually to the exclusion of other parties. Where a party, holds or claims proprietary interests in relation to certain types of property (eg. a creative literary work, or software), that property may also be the subject of intellectual property law (eg. copyright or patents).
Exchange	The trade of things of value between buyer and seller so that each is better off after the trade is called the exchange.
Cost structure	The relative proportion of an organization's fixed, variable, and mixed costs is referred to as cost structure.
Brand	A name, symbol, or design that identifies the goods or services of one seller or group of sellers and distinguishes them from the goods and services of competitors is a brand.
Credibility	The extent to which a source is perceived as having knowledge, skill, or experience relevant to a communication topic and can be trusted to give an unbiased opinion or present objective information on the issue is called credibility.
Distribution channel	A distribution channel is a chain of intermediaries, each passing a product down the chain to the next organization, before it finally reaches the consumer or end-user.
Distribution	Distribution in economics, the manner in which total output and income is distributed among individuals or factors.
Restructuring	Restructuring is the corporate management term for the act of partially dismantling and reorganizing a company for the purpose of making it more efficient and therefore more profitable.
Profit	Profit refers to the return to the resource entrepreneurial ability; total revenue minus total cost.
General manager	A manager who is responsible for several departments that perform different functions is called general manager.
Technology	The body of knowledge and techniques that can be used to combine economic resources to produce goods and services is called technology.
Diffusion	Diffusion is the process by which a new idea or new product is accepted by the market. The rate of diffusion is the speed that the new idea spreads from one consumer to the next.
Euro	The common currency of a subset of the countries of the EU, adopted January 1, 1999 is called euro.
Gain	In finance, gain is a profit or an increase in value of an investment such as a stock or bond. Gain is calculated by fair market value or the proceeds from the sale of the investment minus the sum of the purchase price and all costs associated with it.
Purchasing	Purchasing refers to the function in a firm that searches for quality material resources, finds the best suppliers, and negotiates the best price for goods and services.

Product development	In business and engineering, new product development is the complete process of bringing a new product to market. There are two parallel aspects to this process : one involves product engineering ; the other marketing analysis. Marketers see new product development as the first stage in product life cycle management, engineers as part of Product Lifecycle Management.
Supply	Supply is the aggregate amount of any material good that can be called into being at a certain price point; it comprises one half of the equation of supply and demand. In classical economic theory, a curve representing supply is one of the factors that produce price.
Parallel development	An approach to new product development that involves cross-functional team members who conduct the simultaneous development of both the product and the production process, staying with the product from conception to production is a parallel development.
Category management	An organizational system whereby managers have responsibility for the marketing programs for a particular category or line of products is a category management.
Global strategy	Global strategy refers to strategy focusing on increasing profitability by reaping cost reductions from experience curve and location economies.
Entrepreneurship	The assembling of resources to produce new or improved products and technologies is referred to as entrepreneurship.
Matrix structure	An organizational structure which typically crosses a functional approach with a product or service-based design, often resulting in employees having two bosses is the matrix structure.
Market research	Market research is the process of systematic gathering, recording and analyzing of data about customers, competitors and the market. Market research can help create a business plan, launch a new product or service, fine tune existing products and services, expand into new markets etc. It can be used to determine which portion of the population will purchase the product/service, based on variables like age, gender, location and income level. It can be found out what market characteristics your target market has.
Advertising	Advertising refers to paid, nonpersonal communication through various media by organizations and individuals who are in some way identified in the advertising message.
Reorganization	Reorganization occurs, among other instances, when one corporation acquires another in a merger or acquisition, a single corporation divides into two or more entities, or a corporation makes a substantial change in its capital structure.
Bubble economy	Term for an economy in which the presence of one or more bubbles in its asset markets is a dominant feature of its performance. Japan was said to be a bubble economy in the late 1980s.
Acquisition	A company's purchase of the property and obligations of another company is an acquisition.
Product line	A group of products that are physically similar or are intended for a similar market are called the product line.
Chief operating officer	A chief operating officer is a corporate officer responsible for managing the day-to-day activities of the corporation. The chief operating officer is one of the highest ranking members of an organization, monitoring the daily operations of the company and reporting to the chief executive officer directly.
Emerging markets	The term emerging markets is commonly used to describe business and market activity in industrializing or emerging regions of the world. It is sometimes loosely used as a replacement for emerging economies, but really signifies a business phenomenon that is not fully described by or constrained to geography or economic strength; such countries are considered to be in a transitional phase between developing and developed status.
Emerging market	The term emerging market is commonly used to describe business and market activity in

industrializing or emerging regions of the world.

Closing	The finalization of a real estate sales transaction that passes title to the property from the seller to the buyer is referred to as a closing. Closing is a sales term which refers to the process of making a sale. It refers to reaching the final step, which may be an exchange of money or acquiring a signature.
Preparation	Preparation refers to usually the first stage in the creative process. It includes education and formal training.
Globalization	The increasing world-wide integration of markets for goods, services and capital that attracted special attention in the late 1990s is called globalization.
Industry	A group of firms that produce identical or similar products is an industry. It is also used specifically to refer to an area of economic production focused on manufacturing which involves large amounts of capital investment before any profit can be realized, also called "heavy industry".
Status quo	Status quo is a Latin term meaning the present, current, existing state of affairs.
Stock option	A stock option is a specific type of option that uses the stock itself as an underlying instrument to determine the option's pay-off and therefore its value.
Option	A contract that gives the purchaser the option to buy or sell the underlying financial instrument at a specified price, called the exercise price or strike price, within a specific period of time.
Stock	In financial terminology, stock is the capital raized by a corporation, through the issuance and sale of shares.
Advertising agency	A firm that specializes in the creation, production, and placement of advertising messages and may provide other services that facilitate the marketing communications process is an advertising agency.
Expense	In accounting, an expense represents an event in which an asset is used up or a liability is incurred. In terms of the accounting equation, expenses reduce owners' equity.
Business unit	The lowest level of the company which contains the set of functions that carry a product through its life span from concept through manufacture, distribution, sales and service is a business unit.
Market development	Selling existing products to new markets is called market development.
Bureaucracy	Bureaucracy refers to an organization with many layers of managers who set rules and regulations and oversee all decisions.
Developing country	Developing country refers to a country whose per capita income is low by world standards. Same as LDC. As usually used, it does not necessarily connote that the country's income is rising.
Profit center	Responsibility center where the manager is accountable for revenues and costs is referred to as a profit center.
Lead market	Market where products are first introduced is a lead market.
Product innovation	The development and sale of a new or improved product is a product innovation. Production of a new product on a commercial basis.
Product management	Product management is a function within a company dealing with the day-to-day management and welfare of a product or family of products at all stages of the product lifecycle. The product management function is responsible for defining the products in the marketing mix.

Positioning	The art and science of fitting the product or service to one or more segments of the market in such a way as to set it meaningfully apart from competition is called positioning.
Franchise	A contractual right to sell certain products or services, use certain trademarks, or perform activities in a geographical region is called a franchise.
Product concept	The verbal and perhaps pictorial description of the benefits and features of a proposed product; also the early stage of the product development process in which only the product concept exists.
Pricing strategy	The process in which the price of a product can be determined and is decided upon is a pricing strategy.
Premium	Premium refers to the fee charged by an insurance company for an insurance policy. The rate of losses must be relatively predictable: In order to set the premium (prices) insurers must be able to estimate them accurately.
Premium pricing strategy	Premium pricing strategy is the strategy of pricing at, or near, the high end of the possible price range.
Leverage	Leverage is using given resources in such a way that the potential positive or negative outcome is magnified. In finance, this generally refers to borrowing.
Contribution	In business organization law, the cash or property contributed to a business by its owners is referred to as contribution.
Brand image	The advertising metric that measures the type and favorability of consumer perceptions of the brand is referred to as the brand image.
Investment	Investment refers to spending for the production and accumulation of capital and additions to inventories. In a financial sense, buying an asset with the expectation of making a return.
Consultant	A professional that provides expert advice in a particular field or area in which customers occassionaly require this type of knowledge is a consultant.
Service	Service refers to a "non tangible product" that is not embodied in a physical good and that typically effects some change in another product, person, or institution. Contrasts with good.
Marketing strategy	Marketing strategy refers to the means by which a marketing goal is to be achieved, usually characterized by a specified target market and a marketing program to reach it.
Market position	Market position is a measure of the position of a company or product on a market.
Users	Users refer to people in the organization who actually use the product or service purchased by the buying center.
Clinique	In 1968 Clinique was the first dermatologist-guided, allergy-tested, and fragrance-free cosmetic brand. Clinique was at that time different from most cosmetic companies in that its goal was to meet individual skin care needs by categorizing skin types.
Boot	Boot is any type of personal property received in a real property transaction that is not like kind, such as cash, mortgage notes, a boat or stock. The exchanger pays taxes on the boot to the extent of recognized capital gain. In an exchange if any funds are not used in purchasing the replacement property, that also will be called boot.
Startup	Any new company can be considered a startup, but the description is usually applied to aggressive young companies that are actively courting private financing from venture capitalists, including wealthy individuals and investment companies.
Promotion	Promotion refers to all the techniques sellers use to motivate people to buy products or services. An attempt by marketers to inform people about products and to persuade them to

	participate in an exchange.
Marketing Plan	Marketing plan refers to a road map for the marketing activities of an organization for a specified future period of time, such as one year or five years.
Framing	Framing refers to the tendency for a decision maker to be swayed by whether a decision is pitched as a positive or negative.
Context	The effect of the background under which a message often takes on more and richer meaning is a context. Context is especially important in cross-cultural interactions because some cultures are said to be high context or low context.
Managing director	Managing director is the term used for the chief executive of many limited companies in the United Kingdom, Commonwealth and some other English speaking countries. The title reflects their role as both a member of the Board of Directors but also as the senior manager.
Firm	An organization that employs resources to produce a good or service for profit and owns and operates one or more plants is referred to as a firm.
Partnership	In the common law, a partnership is a type of business entity in which partners share with each other the profits or losses of the business undertaking in which they have all invested.
Revenue	Revenue is a U.S. business term for the amount of money that a company receives from its activities, mostly from sales of products and/or services to customers.
Experience curve	Experience curve refers to function that measures the decline in cost per unit in various value-chain functions such as manufacturing, marketing, distribution, and so on, as units produced increases.
Industrial goods	Components produced for use in the production of other products are called industrial goods.
Insurance	Insurance refers to a system by which individuals can reduce their exposure to risk of large losses by spreading the risks among a large number of persons.
Bell Labs	In the early 1940s, the photovoltaic cell was developed by Russell Ohl. In 1947, the transistor, probably the most important invention developed by Bell Labs, was invented by John Bardeen, William Bradford Shockley, and Walter Houser Brattain (all of whom subsequently won the Nobel Prize in Physics in 1956).
Hierarchy	A system of grouping people in an organization according to rank from the top down in which all subordinate managers must report to one person is called a hierarchy.
Journal	Book of original entry, in which transactions are recorded in a general ledger system, is referred to as a journal.
Harvard Business Review	Harvard Business Review is a research-based magazine written for business practitioners, it claims a high ranking business readership and enjoys the reverence of academics, executives, and management consultants. It has been the frequent publishing home for well known scholars and management thinkers.
Advertisement	Advertisement is the promotion of goods, services, companies and ideas, usually by an identified sponsor. Marketers see advertising as part of an overall promotional strategy.
Information system	An information system is a system whether automated or manual, that comprises people, machines, and/or methods organized to collect, process, transmit, and disseminate data that represent user information.
Specialist	A specialist is a trader who makes a market in one or several stocks and holds the limit order book for those stocks.
Value system	A value system refers to how an individual or a group of individuals organize their ethical or ideological values. A well-defined value system is a moral code.

Go to Cram101.com for the Practice Tests for this Chapter.

Professional development	Professional development refers to vocational education with specific reference to continuing education of the person undertaking it in the area of employment, it may also provide opportunities for other career paths.
Administrator	Administrator refers to the personal representative appointed by a probate court to settle the estate of a deceased person who died.
Financial institution	A financial institution acts as an agent that provides financial services for its clients. Financial institutions generally fall under financial regulation from a government authority.
Matching	Matching refers to an accounting concept that establishes when expenses are recognized. Expenses are matched with the revenues they helped to generate and are recognized when those revenues are recognized.
Analyst	Analyst refers to a person or tool with a primary function of information analysis, generally with a more limited, practical and short term set of goals than a researcher.
Business analyst	A business analyst is responsible for analyzing the business needs of their clients and stakeholders to help identify business problems and propose solutions.
Growth strategy	A strategy based on investing in companies and sectors which are growing faster than their peers is a growth strategy. The benefits are usually in the form of capital gains rather than dividends.
Mentor	An experienced employee who supervises, coaches, and guides lower-level employees by introducing them to the right people and generally being their organizational sponsor is a mentor.
Deregulation	The lessening or complete removal of government regulations on an industry, especially concerning the price that firms are allowed to charge and leaving price to be determined by market forces a deregulation.
Exporter	A firm that sells its product in another country is an exporter.
Staffing	Staffing refers to a management function that includes hiring, motivating, and retaining the best people available to accomplish the company's objectives.
Export	In economics, an export is any good or commodity, shipped or otherwise transported out of a country, province, town to another part of the world in a legitimate fashion, typically for use in trade or sale.
Channel of communication	The means of conveying a message to a receiver is channel of communication.
Intranet	Intranet refers to a companywide network, closed to public access, that uses Internet-type technology. A set of communications links within one company that travel over the Internet but are closed to public access.
Business marketing	Business marketing is the practice of organizations, including commercial businesses, governments and institutions, facilitating the sale of their products or services to other companies or organizations that in turn resell them, use them as components in products or services they offer, or use them to support their operations.
Pillsbury	Pillsbury the company was the first in the United States to use steam rollers for processing grain. The finished product required transportation, so the Pillsburys assisted in funding railroad development in Minnesota.
Confirmed	When the seller's bank agrees to assume liability on the letter of credit issued by the buyer's bank the transaction is confirmed. The term means that the credit is not only backed up by the issuing foreign bank, but that payment is also guaranteed by the notifying American bank.

204

Go to **Cram101.com** for the Practice Tests for this Chapter.

Go to **Cram101.com** for the Practice Tests for this Chapter.
And, **NEVER** highlight a book again!

Trial	An examination before a competent tribunal, according to the law of the land, of the facts or law put in issue in a cause, for the purpose of determining such issue is a trial. When the court hears and determines any issue of fact or law for the purpose of determining the rights of the parties, it may be considered a trial.
Case study	A case study is a particular method of qualitative research. Rather than using large samples and following a rigid protocol to examine a limited number of variables, case study methods involve an in-depth, longitudinal examination of a single instance or event: a case. They provide a systematic way of looking at events, collecting data, analyzing information, and reporting the results.
Word of mouth	People influencing each other during their face-to-face converzations is called word of mouth.
Forming	The first stage of team development, where the team is formed and the objectives for the team are set is referred to as forming.
Intellectual capital	Intellectual capital makes an organization worth more than its balance sheet value. For many years, intellectual capital and goodwill meant the same thing. Today, intellectual capital management is far broader. It seeks to explain how knowledge, collaboration, and process-engagement create decisions and actions that lead to cost allocations, productivity, and finally financial performance.
Capital	Capital generally refers to financial wealth, especially that used to start or maintain a business. In classical economics, capital is one of four factors of production, the others being land and labor and entrepreneurship.
Chief executive officer	A chief executive officer is the highest-ranking corporate officer or executive officer of a corporation, or agency. In closely held corporations, it is general business culture that the office chief executive officer is also the chairman of the board.
International division	Division responsible for a firm's international activities is an international division.
International Business	International business refers to any firm that engages in international trade or investment.
Reinsurance	An allocation of the portion of the insurance risk to another company in exchange for a portion of the insurance premium is called reinsurance.
Assessment	Collecting information and providing feedback to employees about their behavior, communication style, or skills is an assessment.
Barrier to entry	Anything that prevents the entry of firms into an industry is called a barrier to entry.
Administration	Administration refers to the management and direction of the affairs of governments and institutions; a collective term for all policymaking officials of a government; the execution and implementation of public policy.
Money market	The money market, in macroeconomics and international finance, refers to the equilibration of demand for a country's domestic money to its money supply; market for short-term financial instruments.
Mutual fund	A mutual fund is a form of collective investment that pools money from many investors and invests the money in stocks, bonds, short-term money market instruments, and/or other securities. In a mutual fund, the fund manager trades the fund's underlying securities, realizing capital gains or loss, and collects the dividend or interest income.
Instrument	Instrument refers to an economic variable that is controlled by policy makers and can be used to influence other variables, called targets. Examples are monetary and fiscal policies used

Go to **Cram101.com** for the Practice Tests for this Chapter.

to achieve external and internal balance.

Variable	A variable is something measured by a number; it is used to analyze what happens to other things when the size of that number changes.
Annuity	A contract to make regular payments to a person for life or for a fixed period is an annuity.
Appeal	Appeal refers to the act of asking an appellate court to overturn a decision after the trial court's final judgment has been entered.
Organizational design	The structuring of workers so that they can best accomplish the firm's goals is referred to as organizational design.
Controller	Controller refers to the financial executive primarily responsible for management accounting and financial accounting. Also called chief accounting officer.
Economics	The social science dealing with the use of scarce resources to obtain the maximum satisfaction of society's virtually unlimited economic wants is an economics.
Trust	An arrangement in which shareholders of independent firms agree to give up their stock in exchange for trust certificates that entitle them to a share of the trust's common profits.
Effective manager	Leader of a team that consistently achieves high performance goals is an effective manager.
Core business	The core business of an organization is an idealized construct intended to express that organization's "main" or "essential" activity.
Shareholder	A shareholder is an individual or company (including a corporation) that legally owns one or more shares of stock in a joined stock company.
Entrepreneur	The owner/operator. The person who organizes, manages, and assumes the risks of a firm, taking a new idea or a new product and turning it into a successful business is an entrepreneur.
Annuities	Financial contracts under which a customer pays an annual premium in exchange for a future stream of annual payments beginning at a set age, say 65, and ending when the person dies are annuities.
Intervention	Intervention refers to an activity in which a government buys or sells its currency in the foreign exchange market in order to affect its currency's exchange rate.
Turnover	Turnover in a financial context refers to the rate at which a provider of goods cycles through its average inventory. Turnover in a human resources context refers to the characteristic of a given company or industry, relative to rate at which an employer gains and loses staff.
Agent	A person who makes economic decisions for another economic actor. A hired manager operates as an agent for a firm's owner.
Business model	A business model is the instrument by which a business intends to generate revenue and profits. It is a summary of how a company means to serve its employees and customers, and involves both strategy (what an business intends to do) as well as an implementation.
Foundation	A Foundation is a type of philanthropic organization set up by either individuals or institutions as a legal entity (either as a corporation or trust) with the purpose of distributing grants to support causes in line with the goals of the foundation.
Wholesale	According to the United Nations Statistics Division Wholesale is the resale of new and used goods to retailers, to industrial, commercial, institutional or professional users, or to other wholesalers, or involves acting as an agent or broker in buying merchandise for, or selling merchandise, to such persons or companies.

Go to **Cram101.com** for the Practice Tests for this Chapter.

Broker	In commerce, a broker is a party that mediates between a buyer and a seller. A broker who also acts as a seller or as a buyer becomes a principal party to the deal.
Incentive	An incentive is any factor (financial or non-financial) that provides a motive for a particular course of action, or counts as a reason for preferring one choice to the alternatives.
Market opportunities	Market opportunities refer to areas where a company believes there are favorable demand trends, needs, and/or wants that are not being satisfied, and where it can compete effectively.
Social Security	Social security primarily refers to a field of social welfare concerned with social protection, or protection against socially recognized conditions, including poverty, old age, disability, unemployment, families with children and others.
Demographic	A demographic is a term used in marketing and broadcasting, to describe a demographic grouping or a market segment.
Security	Security refers to a claim on the borrower future income that is sold by the borrower to the lender. A security is a type of transferable interest representing financial value.
Asset management	Asset management is the method that a company uses to track fixed assets, for example factory equipment, desks and chairs, computers, even buildings. Although the exact details of the task varies widely from company to company, asset management often includes tracking the physical location of assets, managing demand for scarce resources, and accounting tasks such as amortization.
Comprehensive	A comprehensive refers to a layout accurate in size, color, scheme, and other necessary details to show how a final ad will look. For presentation only, never for reproduction.
Accounting	A system that collects and processes financial information about an organization and reports that information to decision makers is referred to as accounting.
Contract	A contract is a "promise" or an "agreement" that is enforced or recognized by the law. In the civil law, a contract is considered to be part of the general law of obligations.
Financial transaction	A financial transaction involves a change in the status of the finances of two or more businesses or individuals.
Exchange rate	Exchange rate refers to the price at which one country's currency trades for another, typically on the exchange market.
Termination	The ending of a corporation that occurs only after the winding-up of the corporation's affairs, the liquidation of its assets, and the distribution of the proceeds to the claimants are referred to as a termination.
Balance	In banking and accountancy, the outstanding balance is the amount of money owned, (or due), that remains in a deposit account (or a loan account) at a given date, after all past remittances, payments and withdrawal have been accounted for. It can be positive (then, in the balance sheet of a firm, it is an asset) or negative (a liability).
Ledger	Ledger refers to a specialized accounting book in which information from accounting journals is accumulated into specific categories and posted so that managers can find all the information about one account in the same place.
Business development	Business development emcompasses a number of techniques designed to grow an economic enterprise. Such techniques include, but are not limited to, assessments of marketing opportunities and target markets, intelligence gathering on customers and competitors, generating leads for possible sales, followup sales activity, and formal proposal writing.
Money management	Money management refers to managing a firm's global cash resources efficiently.

Go to **Cram101.com** for the Practice Tests for this Chapter.

211

Financial risk	The risk related to the inability of the firm to meet its debt obligations as they come due is called financial risk.
Regulation	Regulation refers to restrictions state and federal laws place on business with regard to the conduct of its activities.
Prototype	A prototype is built to test the function of a new design before starting production of a product.
Management philosophy	Management philosophy refers to a philosophy that links key goal-related issues with key collaboration issues to come up with general ways by which the firm will manage its affairs.
Electronic mail	Electronic mail refers to electronic written communication between individuals using computers connected to the Internet.
Venue	A requirement distinct from jurisdiction that the court be geographically situated so that it is the most appropriate and convenient court to try the case is the venue.
Financial report	Financial report refers to a written statement-also called an accountant's certificate, accountant's opinion, or audit report-prepared by an independent accountant or auditor after an audit.
Training and development	All attempts to improve productivity by increasing an employee's ability to perform is training and development.
Stock exchange	A stock exchange is a corporation or mutual organization which provides facilities for stock brokers and traders, to trade company stocks and other securities.
Book value	The book value of an asset or group of assets is sometimes the price at which they were originally acquired, in many cases equal to purchase price.
Information technology	Information technology refers to technology that helps companies change business by allowing them to use new methods.
Annual report	An annual report is prepared by corporate management that presents financial information including financial statements, footnotes, and the management discussion and analysis.
Inputs	The inputs used by a firm or an economy are the labor, raw materials, electricity and other resources it uses to produce its outputs.
Financial measure	A financial measure is often used as a very simple mechanism to describe the performance of a business or investment. Because they are easily calculated they can not only be used to compare year on year results but also to compare and set norms for a particular type of business or investment.
Utility	Utility refers to the want-satisfying power of a good or service; the satisfaction or pleasure a consumer obtains from the consumption of a good or service.
Balance sheet	A statement of the assets, liabilities, and net worth of a firm or individual at some given time often at the end of its "fiscal year," is referred to as a balance sheet.
Resource allocation	Resource allocation refers to the manner in which an economy distributes its resources among the potential uses so as to produce a particular set of final goods.
Holding company	A corporation whose purpose or function is to own or otherwise hold the shares of other corporations either for investment or control is called holding company.
Holding	The holding is a court's determination of a matter of law based on the issue presented in the particular case. In other words: under this law, with these facts, this result.
Mistake	In contract law a mistake is incorrect understanding by one or more parties to a contract and may be used as grounds to invalidate the agreement. Common law has identified three different

Go to **Cram101.com** for the Practice Tests for this Chapter.

types of mistake in contract: unilateral mistake, mutual mistake, and common mistake.

Openness	Openness refers to the extent to which an economy is open, often measured by the ratio of its trade to GDP.
Customer service	The ability of logistics management to satisfy users in terms of time, dependability, communication, and convenience is called the customer service.
Credit	Credit refers to a recording as positive in the balance of payments, any transaction that gives rise to a payment into the country, such as an export, the sale of an asset, or borrowing from abroad.
Underwriting	The process of selling securities and, at the same time, assuring the seller a specified price is underwriting. Underwriting is done by investment bankers and represents a form of risk taking.
Generation x	Generation x refers to the 15 percent of the U.S. population born between 1965 and 1976 a period also known as the baby bust.
Downturn	A decline in a stock market or economic cycle is a downturn.
Virtual corporation	A temporary, networked organization made up of replaceable firms that join the network and leave it as needed is called virtual corporation. virtual corporation is a firm that outsources the majority of its functions. Typically, a small group of executives will contract out and then coordinate the designing, making, and selling of products or services.In theory, this allows small groups of knowledgeable executives to find the lowest supplier for any given service, and to concentrate solely on the "big picture". In theory, it also allows firms to be nimble, rapidly ramping up production without having to slowly develop people and competencies. However, as the old saying goes, there's no such thing as a free lunch. In practice, virtual firms are scarce due to the difficulties in constructing elaborate contracts that specify the distributions of profits, and because the short-term profit-centered relationships implied by the virtual structure discourage co-operation among the parts of the organization. Moreover, the contracts often fail to effectively measure the ephemeral quality. As a result, there is a tendency for suppliers to defect (in prisoner's dilemma parlance) by providing products that are "up to specs", but that fall short of rigorous quality standards.The term was a buzzword in the 1990s for several reasons. The concept became popular during the dot-com era, when demand was high for new kind of services that traditionally organized companies relied on outsourcing to perform. In the day of the dot-com related businesses it seemed like everyone was so busy that they had to outsource most of their jobs to someone else. The idea that you actually didn't need to have a large number of regular employees to be a major player caught on, and thus virtual corporation became one of the typical ways of describing this phenomenon. In fact it seemed like business in general was about to restructure into a web of temporary outsourcing deals. The existence of the internet helped facilitate communication and cooperation across this web of contracts.The technology of the time was not up to the task though, now with the advent of web services new virtual corporation possibilities exist.But the structure didn't just apply to trendy fast changing dot-com corporations. Other more traditional producers of consumer goods etc decided that they should sell their own production facilites and convert into making contracts on the fly with whoever could produce their type of product for the lowest price. Instead of managing a large structure of the entire value chain they could focus on marketing and branding their products. Companies like The Walt Disney Company, Nike Inc., and GAP became notorious for production of their goods in sweatshop conditions particularly in Asia.Globewide Network Academy was one of the world's first virtual corporations ever incorporated in real, more than 10 years ago in Texas, Austin http://www.gnacademy.org/.A virtual corporation, virtual organization or virtual enterprise is a manifestation of Collaborative Networks.A large number of researchers in this area are organized around the

	non-profit SOCOLNET - Society of Collaborative Networks. A virtual corporation is also a company which exists in cyberspace and not in the real world.
Administrative cost	An administrative cost is all executive, organizational, and clerical costs associated with the general management of an organization rather than with manufacturing, marketing, or selling
Customer loyalty	Marketers tend to define customer loyalty as making repeat purchases. Some argue that it should be defined attitudinally as a strongly positive feeling about the brand.
Consolidation	The combination of two or more firms, generally of equal size and market power, to form an entirely new entity is a consolidation.
Outsourcing	Outsourcing refers to a production activity that was previously done inside a firm or plant that is now conducted outside that firm or plant.
Discount	The difference between the face value of a bond and its selling price, when a bond is sold for less than its face value it's referred to as a discount.
Trade pact	A trade pact is a wide ranging tax, tariff and trade agreement that often includes investment guarantees. They are frequently politically contentious since they may change economic customs and deepen interdependence with trade partners.
Pact	Pact refers to a set of principles endorsed by 21 of the largest U.S. ad agencies aimed at improving the research used in preparing and testing ads, providing a better creative product for clients, and controlling the cost of TV commercials.
Ford	Ford is an American company that manufactures and sells automobiles worldwide. Ford introduced methods for large-scale manufacturing of cars, and large-scale management of an industrial workforce, especially elaborately engineered manufacturing sequences typified by the moving assembly lines.
Board of directors	The group of individuals elected by the stockholders of a corporation to oversee its operations is a board of directors.
Mission statement	Mission statement refers to an outline of the fundamental purposes of an organization.
Labor relations	The field of labor relations looks at the relationship between management and workers, particularly groups of workers represented by a labor union.
Labor market	Any arrangement that brings buyers and sellers of labor services together to agree on conditions of work and pay is called a labor market.
Best practice	Best practice is a management idea which asserts that there is a technique, method, process, activity, incentive or reward that is more effective at delivering a particular outcome than any other technique, method, process, etc.
Not invented here	Not Invented Here (NIH) is a pejorative term used to describe a persistent corporate or institutional culture that either intentionally or unintentionally avoids using previously performed research or knowledge because the research and developed knowledge was not originally executed in-house.
Remainder	A remainder in property law is a future interest created in a transferee that is capable of becoming possessory upon the natural termination of a prior estate created by the same instrument.
Inception	The date and time on which coverage under an insurance policy takes effect is inception. Also refers to the date at which a stock or mutual fund was first traded.
Joint venture	Joint venture refers to an undertaking by two parties for a specific purpose and duration,

taking any of several legal forms.

Union	A worker association that bargains with employers over wages and working conditions is called a union.
Excess capacity	Excess capacity refers to plant resources that are underused when imperfectly competitive firms produce less output than that associated with purely competitive firms, who by definiation, are achieving minimum average total cost.
Raw material	Raw material refers to a good that has not been transformed by production; a primary product.
Consumption	In Keynesian economics consumption refers to personal consumption expenditure, i.e., the purchase of currently produced goods and services out of income, out of savings (net worth), or from borrowed funds. It refers to that part of disposable income that does not go to saving.
Human resources	Human resources refers to the individuals within the firm, and to the portion of the firm's organization that deals with hiring, firing, training, and other personnel issues.
Grant	Grant refers to an intergovernmental transfer of funds . Since the New Deal, state and local governments have become increasingly dependent upon federal grants for an almost infinite variety of programs.
Performance target	A task established for an employee that provides the comparative basis for performance appraisal is a performance target.
Business plan	A detailed written statement that describes the nature of the business, the target market, the advantages the business will have in relation to competition, and the resources and qualifications of the owner is referred to as a business plan.
Productivity	Productivity refers to the total output of goods and services in a given period of time divided by work hours.
Proactive	To be proactive is to act before a situation becomes a source of confrontation or crisis. It is the opposite of "retroactive," which refers to actions taken after an event.
Regular meeting	A meeting held by the board of directors that is held at regular intervals at the time and place established in the bylaws is called a regular meeting.
Customer focus	Customer focus acknowledges that the more a company understands and meets the real needs of its consumers, the more likely it is to have happy customers who come back for more, and tell their friends.
Facilitator	A facilitator is someone who skilfully helps a group of people understand their common objectives and plan to achieve them without personally taking any side of the argument.
Controlling	A management function that involves determining whether or not an organization is progressing toward its goals and objectives, and taking corrective action if it is not is called controlling.
Production efficiency	A situation in which the economy cannot produce more of one good without producing less of some other good is referred to as production efficiency.
Continuous improvement	The constant effort to eliminate waste, reduce response time, simplify the design of both products and processes, and improve quality and customer service is referred to as continuous improvement.
Foreign subsidiary	A company owned in a foreign country by another company is referred to as foreign subsidiary.
Charismatic leader	A leader who has the ability to motivate subordinates to transcend their expected performance is a charismatic leader.

Strike	The withholding of labor services by an organized group of workers is referred to as a strike.
Hearing	A hearing is a proceeding before a court or other decision-making body or officer. A hearing is generally distinguished from a trial in that it is usually shorter and often less formal.
Main product	Product from a joint production process that has a high sales value compared with the sales values of all other products of the joint production process is referred to as main product.
Argument	The discussion by counsel for the respective parties of their contentions on the law and the facts of the case being tried in order to aid the jury in arriving at a correct and just conclusion is called argument.
Freelance	A freelance worker is a self-employed person working in a profession or trade in which full-time employment is also common.
License	A license in the sphere of Intellectual Property Rights (IPR) is a document, contract or agreement giving permission or the 'right' to a legally-definable entity to do something (such as manufacture a product or to use a service), or to apply something (such as a trademark), with the objective of achieving commercial gain.
Yield	The interest rate that equates a future value or an annuity to a given present value is a yield.
Bid	A bid price is a price offered by a buyer when he/she buys a good. In the context of stock trading on a stock exchange, the bid price is the highest price a buyer of a stock is willing to pay for a share of that given stock.
Volkswagen	Volkswagen or VW is an automobile manufacturer based in Wolfsburg, Germany in the state of Lower Saxony. It forms the core of this Group, one of the world's four largest car producers. Its German tagline is "Aus Liebe zum Automobil", which is translated as "For the love of the car" - or, For Love of the People's Cars,".
Tender	An unconditional offer of payment, consisting in the actual production in money or legal tender of a sum not less than the amount due.
Variance	Variance refers to a measure of how much an economic or statistical variable varies across values or observations. Its calculation is the same as that of the covariance, being the covariance of the variable with itself.
Bankruptcy	Bankruptcy is a legally declared inability or impairment of ability of an individual or organization to pay their creditors.
Success factor	The term success factor refers to the characteristics necessary for high performance; knowledge, skills, abilities, behaviors.
Critical success factor	Critical Success Factor is a business term for an element which is necessary for an organization or project to achieve its mission.
Tangible	Having a physical existence is referred to as the tangible. Personal property other than real estate, such as cars, boats, stocks, or other assets.
Buyer	A buyer refers to a role in the buying center with formal authority and responsibility to select the supplier and negotiate the terms of the contract.
Empowerment	Giving employees the authority and responsibility to respond quickly to customer requests is called empowerment.
Enterprise	Enterprise refers to another name for a business organization. Other similar terms are business firm, sometimes simply business, sometimes simply firm, as well as company, and entity.

Goldman Sachs	Goldman Sachs is widely respected as a financial advisor to some of the most important companies, largest governments, and wealthiest families in the world. It is a primary dealer in the U.S. Treasury securities market. It offers its clients mergers & acquisitions advisory, provides underwriting services, engages in proprietary trading, invests in private equity deals, and also manages the wealth of affluent individuals and families.
Internal integration	The creation of a collective identity and way of working and living together within an organization is referred to as internal integration.
Fragmentation	Fragmentation refers to the splitting of production processes into separate parts that can be done in different locations, including in different countries.
Performance management	The means through which managers ensure that employees' activities and outputs are congruent with the organization's goals is referred to as performance management.
Sony	Sony is a multinational corporation and one of the world's largest media conglomerates founded in Tokyo, Japan. One of its divisions Sony Electronics is one of the leading manufacturers of electronics, video, communications, and information technology products for the consumer and professional markets.
Technological change	The introduction of new methods of production or new products intended to increase the productivity of existing inputs or to raise marginal products is a technological change.
Oracle	In 2004, sales at Oracle grew at a rate of 14.5% to $6.2 billion, giving it 41.3% and the top share of the relational-database market. Their main competitors in the database arena are IBM DB2 and Microsoft SQL Server, and to a lesser extent Sybase, Teradata, Informix, and MySQL. In the applications arena, their main competitor is SAP.
Castrol	Castrol was founded on March 19th 1899 by Charles "Cheers" Wakefield in England. It was originally named the Wakefield Oil Company. In 1909, the company began production of a new automotive lubricant named Castrol. The company developed specific oil applications for various applications of the new internal combustion engine, including automobiles, motorcycles, and aircraft.
Merger	Merger refers to the combination of two firms into a single firm.
Amoco	Amoco was formed as Standard Oil (Indiana) in 1889 by John D. Rockefeller as part of the Standard Oil trust. In 1910, with the rise in popularity of the automobile, Amoco decided to specialize in providing gas to everyday families and their cars. In 1911, the year it became independent from the Standard Oil trust, the company sold 88% of the gasoline and kerosene sold in the midwest.
Direct marketing	Promotional element that uses direct communication with consumers to generate a response in the form of an order, a request for further information, or a visit to a retail outlet is direct marketing.
Galbraith	Galbraith was a prolific author, producing four dozen books and over a thousand articles on various subjects. His most famous works were perhaps a popular trilogy of books on economics, "American Capitalism" (1952), "The Affluent Society (1958)", and "The New Industrial State" (1967).
Middle management	Middle management refers to the level of management that includes general managers, division managers, and branch and plant managers who are responsible for tactical planning and controlling.
Horizontal integration	Horizontal integration refers to production of different varieties of the same product, or different products at the same level of processing, within a single firm. This may, but need not, take place in subsidiaries in different countries.
Standardization	Standardization, in the context related to technologies and industries, is the process of

establishing a technical standard among competing entities in a market, where this will bring benefits without hurting competition.

Knowledge base	Knowledge base refers to a database that includes decision rules for use of the data, which may be qualitative as well as quantitative.
Reengineering	The fundamental rethinking and redesign of business processes to achieve improvements in critical measures of performance, such as cost, quality, service, speed, and customer satisfaction is referred to as reengineering.
Bottleneck	An operation where the work to be performed approaches or exceeds the capacity available to do it is a bottleneck.
Strategic alliance	Strategic alliance refers to a long-term partnership between two or more companies established to help each company build competitive market advantages.
Operating margin	In business, operating margin is the ratio of operating income divided by net sales.
Margin	A deposit by a buyer in stocks with a seller or a stockbroker, as security to cover fluctuations in the market in reference to stocks that the buyer has purchased but for which he has not paid is a margin. Commodities are also traded on margin.
Rationalization	Rationalization in economics is an attempt to change a pre-existing ad-hoc workflow into one that is based on a set of published rules.
Objection	In the trial of a case the formal remonstrance made by counsel to something that has been said or done, in order to obtain the court's ruling thereon is an objection.
Enabling	Enabling refers to giving workers the education and tools they need to assume their new decision-making powers.
Interactive media	A variety of media that allows the consumer to interact with the source of the message, actively receiving information and altering images, responding to questions, and so on is an interactive media.
Mass media	Mass media refers to non-personal channels of communication that allow a message to be sent to many individuals at one time.
Targeting	In advertizing, targeting is to select a demographic or other group of people to advertise to, and create advertisements appropriately.
Actionable	Actionable refers to capable of being remedied by a legal action or claim.
Interactive marketing	Interactive marketing refers to two-way buyer-seller electronic communications in a computer-mediated environment in which the buyer controls the kind and amount of information received from the seller.
Standing	Standing refers to the legal requirement that anyone seeking to challenge a particular action in court must demonstrate that such action substantially affects his legitimate interests before he will be entitled to bring suit.
Management system	A management system is the framework of processes and procedures used to ensure that an organization can fulfill all tasks required to achieve its objectives.
Sandbagging	In the sales environment, sandbagging is holding aside completed sales with the expectation of producing them at a specific time of the week or month when there might be extra incentive or higher commissions.
Alignment	Term that refers to optimal coordination among disparate departments and divisions within a firm is referred to as alignment.
Direct orders	The result of direct marketing offers that contain all the information necessary for a

prospective buyer to make a decision to purchase and complete the transaction are direct orders.

Organizational communication	Thee process by which information is exchanged in the organizational setting is organizational communication.
Teamwork	That which occurs when group members work together in ways that utilize their skills well to accomplish a purpose is called teamwork.
Equity	Equity is the name given to the set of legal principles, in countries following the English common law tradition, which supplement strict rules of law where their application would operate harshly, so as to achieve what is sometimes referred to as "natural justice."
Levy	Levy refers to imposing and collecting a tax or tariff.
Fortune magazine	Fortune magazine is America's longest-running business magazine. Currently owned by media conglomerate Time Warner, it was founded in 1930 by Henry Luce. It is known for its regular features ranking companies by revenue.
Benefactor	A benefactor is a person or other entity providing money or other benefits to another; the person receiving them is called a beneficiary.
Capitalism	Capitalism refers to an economic system in which capital is mostly owned by private individuals and corporations. Contrasts with communism.
Vertical integration	Vertical integration refers to production of different stages of processing of a product within the same firm.
Competitive advantage	A business is said to have a competitive advantage when its unique strengths, often based on cost, quality, time, and innovation, offer consumers a greater percieved value and there by diffentiating it from its competitors.
New product development	New product development is the complete process of bringing a new product to market. There are two parallel aspects to this process : one involves product engineering ; the other marketing analysis.
Honda	With more than 14 million internal combustion engines built each year, Honda is the largest engine-maker in the world. In 2004, the company began to produce diesel motors, which were both very quiet whilst not requiring particulate filters to pass pollution standards. It is arguable, however, that the foundation of their success is the motorcycle division.
Automation	Automation allows machines to do work previously accomplished by people.
Analogy	Analogy is either the cognitive process of transferring information from a particular subject to another particular subject (the target), or a linguistic expression corresponding to such a process. In a narrower sense, analogy is an inference or an argument from a particular to another particular, as opposed to deduction, induction, and abduction, where at least one of the premises or the conclusion is general.
Tacit knowledge	Knowledge that has not been articulated. Tacit knowledge is often subconscious and relatively difficult to communicate to other people. Tacit knowledge consists often of habits and culture that we do not recognize in ourselves.
Market share	That fraction of an industry's output accounted for by an individual firm or group of firms is called market share.
Strategic planning	The process of determining the major goals of the organization and the policies and strategies for obtaining and using resources to achieve those goals is called strategic planning.
Knowledge worker	Employees who own the means of producing a product or service are called a knowledge worker.

Patent	The legal right to the proceeds from and control over the use of an invented product or process, granted for a fixed period of time, usually 20 years. Patent is one form of intellectual property that is subject of the TRIPS agreement.
Process innovation	The development and use of new or improved production or distribution methods is called process innovation. It is an approach in business process reengineering by which radical changes are made through innovations.
Explicit knowledge	Explicit knowledge is knowledge that has been or can be articulated, codified, and stored in certain media. The most common forms of explicit knowledge are manuals, documents, procedures, and stories. Knowledge also can be audio-visual.
Shares	Shares refer to an equity security, representing a shareholder's ownership of a corporation. Shares are one of a finite number of equal portions in the capital of a company, entitling the owner to a proportion of distributed, non-reinvested profits known as dividends and to a portion of the value of the company in case of liquidation.
Financial plan	The financial plan section of a business plan consists of three financial statements (the income statement, the cash flow projection, and the balance sheet) and a brief analysis of these three statements.
Comptroller	A comptroller is an official who supervises expenditures. Comptrollers include both royal-household officials and public comptrollers who audit government accounts and sometimes certify expenditures.
Internalize	Internalize refers to causing, usually by a tax or subsidy, an external cost or benefit of someone's actions to be experienced by them directly, so that they will take it into account in their decisions.
Socialization	Socialization is the process by which human beings or animals learn to adopt the behavior patterns of the community in which they live. For both humans and animals, this is typically thought to occur during the early stages of life, during which individuals develop the skills and knowledge necessary to function within their culture and environment.
Senior executive	Senior executive means a chief executive officer, chief operating officer, chief financial officer and anyone in charge of a principal business unit or function.
Accord	An agreement whereby the parties agree to accept something different in satisfaction of the original contract is an accord.
Division of labor	Division of labor is generally speaking the specialization of cooperative labor in specific, circumscribed tasks and roles, intended to increase efficiency of output.
Market leader	The market leader is dominant in its industry. It has substantial market share and often extensive distribution arrangements with retailers. It typically is the industry leader in developing innovative new business models and new products (although not always).
Task force	A temporary team or committee formed to solve a specific short-term problem involving several departments is the task force.

228

Go to **Cram101.com** for the Practice Tests for this Chapter.

Firm	An organization that employs resources to produce a good or service for profit and owns and operates one or more plants is referred to as a firm.
Competitive advantage	A business is said to have a competitive advantage when its unique strengths, often based on cost, quality, time, and innovation, offer consumers a greater percieved value and there by diffentiating it from its competitors.
Competitor	Other organizations in the same industry or type of business that provide a good or service to the same set of customers is referred to as a competitor.
Value creation	Value creation refers to performing activities that increase the value of goods or services to consumers.
Consideration	Consideration in contract law, a basic requirement for an enforceable agreement under traditional contract principles, defined in this text as legal value, bargained for and given in exchange for an act or promise. In corporation law, cash or property contributed to a corporation in exchange for shares, or a promise to contribute such cash or property.
Appropriation	A privacy tort that consists of using a person's name or likeness for commercial gain without the person's permission is an appropriation.
Strategic alliance	Strategic alliance refers to a long-term partnership between two or more companies established to help each company build competitive market advantages.
Cooperative	A business owned and controlled by the people who use it, producers, consumers, or workers with similar needs who pool their resources for mutual gain is called cooperative.
Market	A market is, as defined in economics, a social arrangement that allows buyers and sellers to discover information and carry out a voluntary exchange of goods or services.
Brief	Brief refers to a statement of a party's case or legal arguments, usually prepared by an attorney. Also used to make legal arguments before appellate courts.
Joint venture	Joint venture refers to an undertaking by two parties for a specific purpose and duration, taking any of several legal forms.
Equity	Equity is the name given to the set of legal principles, in countries following the English common law tradition, which supplement strict rules of law where their application would operate harshly, so as to achieve what is sometimes referred to as "natural justice."
Market access	The ability of firms from one country to sell in another is market access.
Gain	In finance, gain is a profit or an increase in value of an investment such as a stock or bond. Gain is calculated by fair market value or the proceeds from the sale of the investment minus the sum of the purchase price and all costs associated with it.
Scope	Scope of a project is the sum total of all projects products and their requirements or features.
Trend	Trend refers to the long-term movement of an economic variable, such as its average rate of increase or decrease over enough years to encompass several business cycles.
Collaboration	Collaboration occurs when the interaction between groups is very important to goal attainment and the goals are compatible. Wherein people work together —applying both to the work of individuals as well as larger collectives and societies.
Technology	The body of knowledge and techniques that can be used to combine economic resources to produce goods and services is called technology.
Confirmed	When the seller's bank agrees to assume liability on the letter of credit issued by the buyer's bank the transaction is confirmed. The term means that the credit is not only backed up by the issuing foreign bank, but that payment is also guaranteed by the notifying American

bank.

Exchange	The trade of things of value between buyer and seller so that each is better off after the trade is called the exchange.
Innovation	Innovation refers to the first commercially successful introduction of a new product, the use of a new method of production, or the creation of a new form of business organization.
Product life cycle	Product life cycle refers to a series of phases in a product's sales and cash flows over time; these phases, in order of occurrence, are introductory, growth, maturity, and decline.
Investment	Investment refers to spending for the production and accumulation of capital and additions to inventories. In a financial sense, buying an asset with the expectation of making a return.
Payback	A value that indicates the time period required to recoup an initial investment is a payback. The payback does not include the time-value-of-money concept.
Information technology	Information technology refers to technology that helps companies change business by allowing them to use new methods.
Value chain	The sequence of business functions in which usefulness is added to the products or services of a company is a value chain.
Industry	A group of firms that produce identical or similar products is an industry. It is also used specifically to refer to an area of economic production focused on manufacturing which involves large amounts of capital investment before any profit can be realized, also called "heavy industry".
Commercializ-tion	Promoting a product to distributors and retailers to get wide distribution and developing strong advertising and sales campaigns to generate and maintain interest in the product among distributors and consumers is commercialization.
Ford	Ford is an American company that manufactures and sells automobiles worldwide. Ford introduced methods for large-scale manufacturing of cars, and large-scale management of an industrial workforce, especially elaborately engineered manufacturing sequences typified by the moving assembly lines.
Strategic partnership	Strategic partnership refers to an association between two firms by which they agree to work together to achieve a strategic goal. This is often associated with long-term supplier-customer relationships.
Global competition	Global competition exists when competitive conditions across national markets are linked strongly enough to form a true international market and when leading competitors compete head to head in many different countries.
Partnership	In the common law, a partnership is a type of business entity in which partners share with each other the profits or losses of the business undertaking in which they have all invested.
General Electric	In 1876, Thomas Alva Edison opened a new laboratory in Menlo Park, New Jersey. Out of the laboratory was to come perhaps the most famous invention of all—a successful development of the incandescent electric lamp. By 1890, Edison had organized his various businesses into the Edison General Electric Company.
Positioning	The art and science of fitting the product or service to one or more segments of the market in such a way as to set it meaningfully apart from competition is called positioning.
Evaluation	The consumer's appraisal of the product or brand on important attributes is called evaluation.
Subsidiary	A company that is controlled by another company or corporation is a subsidiary.
Market leader	The market leader is dominant in its industry. It has substantial market share and often

extensive distribution arrangements with retailers. It typically is the industry leader in developing innovative new business models and new products (although not always).

Coalition	An informal alliance among managers who support a specific goal is called coalition.
Microsoft	Microsoft is a multinational computer technology corporation with 2004 global annual sales of US$39.79 billion and 71,553 employees in 102 countries and regions as of July 2006. It develops, manufactures, licenses, and supports a wide range of software products for computing devices.
Convergence	The blending of various facets of marketing functions and communication technology to create more efficient and expanded synergies is a convergence.
Artificial intelligence	Computers or computer enhaned machines that can be programmed to think, learn, and make decisions in a manner similar to people is is the subject of artificial intelligence.
Economies of scale	In economics, returns to scale and economies of scale are related terms that describe what happens as the scale of production increases. They are different terms and not to be used interchangeably.
Economy	The income, expenditures, and resources that affect the cost of running a business and household are called an economy.
Toyota	Toyota is a Japanese multinational corporation that manufactures automobiles, trucks and buses. Toyota is the world's second largest automaker by sales. Toyota also provides financial services through its subsidiary, Toyota Financial Services, and participates in other lines of business.
Nissan	Nissan is Japan's second largest car company after Toyota. Nissan is among the top three Asian rivals of the "big three" in the US.
Product development	In business and engineering, new product development is the complete process of bringing a new product to market. There are two parallel aspects to this process : one involves product engineering ; the other marketing analysis. Marketers see new product development as the first stage in product life cycle management, engineers as part of Product Lifecycle Management.
Manufacturing	Production of goods primarily by the application of labor and capital to raw materials and other intermediate inputs, in contrast to agriculture, mining, forestry, fishing, and services a manufacturing.
Distribution	Distribution in economics, the manner in which total output and income is distributed among individuals or factors.
Leadership	Management merely consists of leadership applied to business situations; or in other words: management forms a sub-set of the broader process of leadership.
Synergy	Corporate synergy occurs when corporations interact congruently. A corporate synergy refers to a financial benefit that a corporation expects to realize when it merges with or acquires another corporation.
Acquisition	A company's purchase of the property and obligations of another company is an acquisition.
Merger	Merger refers to the combination of two firms into a single firm.
Mergers and acquisitions	The phrase mergers and acquisitions refers to the aspect of corporate finance strategy and management dealing with the merging and acquiring of different companies as well as other assets. Usually mergers occur in a friendly setting where executives from the respective companies participate in a due diligence process to ensure a successful combination of all parts.

Go to **Cram101.com** for the Practice Tests for this Chapter.

Foreign ownership	Foreign ownership refers to the complete or majority ownership/control of businesses or resources in a country, by individuals who are not citizens of that country, or by companies whose headquarters are not in that country.
Domestic	From or in one's own country. A domestic producer is one that produces inside the home country. A domestic price is the price inside the home country. Opposite of 'foreign' or 'world.'.
Integration	Economic integration refers to reducing barriers among countries to transactions and to movements of goods, capital, and labor, including harmonization of laws, regulations, and standards. Integrated markets theoretically function as a unified market.
Management	Management characterizes the process of leading and directing all or part of an organization, often a business, through the deployment and manipulation of resources. Early twentieth-century management writer Mary Parker Follett defined management as "the art of getting things done through people."
Competitive market	A market in which no buyer or seller has market power is called a competitive market.
Argument	The discussion by counsel for the respective parties of their contentions on the law and the facts of the case being tried in order to aid the jury in arriving at a correct and just conclusion is called argument.
Leverage	Leverage is using given resources in such a way that the potential positive or negative outcome is magnified. In finance, this generally refers to borrowing.
Marketing	Promoting and selling products or services to customers, or prospective customers, is referred to as marketing.
Tactic	A short-term immediate decision that, in its totality, leads to the achievement of strategic goals is called a tactic.
Trust	An arrangement in which shareholders of independent firms agree to give up their stock in exchange for trust certificates that entitle them to a share of the trust's common profits.
Complexity	The technical sophistication of the product and hence the amount of understanding required to use it is referred to as complexity. It is the opposite of simplicity.
Operation	A standardized method or technique that is performed repetitively, often on different materials resulting in different finished goods is called an operation.
Accounting	A system that collects and processes financial information about an organization and reports that information to decision makers is referred to as accounting.
Takeover	A takeover in business refers to one company (the acquirer) purchasing another (the target). Such events resemble mergers, but without the formation of a new company.
Stock	In financial terminology, stock is the capital raized by a corporation, through the issuance and sale of shares.
Bid	A bid price is a price offered by a buyer when he/she buys a good. In the context of stock trading on a stock exchange, the bid price is the highest price a buyer of a stock is willing to pay for a share of that given stock.
Competitive Strategy	An outline of how a business intends to compete with other firms in the same industry is called competitive strategy.
Negotiation	Negotiation is the process whereby interested parties resolve disputes, agree upon courses of action, bargain for individual or collective advantage, and/or attempt to craft outcomes which serve their mutual interests.

Go to **Cram101.com** for the Practice Tests for this Chapter.

Reciprocity	An industrial buying practice in which two organizations agree to purchase each other's products and services is called reciprocity.
Foundation	A Foundation is a type of philanthropic organization set up by either individuals or institutions as a legal entity (either as a corporation or trust) with the purpose of distributing grants to support causes in line with the goals of the foundation.
Escalating commitment	The tendency to continue a previously chosen course of action even when feedback suggests that it is failing is an escalating commitment.
Brand	A name, symbol, or design that identifies the goods or services of one seller or group of sellers and distinguishes them from the goods and services of competitors is a brand.
Physical asset	A physical asset is an item of economic value that has a tangible or material existence. A physical asset usually refers to cash, equipment, inventory and properties owned by a business.
Productivity	Productivity refers to the total output of goods and services in a given period of time divided by work hours.
Loyalty	Marketers tend to define customer loyalty as making repeat purchases. Some argue that it should be defined attitudinally as a strongly positive feeling about the brand.
Asset	An item of property, such as land, capital, money, a share in ownership, or a claim on others for future payment, such as a bond or a bank deposit is an asset.
Assessment	Collecting information and providing feedback to employees about their behavior, communication style, or skills is an assessment.
Xerox	Xerox was founded in 1906 as "The Haloid Company" manufacturing photographic paper and equipment. The company came to prominence in 1959 with the introduction of the first plain paper photocopier using the process of xerography (electrophotography) developed by Chester Carlson, the Xerox 914.
Harvard Business Review	Harvard Business Review is a research-based magazine written for business practitioners, it claims a high ranking business readership and enjoys the reverence of academics, executives, and management consultants. It has been the frequent publishing home for well known scholars and management thinkers.
Ad hoc	Ad hoc is a Latin phrase which means "for this purpose." It generally signifies a solution that has been tailored to a specific purpose and is makeshift and non-general, such as a handcrafted network protocol or a specific-purpose equation, as opposed to general solutions.
Business intelligence	Business intelligence refers to data about the past history, present status, or future projections for a business organization.
Escalation	Regarding the structure of tariffs. In the context of a trade war, escalation refers to the increase in tariffs that occurs as countries retaliate again and again.
Strategic goal	A strategic goal is a broad statement of where an organization wants to be in the future; pertains to the organization as a whole rather than to specific divisions or departments.
Limited partnership	A partnership in which some of the partners are limited partners. At least one of the partners in a limited partnership must be a general partner.
Union	A worker association that bargains with employers over wages and working conditions is called a union.
Administrative controls	Procedures designed to evaluate performance and the degree of compliance with a firm's policies and public laws are administrative controls.
Administrative	Administrative control is any procedure or method used by an employer to decrease exposure to

Go to **Cram101.com** for the Practice Tests for this Chapter.

Go to **Cram101.com** for the Practice Tests for this Chapter.
And, **NEVER** highlight a book again!

control	risk factors by changing the way a job is performed.
Committee	A long-lasting, sometimes permanent team in the organization structure created to deal with tasks that recur regularly is the committee.
Users	Users refer to people in the organization who actually use the product or service purchased by the buying center.
Gatekeeper	Gatekeeper refers to an individual who has a strategic position in the network that allows him or her to control information moving in either direction through a channel.
Credibility	The extent to which a source is perceived as having knowledge, skill, or experience relevant to a communication topic and can be trusted to give an unbiased opinion or present objective information on the issue is called credibility.
Proprietary	Proprietary indicates that a party, or proprietor, exercises private ownership, control or use over an item of property, usually to the exclusion of other parties. Where a party, holds or claims proprietary interests in relation to certain types of property (eg. a creative literary work, or software), that property may also be the subject of intellectual property law (eg. copyright or patents).
Strategic control	Strategic control processes allow managers to evaluate a company's marketing program from a critical long-term perspective. This involves a detailed and objective analysis of a company's organization and its ability to maximize its strengths and market opportunities.
Conflict resolution	Conflict resolution is the process of resolving a dispute or a conflict. Successful conflict resolution occurs by providing each side's needs, and adequately addressing their interests so that they are each satisfied with the outcome. Conflict resolution aims to end conflicts before they start or lead to physical fighting.
Option	A contract that gives the purchaser the option to buy or sell the underlying financial instrument at a specified price, called the exercise price or strike price, within a specific period of time.
Recovery	Characterized by rizing output, falling unemployment, rizing profits, and increasing economic activity following a decline is a recovery.
Scarcity	Scarcity is defined as not having sufficient resources to produce enough to fulfill unlimited subjective wants. Alternatively, scarcity implies that not all of society's goals can be attained at the same time, so that trade-offs one good against others are made.
Dissolution	Dissolution is the process of admitting or removing a partner in a partnership.
Corporation	A legal entity chartered by a state or the Federal government that is distinct and separate from the individuals who own it is a corporation. This separation gives the corporation unique powers which other legal entities lack.
Revenue	Revenue is a U.S. business term for the amount of money that a company receives from its activities, mostly from sales of products and/or services to customers.
Contribution	In business organization law, the cash or property contributed to a business by its owners is referred to as contribution.
Task force	A temporary team or committee formed to solve a specific short-term problem involving several departments is the task force.
Restructuring	Restructuring is the corporate management term for the act of partially dismantling and reorganizing a company for the purpose of making it more efficient and therefore more profitable.
Licensing	Licensing is a form of strategic alliance which involves the sale of a right to use certain

Go to **Cram101.com** for the Practice Tests for this Chapter.

proprietary knowledge (so called intellectual property) in a defined way.

Contract	A contract is a "promise" or an "agreement" that is enforced or recognized by the law. In the civil law, a contract is considered to be part of the general law of obligations.
Net income	Net income is equal to the income that a firm has after subtracting costs and expenses from the total revenue. Expenses will typically include tax expense.
Fund	Independent accounting entity with a self-balancing set of accounts segregated for the purposes of carrying on specific activities is referred to as a fund.
Profit	Profit refers to the return to the resource entrepreneurial ability; total revenue minus total cost.
Diversification	Investing in a collection of assets whose returns do not always move together, with the result that overall risk is lower than for individual assets is referred to as diversification.
License	A license in the sphere of Intellectual Property Rights (IPR) is a document, contract or agreement giving permission or the 'right' to a legally-definable entity to do something (such as manufacture a product or to use a service), or to apply something (such as a trademark), with the objective of achieving commercial gain.
Regulation	Regulation refers to restrictions state and federal laws place on business with regard to the conduct of its activities.
Licensee	A person lawfully on land in possession of another for purposes unconnected with the business interests of the possessor is referred to as the licensee.
Contracting party	Contracting party refers to a country that has signed the GATT.
Patent	The legal right to the proceeds from and control over the use of an invented product or process, granted for a fixed period of time, usually 20 years. Patent is one form of intellectual property that is subject of the TRIPS agreement.
Licensing agreement	Detailed and comprehensive written agreement between the licensor and licensee that sets forth the express terms of their agreement is called a licensing agreement.
Managing director	Managing director is the term used for the chief executive of many limited companies in the United Kingdom, Commonwealth and some other English speaking countries. The title reflects their role as both a member of the Board of Directors but also as the senior manager.
Core	A core is the set of feasible allocations in an economy that cannot be improved upon by subset of the set of the economy's consumers (a coalition). In construction, when the force in an element is within a certain center section, the core, the element will only be under compression.
Policy	Similar to a script in that a policy can be a less than completely rational decision-making method. Involves the use of a pre-existing set of decision steps for any problem that presents itself.
Direct relationship	Direct relationship refers to the relationship between two variables that change in the same direction, for example, product price and quantity supplied.
Organizational structure	Organizational structure is the way in which the interrelated groups of an organization are constructed. From a managerial point of view the main concerns are ensuring effective communication and coordination.
Production	The creation of finished goods and services using the factors of production: land, labor, capital, entrepreneurship, and knowledge.

Go to **Cram101.com** for the Practice Tests for this Chapter.

Supply	Supply is the aggregate amount of any material good that can be called into being at a certain price point; it comprises one half of the equation of supply and demand. In classical economic theory, a curve representing supply is one of the factors that produce price.
Financial institution	A financial institution acts as an agent that provides financial services for its clients. Financial institutions generally fall under financial regulation from a government authority.
Trademark	A distinctive word, name, symbol, device, or combination thereof, which enables consumers to identify favored products or services and which may find protection under state or federal law is a trademark.
Product line	A group of products that are physically similar or are intended for a similar market are called the product line.
Monopoly	A monopoly is defined as a persistent market situation where there is only one provider of a kind of product or service.
Shareholder	A shareholder is an individual or company (including a corporation) that legally owns one or more shares of stock in a joined stock company.
Manufacturing costs	Costs incurred in a manufacturing process, which consist of direct material, direct labor, and manufacturing overhead are referred to as manufacturing costs.
Prototype	A prototype is built to test the function of a new design before starting production of a product.
Just In Time	Just In Time is an inventory strategy implemented to improve the return on investment of a business by reducing in-process inventory and its associated costs. The process is driven by a series of signals, or Kanban that tell production processes to make the next part.
Case study	A case study is a particular method of qualitative research. Rather than using large samples and following a rigid protocol to examine a limited number of variables, case study methods involve an in-depth, longitudinal examination of a single instance or event: a case. They provide a systematic way of looking at events, collecting data, analyzing information, and reporting the results.
Toshiba	Toshiba is a Japanese high technology electrical and electronics manufacturing firm, headquartered in Tokyo, Japan. It is the 7th largest integrated manufacturer of electric and electronic equipment in the world.
Incentive	An incentive is any factor (financial or non-financial) that provides a motive for a particular course of action, or counts as a reason for preferring one choice to the alternatives.
Total quality control	A product-quality program in which the objective is complete elimination of product defects is called total quality control.
Quality control	The measurement of products and services against set standards is referred to as quality control.
Recession	A significant decline in economic activity. In the U.S., recession is approximately defined as two successive quarters of falling GDP, as judged by NBER.
Quality management	Quality management is a method for ensuring that all the activities necessary to design, develop and implement a product or service are effective and efficient with respect to the system and its performance.
Deming prize	Japanese quality award for individuals and groups that have contributed to the field of quality control is called the deming prize.
Deming	Deming is widely credited with improving production in the United States during World War II,

Go to **Cram101.com** for the Practice Tests for this Chapter.

	although he is perhaps best known for his work in Japan. There, from 1950 onward he taught top management how to improve design (and thus service), product quality, testing and sales (the latter through global markets).
Gap	In December of 1995, Gap became the first major North American retailer to accept independent monitoring of the working conditions in a contract factory producing its garments. Gap is the largest specialty retailer in the United States.
Vendor	A person who sells property to a vendee is a vendor. The words vendor and vendee are more commonly applied to the seller and purchaser of real estate, and the words seller and buyer are more commonly applied to the seller and purchaser of personal property.
Dealer	People who link buyers with sellers by buying and selling securities at stated prices are referred to as a dealer.
Service	Service refers to a "non tangible product" that is not embodied in a physical good and that typically effects some change in another product, person, or institution. Contrasts with good.
Eastman Kodak	Eastman Kodak Company is an American multinational public company producing photographic materials and equipment. Long known for its wide range of photographic film products, it has focused in recent years on three main businesses: digital photography, health imaging, and printing. This company remains the largest supplier of films in the world, both for the amateur and professional markets.
Market share	That fraction of an industry's output accounted for by an individual firm or group of firms is called market share.
Marketing strategy	Marketing strategy refers to the means by which a marketing goal is to be achieved, usually characterized by a specified target market and a marketing program to reach it.
General manager	A manager who is responsible for several departments that perform different functions is called general manager.
Export	In economics, an export is any good or commodity, shipped or otherwise transported out of a country, province, town to another part of the world in a legitimate fashion, typically for use in trade or sale.
Patent infringement	Patent infringement refers to unauthorized use of another's patent. A patent holder may recover damages and other remedies against a patent infringer.
Antitrust	Government intervention to alter market structure or prevent abuse of market power is called antitrust.
Damages	The sum of money recoverable by a plaintiff who has received a judgment in a civil case is called damages.
Federal trade commission	The commission of five members established by the Federal Trade Commission Act of 1914 to investigate unfair competitive practices of firms, to hold hearings on the complaints of such practices, and to issue cease-and-desist orders when firms were found guilty of unfair practices.
Sherman Antitrust Act	The Sherman Antitrust Act, formally known as the Act of July 2, 1890 was the first United States federal government action to limit monopolies.
Royalties	Remuneration paid to the owners of technology, patents, or trade names for the use of same name are called royalties.
Transfer pricing	Transfer pricing refers to the pricing of goods and services within a multi-divisional organization. Goods from the production division may be sold to the marketing division, or goods from a parent company may be sold to a foreign subsidiary.

Go to **Cram101.com** for the Practice Tests for this Chapter.

Benchmarking	The continuous process of comparing the levels of performance in producing products and services and executing activities against the best levels of performance is benchmarking.
Consultant	A professional that provides expert advice in a particular field or area in which customers occassionaly require this type of knowledge is a consultant.
Competitive benchmarking	Rating an organization's practices, processes, and products against the world's best is referred to as competitive benchmarking.
Market research	Market research is the process of systematic gathering, recording and analyzing of data about customers, competitors and the market. Market research can help create a business plan, launch a new product or service, fine tune existing products and services, expand into new markets etc. It can be used to determine which portion of the population will purchase the product/service, based on variables like age, gender, location and income level. It can be found out what market characteristics your target market has.
Points	Loan origination fees that may be deductible as interest by a buyer of property. A seller of property who pays points reduces the selling price by the amount of the points paid for the buyer.
Malcolm Baldrige National Quality Award	Malcolm Baldrige national quality award refers to U.S. national quality award sponsored by the U.S. Department of Commerce and private industry. The program aims to reward quality in the business sector, health care, and education, and was inspired by the ideas of Total Quality Management.
Commerce	Commerce is the exchange of something of value between two entities. It is the central mechanism from which capitalism is derived.
Analyst	Analyst refers to a person or tool with a primary function of information analysis, generally with a more limited, practical and short term set of goals than a researcher.
Net earnings	Another name for net income is net earnings. That part of a company's profits remaining after all expenses and taxes have been paid and out of which dividends may be paid.
Interest	In finance and economics, interest is the price paid by a borrower for the use of a lender's money. In other words, interest is the amount of paid to "rent" money for a period of time.
Agent	A person who makes economic decisions for another economic actor. A hired manager operates as an agent for a firm's owner.
Context	The effect of the background under which a message often takes on more and richer meaning is a context. Context is especially important in cross-cultural interactions because some cultures are said to be high context or low context.
Profit margin	Profit margin is a measure of profitability. It is calculated using a formula and written as a percentage or a number. Profit margin = Net income before tax and interest / Revenue.
Margin	A deposit by a buyer in stocks with a seller or a stockbroker, as security to cover fluctuations in the market in reference to stocks that the buyer has purchased but for which he has not paid is a margin. Commodities are also traded on margin.
Gross profit	Net sales less cost of goods sold is called gross profit.
Chrysler	The Chrysler Corporation was an American automobile manufacturer that existed independently from 1925–1998. The company was formed by Walter Percy Chrysler on June 6, 1925, with the remaining assets of Maxwell Motor Company.
DaimlerChrysler	In 2002, the merged company, DaimlerChrysler, appeared to run two independent product lines, with few signs of corporate integration. In 2003, however, it was alleged by the Detroit News that the "merger of equals" was, in fact, a takeover.

Go to **Cram101.com** for the Practice Tests for this Chapter.

Volkswagen	Volkswagen or VW is an automobile manufacturer based in Wolfsburg, Germany in the state of Lower Saxony. It forms the core of this Group, one of the world's four largest car producers. Its German tagline is "Aus Liebe zum Automobil", which is translated as "For the love of the car" - or, For Love of the People's Cars,".
A share	In finance the term A share has two distinct meanings, both relating to securities. The first is a designation for a 'class' of common or preferred stock. A share of common or preferred stock typically has enhanced voting rights or other benefits compared to the other forms of shares that may have been created. The equity structure, or how many types of shares are offered, is determined by the corporate charter.
Industrial policy	Industrial policy refers to government policy to influence which industries expand and, perhaps implicitly, which contract, via subsidies, tax breaks, and other aids for favored industries.
Authority	Authority in agency law, refers to an agent's ability to affect his principal's legal relations with third parties. Also used to refer to an actor's legal power or ability to do something. In addition, sometimes used to refer to a statute, case, or other legal source that justifies a particular result.
Balance	In banking and accountancy, the outstanding balance is the amount of money owned, (or due), that remains in a deposit account (or a loan account) at a given date, after all past remittances, payments and withdrawal have been accounted for. It can be positive (then, in the balance sheet of a firm, it is an asset) or negative (a liability).
Mitsubishi	In a statement, the Mitsubishi says that forced labor is inconsistent with the company's values, and that the various lawsuits targeting Mitsubishi are misdirected. Instead, a spokesman says the Mitsubishi of World War II is not the same Mitsubishi of today. The conglomerate also rejected a Chinese slave labor lawsuit demand by saying it bore no responsibility since it was national policy to employ Chinese laborers."
Strategic choice	Strategic choice refers to an organization's strategy; the ways an organization will attempt to fulfill its mission and achieve its long-term goals.
Strategic planning	The process of determining the major goals of the organization and the policies and strategies for obtaining and using resources to achieve those goals is called strategic planning.
Honda	With more than 14 million internal combustion engines built each year, Honda is the largest engine-maker in the world. In 2004, the company began to produce diesel motors, which were both very quiet whilst not requiring particulate filters to pass pollution standards. It is arguable, however, that the foundation of their success is the motorcycle division.
Samsung	On November 30, 2005 Samsung pleaded guilty to a charge it participated in a worldwide DRAM price fixing conspiracy during 1999-2002 that damaged competition and raized PC prices.
Forming	The first stage of team development, where the team is formed and the objectives for the team are set is referred to as forming.
Quota	A government-imposed restriction on quantity, or sometimes on total value, used to restrict the import of something to a specific quantity is called a quota.
Strategic plan	The formal document that presents the ways and means by which a strategic goal will be achieved is a strategic plan. A long-term flexible plan that does not regulate activities but rather outlines the means to achieve certain results, and provides the means to alter the course of action should the desired ends change.
Assignment	A transfer of property or some right or interest is referred to as assignment.
Delegation	Delegation is the handing of a task over to another person, usually a subordinate. It is the

	assignment of authority and responsibility to another person to carry out specific activities.
General Motors	General Motors is the world's largest automaker. Founded in 1908, today it employs about 327,000 people around the world. With global headquarters in Detroit, it manufactures its cars and trucks in 33 countries.
Finance director	Finance director refers to see chief financial officer in charge of financial accounting. Measures and records business transactions and provides financial statements that are based on generally accepted accounting principles.
Global strategy	Global strategy refers to strategy focusing on increasing profitability by reaping cost reductions from experience curve and location economies.
Purchasing	Purchasing refers to the function in a firm that searches for quality material resources, finds the best suppliers, and negotiates the best price for goods and services.
Euro	The common currency of a subset of the countries of the EU, adopted January 1, 1999 is called euro.
Keiretsu	Keiretsu is a set of companies with interlocking business relationships and shareholdings. It is a type of business group.
Promotion	Promotion refers to all the techniques sellers use to motivate people to buy products or services. An attempt by marketers to inform people about products and to persuade them to participate in an exchange.
Bankruptcy	Bankruptcy is a legally declared inability or impairment of ability of an individual or organization to pay their creditors.
Credit	Credit refers to a recording as positive in the balance of payments, any transaction that gives rise to a payment into the country, such as an export, the sale of an asset, or borrowing from abroad.
Fiscal year	A fiscal year is a 12-month period used for calculating annual ("yearly") financial reports in businesses and other organizations. In many jurisdictions, regulatory laws regarding accounting require such reports once per twelve months, but do not require that the twelve months constitute a calendar year (i.e. January to December).
Expense	In accounting, an expense represents an event in which an asset is used up or a liability is incurred. In terms of the accounting equation, expenses reduce owners' equity.
Bail	Bail refers to an amount of money the defendant pays to the court upon release from custody as security that he or she will return for trial.
Collective responsibility	Cabinet collective responsibility is constitutional convention in the states that use the Westminster System. It means that members of the Cabinet must publicly support all governmental decisions made in Cabinet, even if they do not privately agree with them.
Corporate governance	Corporate governance is the set of processes, customs, policies, laws and institutions affecting the way a corporation is directed, administered or controlled.
Levy	Levy refers to imposing and collecting a tax or tariff.
Deficit	The deficit is the amount by which expenditure exceed revenue.
Public company	A public company is a company owned by the public rather than by a relatively few individuals. There are two different meanings for this term: (1) A company that is owned by stockholders who are members of the general public and trade shares publicly, often through a listing on a stock exchange. Ownership is open to anyone that has the money and inclination to buy shares in the company. It is differentiated from privately held companies where the

253

shares are held by a small group of individuals, who are often members of one or a small group of families or otherwise related individuals, or other companies. The variant of this type of company in the United Kingdom and Ireland is known as a public limited compan, and (2) A government-owned corporation. This meaning of a "public company" comes from the fact that government debt is sometimes referred to as "public debt" although there are no "public bonds", government finance is sometimes called "public finance", among similar uses. This is the less-common meaning.

Cost management	The approaches and activities of managers in short-run and long-run planning and control decisions that increase value for customers and lower costs of products and services are called cost management.
Board of directors	The group of individuals elected by the stockholders of a corporation to oversee its operations is a board of directors.
Chief financial officer	Chief financial officer refers to executive responsible for overseeing the financial operations of an organization.
Draft	A signed, written order by which one party instructs another party to pay a specified sum to a third party, at sight or at a specific date is a draft.
Capital	Capital generally refers to financial wealth, especially that used to start or maintain a business. In classical economics, capital is one of four factors of production, the others being land and labor and entrepreneurship.
Absorption	Total demand for goods and services by all residents of a country is absorption. The term was introduced as part of the Absorption Approach.
Holding	The holding is a court's determination of a matter of law based on the issue presented in the particular case. In other words: under this law, with these facts, this result.
Due diligence	Due diligence is the effort made by an ordinarily prudent or reasonable party to avoid harm to another party or himself. Failure to make this effort is considered negligence. Failure to make this effort is considered negligence.
Datsun	Datsun was originally founded in 1911 by Sotaro Hashimoto and named DAT. It was the first Japanese automobile manufacturer.
Assembly line	An assembly line is a manufacturing process in which interchangeable parts are added to a product in a sequential manner to create a finished product.
Buyer	A buyer refers to a role in the buying center with formal authority and responsibility to select the supplier and negotiate the terms of the contract.
Environmental protection agency	An administrative agency created by Congress in 1970 to coordinate the implementation and enforcement of the federal environmental protection laws is referred to as the Environmental Protection Agency or EPA.
Advertising slogan	A advertising slogan is claimed to be, and often is proven to be, the most effective means of drawing attention to one or more aspects of a product or products. Typically they make claims about being the best quality, the tastiest, cheapest, most nutritious, providing an important benefit or solution, or being most suitable for the potential customer.
Advertising	Advertising refers to paid, nonpersonal communication through various media by organizations and individuals who are in some way identified in the advertising message.
Automation	Automation allows machines to do work previously accomplished by people.
Domestic price	The price of a good or service within a country, determined by domestic demand and supply is referred to as domestic price.

Go to Cram101.com for the Practice Tests for this Chapter.

255

Brand image	The advertising metric that measures the type and favorability of consumer perceptions of the brand is referred to as the brand image.
Bubble economy	Term for an economy in which the presence of one or more bubbles in its asset markets is a dominant feature of its performance. Japan was said to be a bubble economy in the late 1980s.
Customer orientation	Customer orientation is a set of beliefs/ strategy that customer needs and satisfaction are the priority of an organization. It focuses on dynamic interactions between the organization and customers as well as competitors in the market and its internal stakeholders.
Marketable securities	Marketable securities refer to securities that are readily traded in the secondary securities market.
Portfolio	In finance, a portfolio is a collection of investments held by an institution or a private individual. Holding but not always a portfolio is part of an investment and risk-limiting strategy called diversification. By owning several assets, certain types of risk (in particular specific risk) can be reduced.
Security	Security refers to a claim on the borrower future income that is sold by the borrower to the lender. A security is a type of transferable interest representing financial value.
Lease	A contract for the possession and use of land or other property, including goods, on one side, and a recompense of rent or other income on the other is the lease.
Operating profit	Operating profit is a measure of a company's earning power from ongoing operations, equal to earnings before the deduction of interest payments and income taxes.
Press release	A written public news announcement normally distributed to major news services is referred to as press release.
Channel	Channel, in communications (sometimes called communications channel), refers to the medium used to convey information from a sender (or transmitter) to a receiver.
Mercosur	Pact between Argentina, Brazil, Paraguay, and Uruguay to establish a free trade area is called mercosur.
Corporate level	Corporate level refers to level at which top management directs overall strategy for the entire organization.
Market position	Market position is a measure of the position of a company or product on a market.
Strategic group	A strategic group is a concept used in strategic management that groups companies within an industry that have similar business models or similar combinations of strategies.
Best practice	Best practice is a management idea which asserts that there is a technique, method, process, activity, incentive or reward that is more effective at delivering a particular outcome than any other technique, method, process, etc.
Cost structure	The relative proportion of an organization's fixed, variable, and mixed costs is referred to as cost structure.
Business opportunity	A business opportunity involves the sale or lease of any product, service, equipment, etc. that will enable the purchaser-licensee to begin a business
Comprehensive	A comprehensive refers to a layout accurate in size, color, scheme, and other necessary details to show how a final ad will look. For presentation only, never for reproduction.
Downturn	A decline in a stock market or economic cycle is a downturn.
Subsidy	Subsidy refers to government financial assistance to a domestic producer.
Aid	Assistance provided by countries and by international institutions such as the World Bank to developing countries in the form of monetary grants, loans at low interest rates, in kind, or

Go to **Cram101.com** for the Practice Tests for this Chapter.

	a combination of these is called aid. Aid can also refer to assistance of any type rendered to benefit some group or individual.
Deregulation	The lessening or complete removal of government regulations on an industry, especially concerning the price that firms are allowed to charge and leaving price to be determined by market forces a deregulation.
Price competition	Price competition is where a company tries to distinguish its product or service from competing products on the basis of low price.
Bilateral agreement	A bilateral agreement is between two countries or organizations, as opposed to several countries.
Frequency	Frequency refers to the speed of the up and down movements of a fluctuating economic variable; that is, the number of times per unit of time that the variable completes a cycle of up and down movement.
Free market	A free market is a market where price is determined by the unregulated interchange of supply and demand rather than set by artificial means.
Immunity	Granted by law, immunity is the assurance that someone will be exempt from prosectution.
Annual report	An annual report is prepared by corporate management that presents financial information including financial statements, footnotes, and the management discussion and analysis.
Standstill	Standstill refers to a commitment to refrain from introducing new measures such as trade barriers that are not consistent with an agreement. Such commitments are usually offered at the start of multilateral trade negotiations as an indication of good faith.
Pan Am	Pan Am was the principal international airline of the United States from the 1930s until its collapse in 1991. Originally founded as a seaplane service out of Key West, Florida, the airline became a major company credited with many innovations that shaped the international airline industry, including the widespread use of jet aircraft, jumbo jets, and computerized reservation systems. Identified by its blue globe logo and the use of the word "Clipper" in aircraft names and call signs, the airline was a cultural icon of the 20th century, and the unofficial flag carrier of the United States.
Net profit	Net profit is an accounting term which is commonly used in business. It is equal to the gross revenue for a given time period minus associated expenses.
Senior executive	Senior executive means a chief executive officer, chief operating officer, chief financial officer and anyone in charge of a principal business unit or function.
US airways	US Airways is an airline based in Tempe, Arizona, owned by US Airways Group, Inc.. As of May 2006, the combined airline is the fifth largest airline in the United States and has a fleet of 358 mainline jet aircraft and 295 express aircraft connecting 237 destinations in North America, Central America, the Caribbean, Hawaii, and Europe.
Mistake	In contract law a mistake is incorrect understanding by one or more parties to a contract and may be used as grounds to invalidate the agreement. Common law has identified three different types of mistake in contract: unilateral mistake, mutual mistake, and common mistake.
Excess capacity	Excess capacity refers to plant resources that are underused when imperfectly competitive firms produce less output than that associated with purely competitive firms, who by definiation, are achieving minimum average total cost.
Budget	Budget refers to an account, usually for a year, of the planned expenditures and the expected receipts of an entity. For a government, the receipts are tax revenues.
Boeing	Boeing is the world's largest aircraft manufacturer by revenue. Headquartered in Chicago, Illinois, Boeing is the second-largest defense contractor in the world. In 2005, the company

Go to **Cram101.com** for the Practice Tests for this Chapter.

was the world's largest civil aircraft manufacturer in terms of value.

Niche

In industry, a niche is a situation or an activity perfectly suited to a person. A niche can imply a working position or an area suited to a person who occupies it. Basically, a job where a person is able to succeed and thrive.

Intermediaries

Intermediaries specialize in information either to bring together two parties to a transaction or to buy in order to sell again.

Lufthansa

Lufthansa is a founding member of Star Alliance, the largest airline alliance in the world. The Lufthansa Group operates more than 400 aircraft and employs nearly 100,000 people world-wide.

Competitiveness

Competitiveness usually refers to characteristics that permit a firm to compete effectively with other firms due to low cost or superior technology, perhaps internationally.

Procurement

Procurement is the acquisition of goods or services at the best possible total cost of ownership, in the right quantity, at the right time, in the right place for the direct benefit or use of the governments, corporations, or individuals generally via, but not limited to a contract.

Personnel

A collective term for all of the employees of an organization. Personnel is also commonly used to refer to the personnel management function or the organizational unit responsible for administering personnel programs.

American Airlines

American Airlines developed from a conglomeration of about 82 small airlines through a series of corporate acquisitions and reorganizations: initially, the name American Airways was used as a common brand by a number of independent air carriers. American Airlines is the largest airline in the world in terms of total passengers transported and fleet size, and the second-largest airline in the world.

British Airways

British Airways is the largest airline of the United Kingdom. It is also one of the largest airlines in the world, with the greatest number of flights from Europe to North America. Its main bases are London Heathrow (LHR) and London Gatwick (LGW).

Delta Air Lines

Delta Air Lines currently has the largest route network "footprint" of any airline. The airline also serves Puerto Rico, and the U.S. Virgin Islands, in addition to 95 countries.

Air France

Air France took over the Dutch company KLM in May 2004, resulting in the creation of Air France -KLM. Air France -KLM is the largest airline company in the world in terms of operating revenues, and the third-largest in the world in terms of passengers-kilometers.

Continental Airlines

Continental Airlines is an airline of the United States. Based in Houston, Texas, it is the 6th largest airline in the U.S. and the 8th largest in the world. Continental's tagline, since 1998, has been Work Hard, Fly Right.

Premium

Premium refers to the fee charged by an insurance company for an insurance policy. The rate of losses must be relatively predictable: In order to set the premium (prices) insurers must be able to estimate them accurately.

Affiliates

Local television stations that are associated with a major network are called affiliates. Affiliates agree to preempt time during specified hours for programming provided by the network and carry the advertising contained in the program.

Limited liability company

Limited liability company refers to a form of entity allowed by all of the states. The entity is taxed as a partnership in which all members or owners of the limited liability company are treated much like limited partners.

Limited liability

Limited liability is a liability that is limited to a partner or investor's investment. Shareholders in a corporation or in a limited liability company cannot lose more money than

Go to Cram101.com for the Practice Tests for this Chapter.

the value of their shares if the corporation runs into debt, as they are not personally responsible for the corporation's obligations.

Liability	A liability is a present obligation of the enterprise arizing from past events, the settlement of which is expected to result in an outflow from the enterprise of resources embodying economic benefits.
Project management	Project management is the discipline of organizing and managing resources in such a way that these resources deliver all the work required to complete a project within defined scope, time, and cost constraints.
Continuous process	An uninterrupted production process in which long production runs turn out finished goods over time is called continuous process.
Product design	Product Design is defined as the idea generation, concept development, testing and manufacturing or implementation of a physical object or service. It is possibly the evolution of former discipline name - Industrial Design.
Closing	The finalization of a real estate sales transaction that passes title to the property from the seller to the buyer is referred to as a closing. Closing is a sales term which refers to the process of making a sale. It refers to reaching the final step, which may be an exchange of money or acquiring a signature.
Performance target	A task established for an employee that provides the comparative basis for performance appraisal is a performance target.
Consolidation	The combination of two or more firms, generally of equal size and market power, to form an entirely new entity is a consolidation.
Tangible	Having a physical existence is referred to as the tangible. Personal property other than real estate, such as cars, boats, stocks, or other assets.
Maturity	Maturity refers to the final payment date of a loan or other financial instrument, after which point no further interest or principal need be paid.
Insurance	Insurance refers to a system by which individuals can reduce their exposure to risk of large losses by spreading the risks among a large number of persons.
Collateral	Property that is pledged to the lender to guarantee payment in the event that the borrower is unable to make debt payments is called collateral.
Tagline	A tagline is a variant of an advertising slogan typically used in movie marketing, commercials, and websites. The idea behind the concept is to create a memorable phrase that will sum up the tone and premise of a film, or to reinforce the subject's memory of a product or website.
Optimum	Optimum refers to the best. Usually refers to a most preferred choice by consumers subject to a budget constraint or a profit maximizing choice by firms or industry subject to a technological constraint.
Business philosophy	A business philosophy is any of a range of approaches to accounting, marketing, public relations, operations, training, labor relations, executive time management, investment, and/or corporate governance claimed to improve business performance in some measurable or otherwise provable way.
Analogy	Analogy is either the cognitive process of transferring information from a particular subject to another particular subject (the target), or a linguistic expression corresponding to such a process. In a narrower sense, analogy is an inference or an argument from a particular to another particular, as opposed to deduction, induction, and abduction, where at least one of the premises or the conclusion is general.

Halo effect	A halo effect is one where the perceived positive features of a particular item extend to a broader brand.
Specialist	A specialist is a trader who makes a market in one or several stocks and holds the limit order book for those stocks.
Strike	The withholding of labor services by an organized group of workers is referred to as a strike.
Publicity	Publicity refers to any information about an individual, product, or organization that's distributed to the public through the media and that's not paid for or controlled by the seller.
Middle class	Colloquially, the term is often applied to people who have a degree of economic independence, but not a great deal of social influence or power in their society. The term often encompasses merchants and professionals, bureaucrats, and some farmers and skilled workers[citation needed]. While most Americans identify themselves as middle class, only 20% live the lifestyle indicative of the American middle class.
Foreign exchange	In finance, foreign exchange means currencies, such as U.S. Dollars and Euros. These are traded on foreign exchange markets.
Average revenue	Average revenue refers to total revenue from the sale of a product divided by the quantity of the product sold ; equal to the price at which the product is sold when all units of the product are sold at the same price.
Yield	The interest rate that equates a future value or an annuity to a given present value is a yield.
Compromise	Compromise occurs when the interaction is moderately important to meeting goals and the goals are neither completely compatible nor completely incompatible.
Protectionism	Protectionism refers to advocacy of protection. The word has a negative connotation, and few advocates of protection in particular situations will acknowledge being protectionists.
Fixed cost	The cost that a firm bears if it does not produce at all and that is independent of its output. The presence of a fixed cost tends to imply increasing returns to scale. Contrasts with variable cost.
Globalization	The increasing world-wide integration of markets for goods, services and capital that attracted special attention in the late 1990s is called globalization.
Preference	The act of a debtor in paying or securing one or more of his creditors in a manner more favorable to them than to other creditors or to the exclusion of such other creditors is a preference. In the absence of statute, a preference is perfectly good, but to be legal it must be bona fide, and not a mere subterfuge of the debtor to secure a future benefit to himself or to prevent the application of his property to his debts.
Economic nationalism	Economic nationalism is a term used to describe policies which are guided by the idea of protecting domestic consumption, labor and capital formation, even if this requires the imposition of tariffs and other restrictions on the movement of labor, goods and capital. Economic nationalism may include such doctrines as protectionism and import substitution.
Adidas	Adidas is a German sports apparel manufacturer, part of the Adidas Group. The company was named after its founder, Adolf Dassler, who started producing shoes in the 1920s in Herzogenaurach near Nuremberg with the help of his brother Rudolf Dassler who later formed rival shoe company PUMA AG.
Appeal	Appeal refers to the act of asking an appellate court to overturn a decision after the trial court's final judgment has been entered.

Go to **Cram101.com** for the Practice Tests for this Chapter.

265

Industrial robot	An industrial robot is officially defined by ISO as an automatically controlled, reprogrammable, multipurpose manipulator programmable in three or more axes.
Intel	Intel Corporation, founded in 1968 and based in Santa Clara, California, USA, is the world's largest semiconductor company. Intel is best known for its PC microprocessors, where it maintains roughly 80% market share.
External customers	Dealers, who buy products to sell to others, and ultimate customers, who buy products for their own personal use are referred to as external customers.
Sustainable competitive advantage	A strength, relative to competitors, in the markets served and the products offered is referred to as the sustainable competitive advantage.
Labor	People's physical and mental talents and efforts that are used to help produce goods and services are called labor.
Variable	A variable is something measured by a number; it is used to analyze what happens to other things when the size of that number changes.
Management information system	A computer-based system that provides information and support for effective managerial decision makin is referred to as a management information system.
Information system	An information system is a system whether automated or manual, that comprises people, machines, and/or methods organized to collect, process, transmit, and disseminate data that represent user information.
Capital expenditure	A substantial expenditure that is used by a company to acquire or upgrade physical assets such as equipment, property, industrial buildings, including those which improve the quality and life of an asset is referred to as a capital expenditure.
Wage	The payment for the service of a unit of labor, per unit time. In trade theory, it is the only payment to labor, usually unskilled labor. In empirical work, wage data may exclude other compenzation, which must be added to get the total cost of employment.
Return on investment	Return on investment refers to the return a businessperson gets on the money he and other owners invest in the firm; for example, a business that earned $100 on a $1,000 investment would have a ROI of 10 percent: 100 divided by 1000.
Capitalism	Capitalism refers to an economic system in which capital is mostly owned by private individuals and corporations. Contrasts with communism.
Instrument	Instrument refers to an economic variable that is controlled by policy makers and can be used to influence other variables, called targets. Examples are monetary and fiscal policies used to achieve external and internal balance.
Dividend	Amount of corporate profits paid out for each share of stock is referred to as dividend.
Holder	A person in possession of a document of title or an instrument payable or indorsed to him, his order, or to bearer is a holder.
Welfare	Welfare refers to the economic well being of an individual, group, or economy. For individuals, it is conceptualized by a utility function. For groups, including countries and the world, it is a tricky philosophical concept, since individuals fare differently.
Swap	In finance a swap is a derivative, where two counterparties exchange one stream of cash flows against another stream. These streams are called the legs of the swap. The cash flows are calculated over a notional principal amount. Swaps are often used to hedge certain risks, for instance interest rate risk. Another use is speculation.

Go to **Cram101.com** for the Practice Tests for this Chapter.

Eli Lilly	Eli Lilly is a global pharmaceutical company and one of the world's largest corporations. Eli Lilly was the first distributor of methadone, an analgesic used frequently in the treatment of heroin, opium and other opioid and narcotic drug addictions.
Bayer	Bayer is a German chemical and pharmaceutical company founded in 1863. By 1899, their trademark Aspirin was registered worldwide for the Bayer brand of acetylsalicylic acid, but through the widespread use to describe all brands of the compound, and Bayer's inability to protect its trademark the word "aspirin" lost its trademark status in the United States and some other countries.
Siemens	Siemens is the world's largest conglomerate company. Worldwide, Siemens and its subsidiaries employs 461,000 people (2005) in 190 countries and reported global sales of €75.4 billion in fiscal year 2005.
Entrepreneurship	The assembling of resources to produce new or improved products and technologies is referred to as entrepreneurship.
Logistics	Those activities that focus on getting the right amount of the right products to the right place at the right time at the lowest possible cost is referred to as logistics.
Below the line	Below the line is an advertising technique. It uses less conventional methods than the usual specific channels of advertising to promote products, services, etc. than ATL (Above the line) strategy.
Merrill Lynch	Merrill Lynch through its subsidiaries and affiliates, provides capital markets services, investment banking and advisory services, wealth management, asset management, insurance, banking and related products and services on a global basis. It is best known for its Global Private Client services and its strong sales force.
Asset stripping	Asset stripping is the practice of buying a company in order to sell its assets individually at a profit. Asset stripping is also sometimes used to describe the practice of investors dealing directly with armed militant groups in developing nations to take direct control of assets that legally belong to the state or commons or any group in society that the investor and armed militant can effectively coerce.
Junk bond	In finance, a junk bond is a bond that is rated below investment grade. These bonds have a higher risk of defaulting, but typically pay high yields in order to make them attractive to investors.
Bond	Bond refers to a debt instrument, issued by a borrower and promising a specified stream of payments to the purchaser, usually regular interest payments plus a final repayment of principal.
Affiliation	A relationship with other websites in which a company can cross-promote and is credited for sales that accrue through their site is an affiliation.
Stockholder	A stockholder is an individual or company (including a corporation) that legally owns one or more shares of stock in a joined stock company. The shareholders are the owners of a corporation. Companies listed at the stock market strive to enhance shareholder value.
Stock market	An organized marketplace in which common stocks are traded. In the United States, the largest stock market is the New York Stock Exchange, on which are traded the stocks of the largest U.S. companies.
Market price	Market price is an economic concept with commonplace familiarity; it is the price that a good or service is offered at, or will fetch, in the marketplace; it is of interest mainly in the study of microeconomics.
Capital gain	Capital gain refers to the gain in value that the owner of an asset experiences when the price of the asset rises, including when the currency in which the asset is denominated

Go to **Cram101.com** for the Practice Tests for this Chapter.

	appreciates.
Nabisco	In 2000 Philip Morris Companies acquired Nabisco; that acquisition was approved by the Federal Trade Commission subject to the divestiture of products in five areas: three Jell-O and Royal brands types of products (dry-mix gelatin dessert, dry-mix pudding, no-bake desserts), intense mints (such as Altoids), and baking powder. Kraft later purchased the company.
Shares	Shares refer to an equity security, representing a shareholder's ownership of a corporation. Shares are one of a finite number of equal portions in the capital of a company, entitling the owner to a proportion of distributed, non-reinvested profits known as dividends and to a portion of the value of the company in case of liquidation.
Transnational	Transnational focuses on the heightened interconnectivity between people all around the world and the loosening of boundaries between countries.
Motorola	The Six Sigma quality system was developed at Motorola even though it became most well known because of its use by General Electric. It was created by engineer Bill Smith, under the direction of Bob Galvin (son of founder Paul Galvin) when he was running the company.
Production efficiency	A situation in which the economy cannot produce more of one good without producing less of some other good is referred to as production efficiency.
Strategic intent	Strategic intent is when a firm relentlessly pursues a difficult strategic goa and concentrates its competitive actions and energies on achieving that goal.
Honeywell	Honeywell is a major American multinational corporation that produces electronic control systems and automation equipment. It is a major supplier of engineering services and avionics for NASA, Boeing and the United States Department of Defense.
Complement	A good that is used in conjunction with another good is a complement. For example, cameras and film would complement eachother.
Cost center	A cost center is a division that adds to the cost of the organization, but only indirectly adds to the profit of the company. Examples include Research and Development, Marketing and Customer service. A cost center is often identified with a speed type number.
Outsourcing	Outsourcing refers to a production activity that was previously done inside a firm or plant that is now conducted outside that firm or plant.
Laggards	Laggards refer to the 16 percent of the market who have fear of debt, use friends for information sources, and accept ideas and products only after they have been long established in the market.
Market power	The ability of a single economic actor to have a substantial influence on market prices is market power.
Basic research	Involves discovering new knowledge rather than solving specific problems is called basic research.
Transparency	Transparency refers to a concept that describes a company being so open to other companies working with it that the once-solid barriers between them become see-through and electronic information is shared as if the companies were one.
Internalize	Internalize refers to causing, usually by a tax or subsidy, an external cost or benefit of someone's actions to be experienced by them directly, so that they will take it into account in their decisions.
Quality circle	A quality circle is a volunteer group composed of workers who meet together to discuss workplace improvement, and make presentations to management with their ideas.

Go to **Cram101.com** for the Practice Tests for this Chapter.

Inventory	Tangible property held for sale in the normal course of business or used in producing goods or services for sale is an inventory.
Statistical process control	Statistical process control is a method for achieving quality control in manufacturing processes. It is a set of methods using statistical tools such as mean, variance and others, to detect whether the process observed is under control.
Value engineering	Systematic evaluation of all aspects of the value-chain business functions, with the objective of reducing costs while satisfying customer needs is referred to as value engineering.
Design for manufacture	Design for manufacture refers to the principle of designing products so that they are cost effective and easy to make.
Useful life	The length of service of a productive facility or piece of equipment is its useful life. The period of time during which an asset will have economic value and be usable.
Complaint	The pleading in a civil case in which the plaintiff states his claim and requests relief is called complaint. In the common law, it is a formal legal document that sets out the basic facts and legal reasons that the filing party (the plaintiffs) believes are sufficient to support a claim against another person, persons, entity or entities (the defendants) that entitles the plaintiff(s) to a remedy (either money damages or injunctive relief).
Openness	Openness refers to the extent to which an economy is open, often measured by the ratio of its trade to GDP.
Senior management	Senior management is generally a team of individuals at the highest level of organizational management who have the day-to-day responsibilities of managing a corporation.
Financial risk	The risk related to the inability of the firm to meet its debt obligations as they come due is called financial risk.
Competitor analysis	Competitor analysis in marketing and strategic management is an assessment of the strengths and weaknesses of current and potential competitors.
Regular meeting	A meeting held by the board of directors that is held at regular intervals at the time and place established in the bylaws is called a regular meeting.

Technology life cycle	Most new technologies follow a similar technology life cycle. This is similar to a product life cycle, but applies to an entire technology, or a generation of a technology. Technology adoption is the most common phenomenon driving the evolution of industries along the industry lifecycle.
Global competition	Global competition exists when competitive conditions across national markets are linked strongly enough to form a true international market and when leading competitors compete head to head in many different countries.
Globalization	The increasing world-wide integration of markets for goods, services and capital that attracted special attention in the late 1990s is called globalization.
Acceleration	Acceleration refers to the shortening of the time for the performance of a contract or the payment of a note by the operation of some provision in the contract or note itself.
Complexity	The technical sophistication of the product and hence the amount of understanding required to use it is referred to as complexity. It is the opposite of simplicity.
Technology	The body of knowledge and techniques that can be used to combine economic resources to produce goods and services is called technology.
Market	A market is, as defined in economics, a social arrangement that allows buyers and sellers to discover information and carry out a voluntary exchange of goods or services.
Globalization of markets	Moving away from an economic system in which national markets are distinct entities, isolated by trade barriers and barriers of distance, time, and culture, and toward a system in which national markets are merging into one global market is globalization of markets.
Transnational	Transnational focuses on the heightened interconnectivity between people all around the world and the loosening of boundaries between countries.
Management	Management characterizes the process of leading and directing all or part of an organization, often a business, through the deployment and manipulation of resources. Early twentieth-century management writer Mary Parker Follett defined management as "the art of getting things done through people."
Asset	An item of property, such as land, capital, money, a share in ownership, or a claim on others for future payment, such as a bond or a bank deposit is an asset.
Global strategy	Global strategy refers to strategy focusing on increasing profitability by reaping cost reductions from experience curve and location economies.
Consultant	A professional that provides expert advice in a particular field or area in which customers occassionaly require this type of knowledge is a consultant.
Core	A core is the set of feasible allocations in an economy that cannot be improved upon by subset of the set of the economy's consumers (a coalition). In construction, when the force in an element is within a certain center section, the core, the element will only be under compression.
Competitive advantage	A business is said to have a competitive advantage when its unique strengths, often based on cost, quality, time, and innovation, offer consumers a greater percieved value and there by differtiating it from its competitors.
Competitiveness	Competitiveness usually refers to characteristics that permit a firm to compete effectively with other firms due to low cost or superior technology, perhaps internationally.
Positioning	The art and science of fitting the product or service to one or more segments of the market in such a way as to set it meaningfully apart from competition is called positioning.
Economy	The income, expenditures, and resources that affect the cost of running a business and

Go to **Cram101.com** for the Practice Tests for this Chapter.

household are called an economy.

Scope	Scope of a project is the sum total of all projects products and their requirements or features.
Balance	In banking and accountancy, the outstanding balance is the amount of money owned, (or due), that remains in a deposit account (or a loan account) at a given date, after all past remittances, payments and withdrawal have been accounted for. It can be positive (then, in the balance sheet of a firm, it is an asset) or negative (a liability).
Functional manager	A manager who is responsible for a department that performs a single functional task and has employees with similar training and skills is referred to as a functional manager.
Interest	In finance and economics, interest is the price paid by a borrower for the use of a lender's money. In other words, interest is the amount of paid to "rent" money for a period of time.
Corporate Strategy	Corporate strategy is concerned with the firm's choice of business, markets and activities and thus it defines the overall scope and direction of the business.
Business strategy	Business strategy, which refers to the aggregated operational strategies of single business firm or that of an SBU in a diversified corporation refers to the way in which a firm competes in its chosen arenas.
Domestic	From or in one's own country. A domestic producer is one that produces inside the home country. A domestic price is the price inside the home country. Opposite of 'foreign' or 'world.'.
Product development	In business and engineering, new product development is the complete process of bringing a new product to market. There are two parallel aspects to this process : one involves product engineering ; the other marketing analysis. Marketers see new product development as the first stage in product life cycle management, engineers as part of Product Lifecycle Management.
Subsidiary	A company that is controlled by another company or corporation is a subsidiary.
Asea Brown Boveri	Asea Brown Boveri, is a multinational corporation headquartered in Zürich, Switzerland, operating mainly in the power and automation technology areas. It operates in around 100 countries, with about 104,000 employees.
Leverage	Leverage is using given resources in such a way that the potential positive or negative outcome is magnified. In finance, this generally refers to borrowing.
Distribution	Distribution in economics, the manner in which total output and income is distributed among individuals or factors.
Configuration	An organization's shape, which reflects the division of labor and the means of coordinating the divided tasks is configuration.
Committee	A long-lasting, sometimes permanent team in the organization structure created to deal with tasks that recur regularly is the committee.
Policy	Similar to a script in that a policy can be a less than completely rational decision-making method. Involves the use of a pre-existing set of decision steps for any problem that presents itself.
Operation	A standardized method or technique that is performed repetitively, often on different materials resulting in different finished goods is called an operation.
Supply	Supply is the aggregate amount of any material good that can be called into being at a certain price point; it comprises one half of the equation of supply and demand. In classical economic theory, a curve representing supply is one of the factors that produce price.

Go to **Cram101.com** for the Practice Tests for this Chapter.

Labor	People's physical and mental talents and efforts that are used to help produce goods and services are called labor.
Product manager	Product manager refers to a person who plans, implements, and controls the annual and long-range plans for the products for which he or she is responsible.
Commodity	Could refer to any good, but in trade a commodity is usually a raw material or primary product that enters into international trade, such as metals or basic agricultural products.
Pfizer	Pfizer is the world's largest pharmaceutical company based in New York City. It produces the number-one selling drug Lipitor (atorvastatin, used to lower blood cholesterol).
Product design	Product Design is defined as the idea generation, concept development, testing and manufacturing or implementation of a physical object or service. It is possibly the evolution of former discipline name - Industrial Design.
Marketing	Promoting and selling products or services to customers, or prospective customers, is referred to as marketing.
Chief information officer	The chief information officer is a job title for the head of information technology group within an organization. They often report to the chief executive officer or chief financial officer.
Manufacturing	Production of goods primarily by the application of labor and capital to raw materials and other intermediate inputs, in contrast to agriculture, mining, forestry, fishing, and services a manufacturing.
Chief financial officer	Chief financial officer refers to executive responsible for overseeing the financial operations of an organization.
Best practice	Best practice is a management idea which asserts that there is a technique, method, process, activity, incentive or reward that is more effective at delivering a particular outcome than any other technique, method, process, etc.
Innovation	Innovation refers to the first commercially successful introduction of a new product, the use of a new method of production, or the creation of a new form of business organization.
Retailing	All activities involved in selling, renting, and providing goods and services to ultimate consumers for personal, family, or household use is referred to as retailing.
Industry	A group of firms that produce identical or similar products is an industry. It is also used specifically to refer to an area of economic production focused on manufacturing which involves large amounts of capital investment before any profit can be realized, also called "heavy industry".
Regulation	Regulation refers to restrictions state and federal laws place on business with regard to the conduct of its activities.
Trend	Trend refers to the long-term movement of an economic variable, such as its average rate of increase or decrease over enough years to encompass several business cycles.
Competitor	Other organizations in the same industry or type of business that provide a good or service to the same set of customers is referred to as a competitor.
Foreign subsidiary	A company owned in a foreign country by another company is referred to as foreign subsidiary.
Line organization	An organization that has direct two-way lines of responsibility, authority, and communication running from the top to the bottom of the organization, with all people reporting to only one supervisor is referred to as line organization.
Specialist	A specialist is a trader who makes a market in one or several stocks and holds the limit

order book for those stocks.

Production	The creation of finished goods and services using the factors of production: land, labor, capital, entrepreneurship, and knowledge.
Channel	Channel, in communications (sometimes called communications channel), refers to the medium used to convey information from a sender (or transmitter) to a receiver.
Corporate level	Corporate level refers to level at which top management directs overall strategy for the entire organization.
Facilitator	A facilitator is someone who skilfully helps a group of people understand their common objectives and plan to achieve them without personally taking any side of the argument.
Caterpillar	Caterpillar is a United States based corporation headquartered in Peoria, Illinois. Caterpillar is "the world's largest manufacturer of construction and mining equipment, diesel and natural gas engines, and industrial gas turbines."
Flexible manufacturing	Flexible manufacturing refers to designing machines to do multiple tasks so that they can produce a variety of products.
Evaluation	The consumer's appraisal of the product or brand on important attributes is called evaluation.
Brand	A name, symbol, or design that identifies the goods or services of one seller or group of sellers and distinguishes them from the goods and services of competitors is a brand.
Parent company	Parent company refers to the entity that has a controlling influence over another company. It may have its own operations, or it may have been set up solely for the purpose of owning the Subject Company.
International Business	International business refers to any firm that engages in international trade or investment.
Business unit	The lowest level of the company which contains the set of functions that carry a product through its life span from concept through manufacture, distribution, sales and service is a business unit.
Jurisdiction	The power of a court to hear and decide a case is called jurisdiction. It is the practical authority granted to a formally constituted body or to a person to deal with and make pronouncements on legal matters and, by implication, to administer justice within a defined area of responsibility.
Authority	Authority in agency law, refers to an agent's ability to affect his principal's legal relations with third parties. Also used to refer to an actor's legal power or ability to do something. In addition, sometimes used to refer to a statute, case, or other legal source that justifies a particular result.
Market position	Market position is a measure of the position of a company or product on a market.
Broker	In commerce, a broker is a party that mediates between a buyer and a seller. A broker who also acts as a seller or as a buyer becomes a principal party to the deal.
Corporate culture	The whole collection of beliefs, values, and behaviors of a firm that send messages to those within and outside the company about how business is done is the corporate culture.
Corporation	A legal entity chartered by a state or the Federal government that is distinct and separate from the individuals who own it is a corporation. This separation gives the corporation unique powers which other legal entities lack.
Transnational strategy	Plan to exploit experience-based cost and location economies, transfer core competencies with the firm, and pay attention to local responsiveness is called transnational strategy.

Go to **Cram101.com** for the Practice Tests for this Chapter.

281

Mentor	An experienced employee who supervises, coaches, and guides lower-level employees by introducing them to the right people and generally being their organizational sponsor is a mentor.
Union	A worker association that bargains with employers over wages and working conditions is called a union.
Negotiation	Negotiation is the process whereby interested parties resolve disputes, agree upon courses of action, bargain for individual or collective advantage, and/or attempt to craft outcomes which serve their mutual interests.
Transnational corporation	A firm that tries to simultaneously realize gains from experience curve economies, location economies, and global learning, while remaining locally responsive is called transnational corporation.
Senior executive	Senior executive means a chief executive officer, chief operating officer, chief financial officer and anyone in charge of a principal business unit or function.
Integration	Economic integration refers to reducing barriers among countries to transactions and to movements of goods, capital, and labor, including harmonization of laws, regulations, and standards. Integrated markets theoretically function as a unified market.
Leadership	Management merely consists of leadership applied to business situations; or in other words: management forms a sub-set of the broader process of leadership.
Continuity	A media scheduling strategy where a continuous pattern of advertising is used over the time span of the advertising campaign is continuity.
Budget	Budget refers to an account, usually for a year, of the planned expenditures and the expected receipts of an entity. For a government, the receipts are tax revenues.
Stakeholder	A stakeholder is an individual or group with a vested interest in or expectation for organizational performance. Usually stakeholders can either have an effect on or are affected by an organization.
Proactive	To be proactive is to act before a situation becomes a source of confrontation or crisis. It is the opposite of "retroactive," which refers to actions taken after an event.
Corporate goal	A strategic performance target that the entire organization must reach to pursue its vision is a corporate goal.
Assignment	A transfer of property or some right or interest is referred to as assignment.
Personnel	A collective term for all of the employees of an organization. Personnel is also commonly used to refer to the personnel management function or the organizational unit responsible for administering personnel programs.
Capital	Capital generally refers to financial wealth, especially that used to start or maintain a business. In classical economics, capital is one of four factors of production, the others being land and labor and entrepreneurship.
Portfolio	In finance, a portfolio is a collection of investments held by an institution or a private individual. Holding but not always a portfolio is part of an investment and risk-limiting strategy called diversification. By owning several assets, certain types of risk (in particular specific risk) can be reduced.
Centralization	A structural policy in which decision-making authority is concentrated at the top of the organizational hierarchy is referred to as centralization.
Socialization	Socialization is the process by which human beings or animals learn to adopt the behavior patterns of the community in which they live. For both humans and animals, this is typically

Go to **Cram101.com** for the Practice Tests for this Chapter.

thought to occur during the early stages of life, during which individuals develop the skills and knowledge necessary to function within their culture and environment.

Managing director

Managing director is the term used for the chief executive of many limited companies in the United Kingdom, Commonwealth and some other English speaking countries. The title reflects their role as both a member of the Board of Directors but also as the senior manager.

Nielsen

When TV viewers or entertainment professionals in the United States mention "ratings" they are generally referring to Nielsen Ratings, a system developed by Nielsen Media Research to determine the audience size and composition of television programming. Nielsen Ratings are offered in over forty countries.

Collaboration

Collaboration occurs when the interaction between groups is very important to goal attainment and the goals are compatible. Wherein people work together —applying both to the work of individuals as well as larger collectives and societies.

International strategy

Trying to create value by transferring core competencies to foreign markets where indigenous competitors lack those competencies is called international strategy.

Export

In economics, an export is any good or commodity, shipped or otherwise transported out of a country, province, town to another part of the world in a legitimate fashion, typically for use in trade or sale.

Primary demand

Primary demand refers to desire for the product class rather than for a specific brand.

Consumption

In Keynesian economics consumption refers to personal consumption expenditure, i.e., the purchase of currently produced goods and services out of income, out of savings (net worth), or from borrowed funds. It refers to that part of disposable income that does not go to saving.

Per capita

Per capita refers to per person. Usually used to indicate the average per person of any given statistic, commonly income.

Public corporation

A corporation formed to meet a specific governmental or political purpose is referred to as public corporation.

Distribution channel

A distribution channel is a chain of intermediaries, each passing a product down the chain to the next organization, before it finally reaches the consumer or end-user.

Rationalization

Rationalization in economics is an attempt to change a pre-existing ad-hoc workflow into one that is based on a set of published rules.

Consolidation

The combination of two or more firms, generally of equal size and market power, to form an entirely new entity is a consolidation.

Accounting

A system that collects and processes financial information about an organization and reports that information to decision makers is referred to as accounting.

Wholesale

According to the United Nations Statistics Division Wholesale is the resale of new and used goods to retailers, to industrial, commercial, institutional or professional users, or to other wholesalers, or involves acting as an agent or broker in buying merchandise for, or selling merchandise, to such persons or companies.

Exchange rate

Exchange rate refers to the price at which one country's currency trades for another, typically on the exchange market.

Exporting

Selling products to another country is called exporting.

Exchange

The trade of things of value between buyer and seller so that each is better off after the trade is called the exchange.

Cooperative

A business owned and controlled by the people who use it, producers, consumers, or workers

Go to **Cram101.com** for the Practice Tests for this Chapter.

with similar needs who pool their resources for mutual gain is called cooperative.

Agent	A person who makes economic decisions for another economic actor. A hired manager operates as an agent for a firm's owner.
Acquisition	A company's purchase of the property and obligations of another company is an acquisition.
Purchasing	Purchasing refers to the function in a firm that searches for quality material resources, finds the best suppliers, and negotiates the best price for goods and services.
Property	Assets defined in the broadest legal sense. Property includes the unrealized receivables of a cash basis taxpayer, but not services rendered.
Recession	A significant decline in economic activity. In the U.S., recession is approximately defined as two successive quarters of falling GDP, as judged by NBER.
Slowdown	A slowdown is an industrial action in which employees perform their duties but seek to reduce productivity or efficiency in their performance of these duties. A slowdown may be used as either a prelude or an alternative to a strike, as it is seen as less disruptive as well as less risky and costly for workers and their union.
Merger	Merger refers to the combination of two firms into a single firm.
Fund	Independent accounting entity with a self-balancing set of accounts segregated for the purposes of carrying on specific activities is referred to as a fund.
Profit	Profit refers to the return to the resource entrepreneurial ability; total revenue minus total cost.
Middle management	Middle management refers to the level of management that includes general managers, division managers, and branch and plant managers who are responsible for tactical planning and controlling.
Delegation	Delegation is the handing of a task over to another person, usually a subordinate. It is the assignment of authority and responsibility to another person to carry out specific activities.
Status quo	Status quo is a Latin term meaning the present, current, existing state of affairs.
Mistake	In contract law a mistake is incorrect understanding by one or more parties to a contract and may be used as grounds to invalidate the agreement. Common law has identified three different types of mistake in contract: unilateral mistake, mutual mistake, and common mistake.
Repositioning	Changing the position an offering occupies in a consumer's mind relative to competitive offerings and so expanding or otherwise altering its potential market is called repositioning.
Market share	That fraction of an industry's output accounted for by an individual firm or group of firms is called market share.
Restructuring	Restructuring is the corporate management term for the act of partially dismantling and reorganizing a company for the purpose of making it more efficient and therefore more profitable.
Brand image	The advertising metric that measures the type and favorability of consumer perceptions of the brand is referred to as the brand image.
Market price	Market price is an economic concept with commonplace familiarity; it is the price that a good or service is offered at, or will fetch, in the marketplace; it is of interest mainly in the study of microeconomics.
Price point	A price point is a price for which demand is relatively high.

287

Points	Loan origination fees that may be deductible as interest by a buyer of property. A seller of property who pays points reduces the selling price by the amount of the points paid for the buyer.
Controlling	A management function that involves determining whether or not an organization is progressing toward its goals and objectives, and taking corrective action if it is not is called controlling.
Corporate identity	In marketing, a corporate identity is the "persona" of a corporation which is designed to accord with and facilitate the attainment of business objectives, and is usually visibly manifested by way of branding and the use of trademarks.
Shares	Shares refer to an equity security, representing a shareholder's ownership of a corporation. Shares are one of a finite number of equal portions in the capital of a company, entitling the owner to a proportion of distributed, non-reinvested profits known as dividends and to a portion of the value of the company in case of liquidation.
Decentralization	Decentralization is the process of redistributing decision-making closer to the point of service or action. This gives freedom to managers at lower levels of the organization to make decisions.
Management team	A management team is directly responsible for managing the day-to-day operations (and profitability) of a company.
Proprietary	Proprietary indicates that a party, or proprietor, exercises private ownership, control or use over an item of property, usually to the exclusion of other parties. Where a party, holds or claims proprietary interests in relation to certain types of property (eg. a creative literary work, or software), that property may also be the subject of intellectual property law (eg. copyright or patents).
Appeal	Appeal refers to the act of asking an appellate court to overturn a decision after the trial court's final judgment has been entered.
Buyer	A buyer refers to a role in the buying center with formal authority and responsibility to select the supplier and negotiate the terms of the contract.
Outsourcing	Outsourcing refers to a production activity that was previously done inside a firm or plant that is now conducted outside that firm or plant.
Joint venture	Joint venture refers to an undertaking by two parties for a specific purpose and duration, taking any of several legal forms.
Partnership	In the common law, a partnership is a type of business entity in which partners share with each other the profits or losses of the business undertaking in which they have all invested.
Marketing Plan	Marketing plan refers to a road map for the marketing activities of an organization for a specified future period of time, such as one year or five years.
Trust	An arrangement in which shareholders of independent firms agree to give up their stock in exchange for trust certificates that entitle them to a share of the trust's common profits.
Premium	Premium refers to the fee charged by an insurance company for an insurance policy. The rate of losses must be relatively predictable: In order to set the premium (prices) insurers must be able to estimate them accurately.
Senior management	Senior management is generally a team of individuals at the highest level of organizational management who have the day-to-day responsibilities of managing a corporation.
Context	The effect of the background under which a message often takes on more and richer meaning is a context. Context is especially important in cross-cultural interactions because some cultures are said to be high context or low context.

Go to Cram101.com for the Practice Tests for this Chapter.

289

Financial risk	The risk related to the inability of the firm to meet its debt obligations as they come due is called financial risk.
Investment	Investment refers to spending for the production and accumulation of capital and additions to inventories. In a financial sense, buying an asset with the expectation of making a return.
Inventory	Tangible property held for sale in the normal course of business or used in producing goods or services for sale is an inventory.
Contract	A contract is a "promise" or an "agreement" that is enforced or recognized by the law. In the civil law, a contract is considered to be part of the general law of obligations.
Expense	In accounting, an expense represents an event in which an asset is used up or a liability is incurred. In terms of the accounting equation, expenses reduce owners' equity.
Brand management	Brand management is the application of marketing techniques to a specific product, product line, or brand. It seeks to increase the product's perceived value to the customer and thereby increase brand franchise and brand equity.
Public relations	Public relations refers to the management function that evaluates public attitudes, changes policies and procedures in response to the public's requests, and executes a program of action and information to earn public understanding and acceptance.
Sales management	Planning the selling program and implementing and controlling the personal selling effort of the firm is called sales management.
Best efforts	Best efforts refer to a distribution in which the investment banker agrees to work for a commission rather than actually underwriting the issue for resale. It is a procedure that is used by smaller investment bankers with relatively unknown companies. The investment banker is not directly taking the risk for distribution.
Firm	An organization that employs resources to produce a good or service for profit and owns and operates one or more plants is referred to as a firm.
Board of directors	The group of individuals elected by the stockholders of a corporation to oversee its operations is a board of directors.
Standing	Standing refers to the legal requirement that anyone seeking to challenge a particular action in court must demonstrate that such action substantially affects his legitimate interests before he will be entitled to bring suit.
Holding	The holding is a court's determination of a matter of law based on the issue presented in the particular case. In other words: under this law, with these facts, this result.
Business plan	A detailed written statement that describes the nature of the business, the target market, the advantages the business will have in relation to competition, and the resources and qualifications of the owner is referred to as a business plan.
Standardized product	Standardized product refers to a product whose buyers are indifferent to the seller from whom they purchase it, as long as the price charged by all sellers is the same; a product all units of which are identical and thus are perfect substitutes.
Allowance	Reduction in the selling price of goods extended to the buyer because the goods are defective or of lower quality than the buyer ordered and to encourage a buyer to keep merchandise that would otherwise be returned is the allowance.
Logistics	Those activities that focus on getting the right amount of the right products to the right place at the right time at the lowest possible cost is referred to as logistics.
Tariff	A tax imposed by a nation on an imported good is called a tariff.
Wholly owned	A subsidiary in which the firm owns 100 percent of the stock is a wholly owned subsidiary.

Go to **Cram101.com** for the Practice Tests for this Chapter.

subsidiary	
Revenue	Revenue is a U.S. business term for the amount of money that a company receives from its activities, mostly from sales of products and/or services to customers.
Equity	Equity is the name given to the set of legal principles, in countries following the English common law tradition, which supplement strict rules of law where their application would operate harshly, so as to achieve what is sometimes referred to as "natural justice."
Management control	That aspect of management concerned with the comparison of actual versus planned performance as well as the development and implementation of procedures to correct substandard performance is called management control.
Option	A contract that gives the purchaser the option to buy or sell the underlying financial instrument at a specified price, called the exercise price or strike price, within a specific period of time.
Hierarchy	A system of grouping people in an organization according to rank from the top down in which all subordinate managers must report to one person is called a hierarchy.
Competitor analysis	Competitor analysis in marketing and strategic management is an assessment of the strengths and weaknesses of current and potential competitors.
Benchmarking	The continuous process of comparing the levels of performance in producing products and services and executing activities against the best levels of performance is benchmarking.
Service	Service refers to a "non tangible product" that is not embodied in a physical good and that typically effects some change in another product, person, or institution. Contrasts with good.
Boston Consulting Group	The Boston Consulting Group is a management consulting firm founded by Harvard Business School alum Bruce Henderson in 1963. In 1965 Bruce Henderson thought that to survive, much less grow, in a competitive landscape occupied by hundreds of larger and better-known consulting firms, a distinctive identity was needed, and pioneered "Business Strategy" as a special area of expertise.
Mergers and acquisitions	The phrase mergers and acquisitions refers to the aspect of corporate finance strategy and management dealing with the merging and acquiring of different companies as well as other assets. Usually mergers occur in a friendly setting where executives from the respective companies participate in a due diligence process to ensure a successful combination of all parts.
Hearing	A hearing is a proceeding before a court or other decision-making body or officer. A hearing is generally distinguished from a trial in that it is usually shorter and often less formal.
Complement	A good that is used in conjunction with another good is a complement. For example, cameras and film would complement eachother.
Gain	In finance, gain is a profit or an increase in value of an investment such as a stock or bond. Gain is calculated by fair market value or the proceeds from the sale of the investment minus the sum of the purchase price and all costs associated with it.
Total revenue	Total revenue refers to the total number of dollars received by a firm from the sale of a product; equal to the total expenditures for the product produced by the firm; equal to the quantity sold multiplied by the price at which it is sold.
Frequency	Frequency refers to the speed of the up and down movements of a fluctuating economic variable; that is, the number of times per unit of time that the variable completes a cycle of up and down movement.
Variable	A variable is something measured by a number; it is used to analyze what happens to other

Go to **Cram101.com** for the Practice Tests for this Chapter.

things when the size of that number changes.

Mitsubishi	In a statement, the Mitsubishi says that forced labor is inconsistent with the company's values, and that the various lawsuits targeting Mitsubishi are misdirected. Instead, a spokesman says the Mitsubishi of World War II is not the same Mitsubishi of today. The conglomerate also rejected a Chinese slave labor lawsuit demand by saying it bore no responsibility since it was national policy to employ Chinese laborers."
Fixture	Fixture refers to a thing that was originally personal property and that has been actually or constructively affixed to the soil itself or to some structure legally a part of the land.
Analyst	Analyst refers to a person or tool with a primary function of information analysis, generally with a more limited, practical and short term set of goals than a researcher.
Installations	Support goods, consisting of buildings and fixed equipment are called installations.
Margin	A deposit by a buyer in stocks with a seller or a stockbroker, as security to cover fluctuations in the market in reference to stocks that the buyer has purchased but for which he has not paid is a margin. Commodities are also traded on margin.
Controller	Controller refers to the financial executive primarily responsible for management accounting and financial accounting. Also called chief accounting officer.
Localization	As an element of wireless marketing strategy, transmitting messages that are relevant to the user's current geographical location are referred to as localization.
Expatriate	Employee sent by his or her company to live and manage operations in a different country is called an expatriate.
Transfer price	Transfer price refers to the price one subunit charges for a product or service supplied to another subunit of the same organization.
Security	Security refers to a claim on the borrower future income that is sold by the borrower to the lender. A security is a type of transferable interest representing financial value.
Estate	An estate is the totality of the legal rights, interests, entitlements and obligations attaching to property. In the context of wills and probate, it refers to the totality of the property which the deceased owned or in which some interest was held.
Business opportunity	A business opportunity involves the sale or lease of any product, service, equipment, etc. that will enable the purchaser-licensee to begin a business
Business development	Business development emcompasses a number of techniques designed to grow an economic enterprise. Such techniques include, but are not limited to, assessments of marketing opportunities and target markets, intelligence gathering on customers and competitors, generating leads for possible sales, followup sales activity, and formal proposal writing.
Federal government	Federal government refers to the government of the United States, as distinct from the state and local governments.
Bid	A bid price is a price offered by a buyer when he/she buys a good. In the context of stock trading on a stock exchange, the bid price is the highest price a buyer of a stock is willing to pay for a share of that given stock.
General Electric	In 1876, Thomas Alva Edison opened a new laboratory in Menlo Park, New Jersey. Out of the laboratory was to come perhaps the most famous invention of all—a successful development of the incandescent electric lamp. By 1890, Edison had organized his various businesses into the Edison General Electric Company.
Thomas Edison	Thomas Edison was one of the first inventors to apply the principles of mass production to the process of invention, and can therefore be credited with the creation of the first

Go to **Cram101.com** for the Practice Tests for this Chapter.

295

industrial research laboratory. He developed many devices which greatly influenced life in the 20th century.

Strategic planning	The process of determining the major goals of the organization and the policies and strategies for obtaining and using resources to achieve those goals is called strategic planning.
Jack Welch	In 1986, GE acquired NBC. During the 90s, Jack Welch helped to modernize GE by emphasizing a shift from manufacturing to services. He also made hundreds of acquisitions and made a push to dominate markets abroad. Welch adopted the Six Sigma quality program in late 1995.
Customer focus	Customer focus acknowledges that the more a company understands and meets the real needs of its consumers, the more likely it is to have happy customers who come back for more, and tell their friends.
Empowerment	Giving employees the authority and responsibility to respond quickly to customer requests is called empowerment.
Harvard Business Review	Harvard Business Review is a research-based magazine written for business practitioners, it claims a high ranking business readership and enjoys the reverence of academics, executives, and management consultants. It has been the frequent publishing home for well known scholars and management thinkers.
Financial statement	Financial statement refers to a summary of all the transactions that have occurred over a particular period.
Structural change	Changes in the relative importance of different areas of an economy over time, usually measured in terms of their share of output, employment, or total spending is structural change.
Strategic business unit	Strategic business unit is understood as a business unit within the overall corporate identity which is distinguishable from other business because it serves a defined external market where management can conduct strategic planning in relation to products and markets. When companies become really large, they are best thought of as being composed of a number of businesses
General manager	A manager who is responsible for several departments that perform different functions is called general manager.
Small business	Small business refers to a business that is independently owned and operated, is not dominant in its field of operation, and meets certain standards of size in terms of employees or annual receipts.
Market development	Selling existing products to new markets is called market development.
Integration process	The way information such as product knowledge, meanings, and beliefs is combined to evaluate two or more alternatives is referred to as an integration process.
Shareholder	A shareholder is an individual or company (including a corporation) that legally owns one or more shares of stock in a joined stock company.
Free trade	Free trade refers to a situation in which there are no artificial barriers to trade, such as tariffs and quotas. Usually used, often only implicitly, with frictionless trade, so that it implies that there are no barriers to trade of any kind.
Buyout	A buyout is an investment transaction by which the entire or a controlling part of the stock of a company is sold. A firm buysout the stake of the company to strengthen its influence on the company's decision making body. A buyout can take the forms of a leveraged buyout or a management buyout.

Market opportunities	Market opportunities refer to areas where a company believes there are favorable demand trends, needs, and/or wants that are not being satisfied, and where it can compete effectively.
Utility	Utility refers to the want-satisfying power of a good or service; the satisfaction or pleasure a consumer obtains from the consumption of a good or service.
Audit	An examination of the financial reports to ensure that they represent what they claim and conform with generally accepted accounting principles is referred to as audit.
Credibility	The extent to which a source is perceived as having knowledge, skill, or experience relevant to a communication topic and can be trusted to give an unbiased opinion or present objective information on the issue is called credibility.
Consortia	B2B marketplaces sponsored by a group of otherwise competitive enterprises in a specific industry like automobile manufacturing or airline operations are called a consortia.
Yield	The interest rate that equates a future value or an annuity to a given present value is a yield.
Argument	The discussion by counsel for the respective parties of their contentions on the law and the facts of the case being tried in order to aid the jury in arriving at a correct and just conclusion is called argument.
Genzyme	Genzyme Corporation is a biotechnology company based in Cambridge, Massachusetts. Genzyme specializes in developing and commercializing orphan drugs. Many of its drugs are replacement enzymes which treat lysosomal storage disorders. Genzyme is known for charging extraordinary prices in order to recoup expenses from small patient populations.
Trademark	A distinctive word, name, symbol, device, or combination thereof, which enables consumers to identify favored products or services and which may find protection under state or federal law is a trademark.
Developed country	A developed country is one that enjoys a relatively high standard of living derived through an industrialized, diversified economy. Countries with a very high Human Development Index are generally considered developed countries.
Business model	A business model is the instrument by which a business intends to generate revenue and profits. It is a summary of how a company means to serve its employees and customers, and involves both strategy (what an business intends to do) as well as an implementation.
Raw material	Raw material refers to a good that has not been transformed by production; a primary product.
Cash flow	In finance, cash flow refers to the amounts of cash being received and spent by a business during a defined period of time, sometimes tied to a specific project. Most of the time they are being used to determine gaps in the liquid position of a company.
Foundation	A Foundation is a type of philanthropic organization set up by either individuals or institutions as a legal entity (either as a corporation or trust) with the purpose of distributing grants to support causes in line with the goals of the foundation.
Incidence	The ultimate economic effect of a tax on the real incomes of producers or consumers. Thus a sales tax may be paid by a retailer, but it is likely that the incidence falls upon the consumer.
Protocol	Protocol refers to a statement that, before product development begins, identifies a well-defined target market; specific customers' needs, wants, and preferences; and what the product will be and do.
Trial	An examination before a competent tribunal, according to the law of the land, of the facts or law put in issue in a cause, for the purpose of determining such issue is a trial. When the

Go to **Cram101.com** for the Practice Tests for this Chapter.

court hears and determines any issue of fact or law for the purpose of determining the rights of the parties, it may be considered a trial.

Entrepreneur

The owner/operator. The person who organizes, manages, and assumes the risks of a firm, taking a new idea or a new product and turning it into a successful business is an entrepreneur.

Internally generated funds

Internally generated funds refers to funds generated through the operations of the firm. The principal sources are retained earnings and cash flow added back from depreciation and other noncash deductions.

Value chain

The sequence of business functions in which usefulness is added to the products or services of a company is a value chain.

Internal controls

A company's policies and procedures designed to reduce the opportunity for fraud and to provide reasonable assurance that its objectives will be accomplished are internal controls.

Internal control

Internal control refers to the plan of organization and all the related methods and measures adopted within a business to safeguard its assets and enhance the accuracy and reliability of its accounting records.

Recovery

Characterized by rizing output, falling unemployment, rizing profits, and increasing economic activity following a decline is a recovery.

Entry barrier

An entry barrier or barrier to entry is an obstacle in the path of a potential firm which wants to enter a given market.

Intermediaries

Intermediaries specialize in information either to bring together two parties to a transaction or to buy in order to sell again.

Research and development

The use of resources for the deliberate discovery of new information and ways of doing things, together with the application of that information in inventing new products or processes is referred to as research and development.

Patent

The legal right to the proceeds from and control over the use of an invented product or process, granted for a fixed period of time, usually 20 years. Patent is one form of intellectual property that is subject of the TRIPS agreement.

Amgen

Amgen is an international biotechnology company headquartered in Newbury Park, California. Amgen is the largest independent biotech firm, with approx. 15,000 staff members in 2005.

Diversification

Investing in a collection of assets whose returns do not always move together, with the result that overall risk is lower than for individual assets is referred to as diversification.

Stock

In financial terminology, stock is the capital raized by a corporation, through the issuance and sale of shares.

Burroughs

Burroughs developed three highly innovative architectures, based on the design philosophy of "language directed design". Their machine instruction sets favored one or many high level programming languages, such as ALGOL, COBOL or FORTRAN. All three architectures were considered "main-frame" class machines.

Aid

Assistance provided by countries and by international institutions such as the World Bank to developing countries in the form of monetary grants, loans at low interest rates, in kind, or a combination of these is called aid. Aid can also refer to assistance of any type rendered to benefit some group or individual.

Business Week

Business Week is a business magazine published by McGraw-Hill. It was first published in 1929 under the direction of Malcolm Muir, who was serving as president of the McGraw-Hill Publishing company at the time. It is considered to be the standard both in industry and

Go to **Cram101.com** for the Practice Tests for this Chapter.

	among students.
Insurance	Insurance refers to a system by which individuals can reduce their exposure to risk of large losses by spreading the risks among a large number of persons.
Profit margin	Profit margin is a measure of profitability. It is calculated using a formula and written as a percentage or a number. Profit margin = Net income before tax and interest / Revenue.
Annual report	An annual report is prepared by corporate management that presents financial information including financial statements, footnotes, and the management discussion and analysis.
Promotion	Promotion refers to all the techniques sellers use to motivate people to buy products or services. An attempt by marketers to inform people about products and to persuade them to participate in an exchange.
Emerging markets	The term emerging markets is commonly used to describe business and market activity in industrializing or emerging regions of the world. It is sometimes loosely used as a replacement for emerging economies, but really signifies a business phenomenon that is not fully described by or constrained to geography or economic strength; such countries are considered to be in a transitional phase between developing and developed status.
Emerging market	The term emerging market is commonly used to describe business and market activity in industrializing or emerging regions of the world.
Tactic	A short-term immediate decision that, in its totality, leads to the achievement of strategic goals is called a tactic.
Philanthropy	Philanthropy is the voluntary act of donating money or goods or providing some other support to a charitable cause, usually over an extended period of time. In a more fundamental sense, philanthropy may encompass any activity which is intended to enhance the common good or improve human well being.
Corporate philanthropy	Dimension of social responsibility that includes charitable donations is called corporate philanthropy.
Screening	Screening in economics refers to a strategy of combating adverse selection, one of the potential decision-making complications in cases of asymmetric information.
Quality control	The measurement of products and services against set standards is referred to as quality control.
Health insurance	Health insurance is a type of insurance whereby the insurer pays the medical costs of the insured if the insured becomes sick due to covered causes, or due to accidents. The insurer may be a private organization or a government agency.
Global marketing	A strategy of using a common marketing plan and program for all countries in which a company operates, thus selling the product or services the same way everywhere in the world is called global marketing.
Standardization	Standardization, in the context related to technologies and industries, is the process of establishing a technical standard among competing entities in a market, where this will bring benefits without hurting competition.
Homogeneous	In the context of procurement/purchasing, homogeneous is used to describe goods that do not vary in their essential characteristics irrespective of the source of supply.
Advertising	Advertising refers to paid, nonpersonal communication through various media by organizations and individuals who are in some way identified in the advertising message.
Stock exchange	A stock exchange is a corporation or mutual organization which provides facilities for stock brokers and traders, to trade company stocks and other securities.

Go to **Cram101.com** for the Practice Tests for this Chapter.
And, **NEVER** highlight a book again!

Brand manager	A manager who has direct responsibility for one brand or one product line is called a brand manager.
Household	An economic unit that provides the economy with resources and uses the income received to purchase goods and services that satisfy economic wants is called household.
Point of Sale	Point of sale can mean a retail shop, a checkout counter in a shop, or a variable location where a transaction occurs.
Pluralism	A theory of government that attempts to reaffirm the democratic character of society by asserting that open, multiple, competing, and responsive groups preserve traditional democratic values in a mass industrial state. Pluralism assumes that power will shift from group to group as elements in the mass public transfer their allegiance in response to their perceptions of their individual interests.
Large country	Large country refers to a country that is large enough for its international transactions to affect economic variables abroad, usually for its trade to matter for world prices.
Boycott	To protest by refusing to purchase from someone, or otherwise do business with them. In international trade, a boycott most often takes the form of refusal to import a country's goods.
Patronage	The power of elected and appointed officials to make partisan appointments to office or to confer contracts, honors, or other benefits on their political supporters. Patronage has always been one of the major tools by which political executives consolidate their power and attempt to control a bureaucracy.
Productivity	Productivity refers to the total output of goods and services in a given period of time divided by work hours.
Socialism	An economic system under which the state owns the resources and makes the economic decisions is called socialism.
Absorption	Total demand for goods and services by all residents of a country is absorption. The term was introduced as part of the Absorption Approach.
Multinational corporations	Firms that own production facilities in two or more countries and produce and sell their products globally are referred to as multinational corporations.
Multinational corporation	An organization that manufactures and markets products in many different countries and has multinational stock ownership and multinational management is referred to as multinational corporation.
Automatic teller machine	An automated teller machine is an electronic computerized telecommunications device that allows a financial institution's customers to directly use a secure method of communication to access their bank accounts, order or make cash withdrawals (or cash advances using a credit card) and check their account balances without the need for a human bank teller.
Technological change	The introduction of new methods of production or new products intended to increase the productivity of existing inputs or to raise marginal products is a technological change.
Strategic management	A philosophy of management that links strategic planning with dayto-day decision making. Strategic management seeks a fit between an organization's external and internal environments.
Entrepreneurship	The assembling of resources to produce new or improved products and technologies is referred to as entrepreneurship.
Stockholm school	The Stockholm school, is a school of economic thought. It refers to a loosely organized group of Swedish economists that worked together, in Sweden primarily in the 1930s. They arguably developed Keynesian economics before Keynes.

Go to **Cram101.com** for the Practice Tests for this Chapter.

Economics	The social science dealing with the use of scarce resources to obtain the maximum satisfaction of society's virtually unlimited economic wants is an economics.
Journal	Book of original entry, in which transactions are recorded in a general ledger system, is referred to as a journal.
Product line	A group of products that are physically similar or are intended for a similar market are called the product line.
Serviceability	A dimension of quality that refers to a product's ease of repair is referred to as serviceability.
Principal	In agency law, one under whose direction an agent acts and for whose benefit that agent acts is a principal.
Skunkworks	A separate small, informal, highly autonomous, and often secretive group that focuses on breakthrough ideas for the business is referred to as skunkworks.
Management system	A management system is the framework of processes and procedures used to ensure that an organization can fulfill all tasks required to achieve its objectives.
Process control system	A computer system that monitors and controls ongoing physical processes, such as temperature or pressure changes is called process control system.
Control system	A control system is a device or set of devices that manage the behavior of other devices. Some devices or systems are not controllable.A control system is an interconnection of components connected or related in such a manner as to command, direct, or regulate itself or another system.
Honeywell	Honeywell is a major American multinational corporation that produces electronic control systems and automation equipment. It is a major supplier of engineering services and avionics for NASA, Boeing and the United States Department of Defense.
Charter	Charter refers to an instrument or authority from the sovereign power bestowing the right or power to do business under the corporate form of organization. Also, the organic law of a city or town, and representing a portion of the statute law of the state.
Core business	The core business of an organization is an idealized construct intended to express that organization's "main" or "essential" activity.
Inception	The date and time on which coverage under an insurance policy takes effect is inception. Also refers to the date at which a stock or mutual fund was first traded.
Swap	In finance a swap is a derivative, where two counterparties exchange one stream of cash flows against another stream. These streams are called the legs of the swap. The cash flows are calculated over a notional principal amount. Swaps are often used to hedge certain risks, for instance interest rate risk. Another use is speculation.
Strategic plan	The formal document that presents the ways and means by which a strategic goal will be achieved is a strategic plan. A long-term flexible plan that does not regulate activities but rather outlines the means to achieve certain results, and provides the means to alter the course of action should the desired ends change.
Rate of return	A rate of return is a comparison of the money earned (or lost) on an investment to the amount of money invested.
Expected rate of return	Expected rate of return refers to the increase in profit a firm anticipates it will obtain by purchasing capital ; expressed as a percentage of the total cost of the investment activity.
Ethnocentrism	Ironically, ethnocentrism may be something that all cultures have in common. People often feel this occurring during what some call culture shock. Ethnocentrism often entails the

307

belief that one's own race or ethnic group is the most important and/or that some or all aspects of its culture are superior to those of other groups.

Customer satisfaction

Customer satisfaction is a business term which is used to capture the idea of measuring how satisfied an enterprise's customers are with the organization's efforts in a marketplace.

Capital flow

International capital movement is referred to as capital flow.

Michael Porter

Michael Porter is a leading contributor to strategic management theory, Porter's main academic objectives focus on how a firm or a region, can build a competitive advantage and develop competitive strategy. Porter's strategic system consists primarily of 5 forces analysis, strategic groups, the value chain, and market positioning stratagies.

Competitive Strategy

An outline of how a business intends to compete with other firms in the same industry is called competitive strategy.

Case study

A case study is a particular method of qualitative research. Rather than using large samples and following a rigid protocol to examine a limited number of variables, case study methods involve an in-depth, longitudinal examination of a single instance or event: a case. They provide a systematic way of looking at events, collecting data, analyzing information, and reporting the results.

Contrarian

A contrarian is sometimes thought of as perma-bears—market participants who are permanently biased to a bear market view. However, the contrarian is not biased specifically towards a negative view of the price trend in a market, but rather takes a contrary position to the prevailing market trend, whether that trend is positive or negative.

Intervention

Intervention refers to an activity in which a government buys or sells its currency in the foreign exchange market in order to affect its currency's exchange rate.

Employee empowerment

Employee empowerment is a method of improving customer service in which workers have discretion to do what they believe is necessary, but within reason, to satisfy the customer, even if this means bending some company rules.

Compromise

Compromise occurs when the interaction is moderately important to meeting goals and the goals are neither completely compatible nor completely incompatible.

308

Go to **Cram101.com** for the Practice Tests for this Chapter.

WorldCom	WorldCom was the United States' second largest long distance phone company (AT&T was the largest). WorldCom grew largely by acquiring other telecommunications companies, most notably MCI Communications. It also owned the Tier 1 ISP UUNET, a major part of the Internet backbone.
Boeing	Boeing is the world's largest aircraft manufacturer by revenue. Headquartered in Chicago, Illinois, Boeing is the second-largest defense contractor in the world. In 2005, the company was the world's largest civil aircraft manufacturer in terms of value.
Enron	Enron Corportaion's global reputation was undermined by persistent rumours of bribery and political pressure to secure contracts in Central America, South America, Africa, and the Philippines. Especially controversial was its $3 billion contract with the Maharashtra State Electricity Board in India, where it is alleged that Enron officials used political connections within the Clinton and Bush administrations to exert pressure on the board.
Ford	Ford is an American company that manufactures and sells automobiles worldwide. Ford introduced methods for large-scale manufacturing of cars, and large-scale management of an industrial workforce, especially elaborately engineered manufacturing sequences typified by the moving assembly lines.
Toshiba	Toshiba is a Japanese high technology electrical and electronics manufacturing firm, headquartered in Tokyo, Japan. It is the 7th largest integrated manufacturer of electric and electronic equipment in the world.
Layoff	A layoff is the termination of an employee or (more commonly) a group of employees for business reasons, such as the decision that certain positions are no longer necessary.
Virtual corporation	A temporary, networked organization made up of replaceable firms that join the network and leave it as needed is called virtual corporation. virtual corporation is a firm that outsources the majority of its functions. Typically, a small group of executives will contract out and then coordinate the designing, making, and selling of products or services.In theory, this allows small groups of knowledgeable executives to find the lowest supplier for any given service, and to concentrate solely on the "big picture". In theory, it also allows firms to be nimble, rapidly ramping up production without having to slowly develop people and competencies. However, as the old saying goes, there's no such thing as a free lunch. In practice, virtual firms are scarce due to the difficulties in constructing elaborate contracts that specify the distributions of profits, and because the short-term profit-centered relationships implied by the virtual structure discourage co-operation among the parts of the organization. Moreover, the contracts often fail to effectively measure the ephemeral quality. As a result, there is a tendency for suppliers to defect (in prisoner's dilemma parlance) by providing products that are "up to specs", but that fall short of rigorous quality standards.The term was a buzzword in the 1990s for several reasons. The concept became popular during the dot-com era, when demand was high for new kind of services that traditionally organized companies relied on outsourcing to perform. In the day of the dot-com related businesses it seemed like everyone was so busy that they had to outsource most of their jobs to someone else. The idea that you actually didn't need to have a large number of regular employees to be a major player caught on, and thus virtual corporation became one of the typical ways of describing this phenomenon. In fact it seemed like business in general was about to restructure into a web of temporary outsourcing deals. The existence of the internet helped facilitate communication and cooperation across this web of contracts.The technology of the time was not up to the task though, now with the advent of web services new virtual corporation possibilities exist.But the structure didn't just apply to trendy fast changing dot-com corporations. Other more traditional producers of consumer goods etc decided that they should sell their own production faciltes and convert into making contracts on the fly with whoever could produce their type of product for the lowest price. Instead of managing a large structure of the entire value chain they could focus on

Go to **Cram101.com** for the Practice Tests for this Chapter.

marketing and branding their products. Companies like The Walt Disney Company, Nike Inc., and GAP became notorious for production of their goods in sweatshop conditions particularly in Asia.Globewide Network Academy was one of the world's first virtual corporations ever incorporated in real, more than 10 years ago in Texas, Austin http://www.gnacademy.org/.A virtual corporation, virtual organization or virtual enterprise is a manifestation of Collaborative Networks.A large number of researchers in this area are organized around the non-profit SOCOLNET - Society of Collaborative Networks. A virtual corporation is also a company which exists in cyberspace and not in the real world.

Corporation	A legal entity chartered by a state or the Federal government that is distinct and separate from the individuals who own it is a corporation. This separation gives the corporation unique powers which other legal entities lack.
Specie	Specie refers to coins, normally including only those made of precious metal.
Market	A market is, as defined in economics, a social arrangement that allows buyers and sellers to discover information and carry out a voluntary exchange of goods or services.
Domestic	From or in one's own country. A domestic producer is one that produces inside the home country. A domestic price is the price inside the home country. Opposite of 'foreign' or 'world.'.
Scope	Scope of a project is the sum total of all projects products and their requirements or features.
Context	The effect of the background under which a message often takes on more and richer meaning is a context. Context is especially important in cross-cultural interactions because some cultures are said to be high context or low context.
Transnational	Transnational focuses on the heightened interconnectivity between people all around the world and the loosening of boundaries between countries.
Management	Management characterizes the process of leading and directing all or part of an organization, often a business, through the deployment and manipulation of resources. Early twentieth-century management writer Mary Parker Follett defined management as "the art of getting things done through people."
Environmental complexity	The number of environmental components that impinge on organizational decision-making is called environmental complexity.
Complexity	The technical sophistication of the product and hence the amount of understanding required to use it is referred to as complexity. It is the opposite of simplicity.
Core	A core is the set of feasible allocations in an economy that cannot be improved upon by subset of the set of the economy's consumers (a coalition). In construction, when the force in an element is within a certain center section, the core, the element will only be under compression.
Integration process	The way information such as product knowledge, meanings, and beliefs is combined to evaluate two or more alternatives is referred to as an integration process.
Integration	Economic integration refers to reducing barriers among countries to transactions and to movements of goods, capital, and labor, including harmonization of laws, regulations, and standards. Integrated markets theoretically function as a unified market.
Leverage	Leverage is using given resources in such a way that the potential positive or negative outcome is magnified. In finance, this generally refers to borrowing.
Operation	A standardized method or technique that is performed repetitively, often on different materials resulting in different finished goods is called an operation.

Frontline manager	A lower-level manager who supervises the operational activities of the organization is called a frontline manager.
Controller	Controller refers to the financial executive primarily responsible for management accounting and financial accounting. Also called chief accounting officer.
Jack Welch	In 1986, GE acquired NBC. During the 90s, Jack Welch helped to modernize GE by emphasizing a shift from manufacturing to services. He also made hundreds of acquisitions and made a push to dominate markets abroad. Welch adopted the Six Sigma quality program in late 1995.
Competitive advantage	A business is said to have a competitive advantage when its unique strengths, often based on cost, quality, time, and innovation, offer consumers a greater percieved value and there by diffetiating it from its competitors.
Capital	Capital generally refers to financial wealth, especially that used to start or maintain a business. In classical economics, capital is one of four factors of production, the others being land and labor and entrepreneurship.
Entrepreneur	The owner/operator. The person who organizes, manages, and assumes the risks of a firm, taking a new idea or a new product and turning it into a successful business is an entrepreneur.
Fund	Independent accounting entity with a self-balancing set of accounts segregated for the purposes of carrying on specific activities is referred to as a fund.
Transnational corporation	A firm that tries to simultaneously realize gains from experience curve economies, location economies, and global learning, while remaining locally responsive is called transnational corporation.
Intrapreneurship	Intrapreneurship is the practice of entrepreneurial skills and approaches by or within a company. Employees, perhaps engaged in a special project within a larger firm are supposed to behave as entrepreneurs, even though they have the resources and capabilities of the larger firm to draw upon.
Hierarchical organization	A hierarchical organization is an organization structured in a way such that every entity in the organization, except one, is subordinate to a single other entity. This is the dominant mode of organization among large organizations; most corporations, governments, and organized religions are hierarchical organizations.
Skunk works	A separate small, informal, highly autonomous, and often secretive group that focuses on breakthrough ideas for the business is referred to as skunk works.
Financial control	A process in which a firm periodically compares its actual revenues, costs, and expenses with its projected ones is called financial control.
Instrument	Instrument refers to an economic variable that is controlled by policy makers and can be used to influence other variables, called targets. Examples are monetary and fiscal policies used to achieve external and internal balance.
Resource allocation	Resource allocation refers to the manner in which an economy distributes its resources among the potential uses so as to produce a particular set of final goods.
Budget	Budget refers to an account, usually for a year, of the planned expenditures and the expected receipts of an entity. For a government, the receipts are tax revenues.
Control system	A control system is a device or set of devices that manage the behavior of other devices. Some devices or systems are not controllable.A control system is an interconnection of components connected or related in such a manner as to command, direct, or regulate itself or another system.
Mission	Mission statement refers to an outline of the fundamental purposes of an organization.

Go to Cram101.com for the Practice Tests for this Chapter.

315

statement	
Customer service	The ability of logistics management to satisfy users in terms of time, dependability, communication, and convenience is called the customer service.
Proprietary	Proprietary indicates that a party, or proprietor, exercises private ownership, control or use over an item of property, usually to the exclusion of other parties. Where a party, holds or claims proprietary interests in relation to certain types of property (eg. a creative literary work, or software), that property may also be the subject of intellectual property law (eg. copyright or patents).
Service	Service refers to a "non tangible product" that is not embodied in a physical good and that typically effects some change in another product, person, or institution. Contrasts with good.
Performance parameters	Performance parameters are those mission-critical performance and lifecycle supportability criteria contained in the Requirements Document. They represent the sponsoring organization's translation of the capability shortfall in the Mission Need Statement into critical factors the selected solution must contain in its eventual operational state to satisfy the user's needs.
Bertelsmann	Bertelsmann is a transnational media corporation founded in 1835, based in Gütersloh, Germany. Bertelsmann made headlines on May 17, 2002, when it announced it would acquire the assets of Napster for $8 million.
Technology	The body of knowledge and techniques that can be used to combine economic resources to produce goods and services is called technology.
Internal customer	An individuals or unit within the firm that receives services from other entities within the organization is an internal customer.
Closing	The finalization of a real estate sales transaction that passes title to the property from the seller to the buyer is referred to as a closing. Closing is a sales term which refers to the process of making a sale. It refers to reaching the final step, which may be an exchange of money or acquiring a signature.
Maturity	Maturity refers to the final payment date of a loan or other financial instrument, after which point no further interest or principal need be paid.
Operating profit	Operating profit is a measure of a company's earning power from ongoing operations, equal to earnings before the deduction of interest payments and income taxes.
Profit	Profit refers to the return to the resource entrepreneurial ability; total revenue minus total cost.
Hierarchy	A system of grouping people in an organization according to rank from the top down in which all subordinate managers must report to one person is called a hierarchy.
Variance	Variance refers to a measure of how much an economic or statistical variable varies across values or observations. Its calculation is the same as that of the covariance, being the covariance of the variable with itself.
Firm	An organization that employs resources to produce a good or service for profit and owns and operates one or more plants is referred to as a firm.
Aggregation	Aggregation refers to the combining of two or more things into a single category. Data on international trade necessarily aggregate goods and services into manageable groups.
Entrepreneurship	The assembling of resources to produce new or improved products and technologies is referred to as entrepreneurship.

Go to **Cram101.com** for the Practice Tests for this Chapter.

Strategic choice	Strategic choice refers to an organization's strategy; the ways an organization will attempt to fulfill its mission and achieve its long-term goals.
Category management	An organizational system whereby managers have responsibility for the marketing programs for a particular category or line of products is a category management.
Global competition	Global competition exists when competitive conditions across national markets are linked strongly enough to form a true international market and when leading competitors compete head to head in many different countries.
Asset	An item of property, such as land, capital, money, a share in ownership, or a claim on others for future payment, such as a bond or a bank deposit is an asset.
Toyota	Toyota is a Japanese multinational corporation that manufactures automobiles, trucks and buses. Toyota is the world's second largest automaker by sales. Toyota also provides financial services through its subsidiary, Toyota Financial Services, and participates in other lines of business.
Competitor	Other organizations in the same industry or type of business that provide a good or service to the same set of customers is referred to as a competitor.
Brand	A name, symbol, or design that identifies the goods or services of one seller or group of sellers and distinguishes them from the goods and services of competitors is a brand.
Market share	That fraction of an industry's output accounted for by an individual firm or group of firms is called market share.
Innovation	Innovation refers to the first commercially successful introduction of a new product, the use of a new method of production, or the creation of a new form of business organization.
Authoritarianism	The belief that power and status differences are appropriate within hierarchical social systems such as organizations is referred to as authoritarianism.
Flat structure	Flat structure refers to a management structure characterized by an overall broad span of control and relatively few hierarchical levels.
Partition	Partition refers to proceeding the object of which is to enable those who own property as joint tenants or tenants in common to put an end to the tenancy so as to vest in each a sole estate in specific property or an allotment of the lands and tenements. If a division of the estate is impracticable, the estate ought to be sold and the proceeds divided.
Product development	In business and engineering, new product development is the complete process of bringing a new product to market. There are two parallel aspects to this process : one involves product engineering ; the other marketing analysis. Marketers see new product development as the first stage in product life cycle management, engineers as part of Product Lifecycle Management.
Production	The creation of finished goods and services using the factors of production: land, labor, capital, entrepreneurship, and knowledge.
Inventory	Tangible property held for sale in the normal course of business or used in producing goods or services for sale is an inventory.
Principal	In agency law, one under whose direction an agent acts and for whose benefit that agent acts is a principal.
Information technology	Information technology refers to technology that helps companies change business by allowing them to use new methods.
Information system	An information system is a system whether automated or manual, that comprises people, machines, and/or methods organized to collect, process, transmit, and disseminate data that

Go to **Cram101.com** for the Practice Tests for this Chapter.

319

represent user information.

Distribution	Distribution in economics, the manner in which total output and income is distributed among individuals or factors.
Raw material	Raw material refers to a good that has not been transformed by production; a primary product.
New product development	New product development is the complete process of bringing a new product to market. There are two parallel aspects to this process : one involves product engineering ; the other marketing analysis.
Inventory control	Inventory control, in the field of loss prevention, are systems designed to introduce technical barriers to shoplifting.
Logistics	Those activities that focus on getting the right amount of the right products to the right place at the right time at the lowest possible cost is referred to as logistics.
Supply	Supply is the aggregate amount of any material good that can be called into being at a certain price point; it comprises one half of the equation of supply and demand. In classical economic theory, a curve representing supply is one of the factors that produce price.
Market research	Market research is the process of systematic gathering, recording and analyzing of data about customers, competitors and the market. Market research can help create a business plan, launch a new product or service, fine tune existing products and services, expand into new markets etc. It can be used to determine which portion of the population will purchase the product/service, based on variables like age, gender, location and income level. It can be found out what market characteristics your target market has.
Advertising	Advertising refers to paid, nonpersonal communication through various media by organizations and individuals who are in some way identified in the advertising message.
Marketing	Promoting and selling products or services to customers, or prospective customers, is referred to as marketing.
Complaint	The pleading in a civil case in which the plaintiff states his claim and requests relief is called complaint. In the common law, it is a formal legal document that sets out the basic facts and legal reasons that the filing party (the plaintiffs) believes are sufficient to support a claim against another person, persons, entity or entities (the defendants) that entitles the plaintiff(s) to a remedy (either money damages or injunctive relief).
Rationalization	Rationalization in economics is an attempt to change a pre-existing ad-hoc workflow into one that is based on a set of published rules.
Accumulation	The acquisition of an increasing quantity of something. The accumulation of factors, especially capital, is a primary mechanism for economic growth.
Restructuring	Restructuring is the corporate management term for the act of partially dismantling and reorganizing a company for the purpose of making it more efficient and therefore more profitable.
Continuous improvement	The constant effort to eliminate waste, reduce response time, simplify the design of both products and processes, and improve quality and customer service is referred to as continuous improvement.
Customer satisfaction	Customer satisfaction is a business term which is used to capture the idea of measuring how satisfied an enterprise's customers are with the organization's efforts in a marketplace.
Working capital	The dollar difference between total current assets and total current liabilities is called working capital.
Benchmarking	The continuous process of comparing the levels of performance in producing products and

Go to **Cram101.com** for the Practice Tests for this Chapter.
And, **NEVER** highlight a book again!

services and executing activities against the best levels of performance is benchmarking.

Contribution	In business organization law, the cash or property contributed to a business by its owners is referred to as contribution.
Industry	A group of firms that produce identical or similar products is an industry. It is also used specifically to refer to an area of economic production focused on manufacturing which involves large amounts of capital investment before any profit can be realized, also called "heavy industry".
Nokia	Nokia Corporation is the world's largest manufacturer of mobile telephones (as of June 2006), with a global market share of approximately 34% in Q2 of 2006. It produces mobile phones for every major market and protocol, including GSM, CDMA, and W-CDMA (UMTS).
Stock market	An organized marketplace in which common stocks are traded. In the United States, the largest stock market is the New York Stock Exchange, on which are traded the stocks of the largest U.S. companies.
Stock	In financial terminology, stock is the capital raized by a corporation, through the issuance and sale of shares.
Operating results	Operating results refers to measures that are important to monitoring and tracking the effectiveness of a company's operations.
Investment	Investment refers to spending for the production and accumulation of capital and additions to inventories. In a financial sense, buying an asset with the expectation of making a return.
Credibility	The extent to which a source is perceived as having knowledge, skill, or experience relevant to a communication topic and can be trusted to give an unbiased opinion or present objective information on the issue is called credibility.
Intel	Intel Corporation, founded in 1968 and based in Santa Clara, California, USA, is the world's largest semiconductor company. Intel is best known for its PC microprocessors, where it maintains roughly 80% market share.
Manufacturing	Production of goods primarily by the application of labor and capital to raw materials and other intermediate inputs, in contrast to agriculture, mining, forestry, fishing, and services a manufacturing.
Compatibility	Compatibility refers to used to describe a product characteristic, it means a good fit with other products used by the consumer or with the consumer's lifestyle. Used in a technical context, it means the ability of systems to work together.
Positioning	The art and science of fitting the product or service to one or more segments of the market in such a way as to set it meaningfully apart from competition is called positioning.
Partnership	In the common law, a partnership is a type of business entity in which partners share with each other the profits or losses of the business undertaking in which they have all invested.
Balance	In banking and accountancy, the outstanding balance is the amount of money owned, (or due), that remains in a deposit account (or a loan account) at a given date, after all past remittances, payments and withdrawal have been accounted for. It can be positive (then, in the balance sheet of a firm, it is an asset) or negative (a liability).
Committee	A long-lasting, sometimes permanent team in the organization structure created to deal with tasks that recur regularly is the committee.
Motorola	The Six Sigma quality system was developed at Motorola even though it became most well known because of its use by General Electric. It was created by engineer Bill Smith, under the direction of Bob Galvin (son of founder Paul Galvin) when he was running the company.

Go to **Cram101.com** for the Practice Tests for this Chapter.

Honda	With more than 14 million internal combustion engines built each year, Honda is the largest engine-maker in the world. In 2004, the company began to produce diesel motors, which were both very quiet whilst not requiring particulate filters to pass pollution standards. It is arguable, however, that the foundation of their success is the motorcycle division.
Charisma	A form of interpersonal attraction that inspires support and acceptance from others is charisma. It refers especially to a quality in certain people who easily draw the attention and admiration (or even hatred if the charisma is negative) of others due to a "magnetic" quality of personality and/or appearance.
Tangible	Having a physical existence is referred to as the tangible. Personal property other than real estate, such as cars, boats, stocks, or other assets.
Authority	Authority in agency law, refers to an agent's ability to affect his principal's legal relations with third parties. Also used to refer to an actor's legal power or ability to do something. In addition, sometimes used to refer to a statute, case, or other legal source that justifies a particular result.
Transparency	Transparency refers to a concept that describes a company being so open to other companies working with it that the once-solid barriers between them become see-through and electronic information is shared as if the companies were one.
Openness	Openness refers to the extent to which an economy is open, often measured by the ratio of its trade to GDP.
Action plan	Action plan refers to a written document that includes the steps the trainee and manager will take to ensure that training transfers to the job.
Trust	An arrangement in which shareholders of independent firms agree to give up their stock in exchange for trust certificates that entitle them to a share of the trust's common profits.
Harvard Business Review	Harvard Business Review is a research-based magazine written for business practitioners, it claims a high ranking business readership and enjoys the reverence of academics, executives, and management consultants. It has been the frequent publishing home for well known scholars and management thinkers.
Recession	A significant decline in economic activity. In the U.S., recession is approximately defined as two successive quarters of falling GDP, as judged by NBER.
Economy	The income, expenditures, and resources that affect the cost of running a business and household are called an economy.
Consultant	A professional that provides expert advice in a particular field or area in which customers occassionaly require this type of knowledge is a consultant.
Ad hoc	Ad hoc is a Latin phrase which means "for this purpose." It generally signifies a solution that has been tailored to a specific purpose and is makeshift and non-general, such as a handcrafted network protocol or a specific-purpose equation, as opposed to general solutions.
Economic growth	Economic growth refers to the increase over time in the capacity of an economy to produce goods and services and to improve the well-being of its citizens.
Decentralization	Decentralization is the process of redistributing decision-making closer to the point of service or action. This gives freedom to managers at lower levels of the organization to make decisions.
Globalization	The increasing world-wide integration of markets for goods, services and capital that attracted special attention in the late 1990s is called globalization.
Convergence	The blending of various facets of marketing functions and communication technology to create more efficient and expanded synergies is a convergence.

Go to **Cram101.com** for the Practice Tests for this Chapter.

Globalization of markets	Moving away from an economic system in which national markets are distinct entities, isolated by trade barriers and barriers of distance, time, and culture, and toward a system in which national markets are merging into one global market is globalization of markets.
Subsidiary	A company that is controlled by another company or corporation is a subsidiary.
Private sector	The households and business firms of the economy are referred to as private sector.
Unit cost	Unit cost refers to cost computed by dividing some amount of total costs by the related number of units. Also called average cost.
Bureaucracy	Bureaucracy refers to an organization with many layers of managers who set rules and regulations and oversee all decisions.
Foundation	A Foundation is a type of philanthropic organization set up by either individuals or institutions as a legal entity (either as a corporation or trust) with the purpose of distributing grants to support causes in line with the goals of the foundation.
Leadership	Management merely consists of leadership applied to business situations; or in other words: management forms a sub-set of the broader process of leadership.
Revenue	Revenue is a U.S. business term for the amount of money that a company receives from its activities, mostly from sales of products and/or services to customers.
Merger	Merger refers to the combination of two firms into a single firm.
Shell	One of the original Seven Sisters, Royal Dutch/Shell is the world's third-largest oil company by revenue, and a major player in the petrochemical industry and the solar energy business. Shell has six core businesses: Exploration and Production, Gas and Power, Downstream, Chemicals, Renewables, and Trading/Shipping, and operates in more than 140 countries.
Exxon	Exxon formally replaced the Esso, Enco, and Humble brands on January 1, 1973, in the USA. The name Esso, pronounced S-O, attracted protests from other Standard Oil spinoffs because of its similarity to the name of the parent company, Standard Oil.
Amoco	Amoco was formed as Standard Oil (Indiana) in 1889 by John D. Rockefeller as part of the Standard Oil trust. In 1910, with the rise in popularity of the automobile, Amoco decided to specialize in providing gas to everyday families and their cars. In 1911, the year it became independent from the Standard Oil trust, the company sold 88% of the gasoline and kerosene sold in the midwest.
Market value	Market value refers to the price of an asset agreed on between a willing buyer and a willing seller; the price an asset could demand if it is sold on the open market.
Acquisition	A company's purchase of the property and obligations of another company is an acquisition.
Castrol	Castrol was founded on March 19th 1899 by Charles "Cheers" Wakefield in England. It was originally named the Wakefield Oil Company. In 1909, the company began production of a new automotive lubricant named Castrol. The company developed specific oil applications for various applications of the new internal combustion engine, including automobiles, motorcycles, and aircraft.
Leadership development	In organizational development, leadership development is the strategic investment in, and utilization of, the human capital within the organization. Leader development focuses on the development of the leader, such as the personal attributes desired in a leader, desired ways of behaving, ways of thinking or feeling.
Synergy	Corporate synergy occurs when corporations interact congruently. A corporate synergy refers to a financial benefit that a corporation expects to realize when it merges with or acquires another corporation.

Go to **Cram101.com** for the Practice Tests for this Chapter.

Enterprise	Enterprise refers to another name for a business organization. Other similar terms are business firm, sometimes simply business, sometimes simply firm, as well as company, and entity.
Collective responsibility	Cabinet collective responsibility is constitutional convention in the states that use the Westminster System. It means that members of the Cabinet must publicly support all governmental decisions made in Cabinet, even if they do not privately agree with them.
Managing director	Managing director is the term used for the chief executive of many limited companies in the United Kingdom, Commonwealth and some other English speaking countries. The title reflects their role as both a member of the Board of Directors but also as the senior manager.
Policy	Similar to a script in that a policy can be a less than completely rational decision-making method. Involves the use of a pre-existing set of decision steps for any problem that presents itself.
Management team	A management team is directly responsible for managing the day-to-day operations (and profitability) of a company.
Reorganization	Reorganization occurs, among other instances, when one corporation acquires another in a merger or acquisition, a single corporation divides into two or more entities, or a corporation makes a substantial change in its capital structure.
Business unit	The lowest level of the company which contains the set of functions that carry a product through its life span from concept through manufacture, distribution, sales and service is a business unit.
Regional marketing	Developing marketing plans to reflect specific area differences in taste preferences, perceived needs, or interests is called regional marketing.
Performance management	The means through which managers ensure that employees' activities and outputs are congruent with the organization's goals is referred to as performance management.
Performance measurement	The process by which someone evaluates an employee's work behaviors by measurement and comparison with previously established standards, documents the results, and communicates the results to the employee is called performance measurement.
Shareholder	A shareholder is an individual or company (including a corporation) that legally owns one or more shares of stock in a joined stock company.
Human capital	Human capital refers to the stock of knowledge and skill, embodied in an individual as a result of education, training, and experience that makes them more productive. The stock of knowledge and skill embodied in the population of an economy.
Prejudice	Prejudice is, as the name implies, the process of "pre-judging" something. It implies coming to a judgment on a subject before learning where the preponderance of evidence actually lies, or forming a judgment without direct experience.
Goldman Sachs	Goldman Sachs is widely respected as a financial advisor to some of the most important companies, largest governments, and wealthiest families in the world. It is a primary dealer in the U.S. Treasury securities market. It offers its clients mergers & acquisitions advisory, provides underwriting services, engages in proprietary trading, invests in private equity deals, and also manages the wealth of affluent individuals and families.
Intermediaries	Intermediaries specialize in information either to bring together two parties to a transaction or to buy in order to sell again.
Country risk	Country risk relates to the likelihood that changes in the business environment will occur that reduce the profitability of doing business in a country. These changes can adversely affect operating profits as well as the value of assets.

Case study	A case study is a particular method of qualitative research. Rather than using large samples and following a rigid protocol to examine a limited number of variables, case study methods involve an in-depth, longitudinal examination of a single instance or event: a case. They provide a systematic way of looking at events, collecting data, analyzing information, and reporting the results.
Assessment	Collecting information and providing feedback to employees about their behavior, communication style, or skills is an assessment.
Option	A contract that gives the purchaser the option to buy or sell the underlying financial instrument at a specified price, called the exercise price or strike price, within a specific period of time.
Training and development	All attempts to improve productivity by increasing an employee's ability to perform is training and development.
Intranet	Intranet refers to a companywide network, closed to public access, that uses Internet-type technology. A set of communications links within one company that travel over the Internet but are closed to public access.
Contract	A contract is a "promise" or an "agreement" that is enforced or recognized by the law. In the civil law, a contract is considered to be part of the general law of obligations.
Prototype	A prototype is built to test the function of a new design before starting production of a product.
Frequency	Frequency refers to the speed of the up and down movements of a fluctuating economic variable; that is, the number of times per unit of time that the variable completes a cycle of up and down movement.
Stakeholder	A stakeholder is an individual or group with a vested interest in or expectation for organizational performance. Usually stakeholders can either have an effect on or are affected by an organization.
Word of mouth	People influencing each other during their face-to-face converzations is called word of mouth.
British Petroleum	British Petroleum, is a British energy company with headquarters in London, one of four vertically integrated private sector oil, natural gas, and petrol (gasoline) "supermajors" in the world, along with Royal Dutch Shell, ExxonMobil and Total.
Consumption	In Keynesian economics consumption refers to personal consumption expenditure, i.e., the purchase of currently produced goods and services out of income, out of savings (net worth), or from borrowed funds. It refers to that part of disposable income that does not go to saving.
Points	Loan origination fees that may be deductible as interest by a buyer of property. A seller of property who pays points reduces the selling price by the amount of the points paid for the buyer.
Merchant	Under the Uniform Commercial Code, one who regularly deals in goods of the kind sold in the contract at issue, or holds himself out as having special knowledge or skill relevant to such goods, or who makes the sale through an agent who regularly deals in such goods or claims such knowledge or skill is referred to as merchant.
Boycott	To protest by refusing to purchase from someone, or otherwise do business with them. In international trade, a boycott most often takes the form of refusal to import a country's goods.
Security	Security refers to a claim on the borrower future income that is sold by the borrower to the

Go to **Cram101.com** for the Practice Tests for this Chapter.
And, **NEVER** highlight a book again!

lender. A security is a type of transferable interest representing financial value.

News release	A publicity tool consisting of an announcement regarding changes in the company or the product line is called a news release.
Organizational design	The structuring of workers so that they can best accomplish the firm's goals is referred to as organizational design.
Shareholder value	For a publicly traded company, shareholder value is the part of its capitalization that is equity as opposed to long-term debt. In the case of only one type of stock, this would roughly be the number of outstanding shares times current shareprice.
Public policy	Decision making by government. Governments are constantly concerned about what they should or should not do. And whatever they do or do not do is public policy. public program All those activities designed to implement a public policy; often this calls for the creation of organizations, public agencies, and bureaus.
Public relations	Public relations refers to the management function that evaluates public attitudes, changes policies and procedures in response to the public's requests, and executes a program of action and information to earn public understanding and acceptance.
Intervention	Intervention refers to an activity in which a government buys or sells its currency in the foreign exchange market in order to affect its currency's exchange rate.
Coalition	An informal alliance among managers who support a specific goal is called coalition.
Journal	Book of original entry, in which transactions are recorded in a general ledger system, is referred to as a journal.
Corporate citizenship	A theory of responsibility that says a business has a responsibility to do good is corporate citizenship. Terms used in the business sector to refer to business giving, ie. business relationships and partnerships with not-for-profit organizations.
Corporate branding	Corporate branding refers to the practice of using a company's name as a product brand name. It is an attempt to leverage corporate brand equity to create product brand recognition. It is a type of family branding or umbrella brand.
Specialist	A specialist is a trader who makes a market in one or several stocks and holds the limit order book for those stocks.
Logo	Logo refers to device or other brand name that cannot be spoken.
Analyst	Analyst refers to a person or tool with a primary function of information analysis, generally with a more limited, practical and short term set of goals than a researcher.
Exxon Mobil	Exxon Mobil is the largest publicly traded integrated oil and gas company in the world, formed on November 30, 1999, by the merger of Exxon and Mobil. It is the sixth-largest company in the world as ranked by the Forbes Global 2000 and the largest company in the world (by revenue) as ranked by the Fortune Global 500.
Mobil	Mobil is a major oil company which merged with the Exxon Corporation in 1999. Today Mobil continues as a major brand name within the combined company.
Interest	In finance and economics, interest is the price paid by a borrower for the use of a lender's money. In other words, interest is the amount of paid to "rent" money for a period of time.
Organization structure	The system of task, reporting, and authority relationships within which the organization does its work is referred to as the organization structure.
Organic growth	Organic growth is the rate of business expansion through increasing output and sales as opposed to mergers, acquisitions and take-overs. Typically, the organic growth rate also excludes the impact of foreign exchange. Growth including foreign exchange, but excluding

divestitures and acquistions is often referred to as, core growth.

Mutuality	Reciprocal obligations of the parties required to make a contract binding on either party is referred to as mutuality.
Recruitment	Recruitment refers to the set of activities used to obtain a sufficient number of the right people at the right time; its purpose is to select those who best meet the needs of the organization.
Earnings per share	Earnings per share refers to annual profit of the corporation divided by the number of shares outstanding.
General Electric	In 1876, Thomas Alva Edison opened a new laboratory in Menlo Park, New Jersey. Out of the laboratory was to come perhaps the most famous invention of all—a successful development of the incandescent electric lamp. By 1890, Edison had organized his various businesses into the Edison General Electric Company.
Operating margin	In business, operating margin is the ratio of operating income divided by net sales.
Margin	A deposit by a buyer in stocks with a seller or a stockbroker, as security to cover fluctuations in the market in reference to stocks that the buyer has purchased but for which he has not paid is a margin. Commodities are also traded on margin.
Household	An economic unit that provides the economy with resources and uses the income received to purchase goods and services that satisfy economic wants is called household.
Trend	Trend refers to the long-term movement of an economic variable, such as its average rate of increase or decrease over enough years to encompass several business cycles.
Strategic planning	The process of determining the major goals of the organization and the policies and strategies for obtaining and using resources to achieve those goals is called strategic planning.
Strategic business unit	Strategic business unit is understood as a business unit within the overall corporate identity which is distinguishable from other business because it serves a defined external market where management can conduct strategic planning in relation to products and markets. When companies become really large, they are best thought of as being composed of a number of businesses
Strategic plan	The formal document that presents the ways and means by which a strategic goal will be achieved is a strategic plan. A long-term flexible plan that does not regulate activities but rather outlines the means to achieve certain results, and provides the means to alter the course of action should the desired ends change.
Agglomeration	The phenomenon of economic activity congregating in or close to a single location, rather than being spread out uniformly over space is an agglomeration.
Divestiture	In finance and economics, divestiture is the reduction of some kind of asset, for either financial or social goals. A divestment is the opposite of an investment.
Insurance	Insurance refers to a system by which individuals can reduce their exposure to risk of large losses by spreading the risks among a large number of persons.
Credit	Credit refers to a recording as positive in the balance of payments, any transaction that gives rise to a payment into the country, such as an export, the sale of an asset, or borrowing from abroad.
Reinsurance	An allocation of the portion of the insurance risk to another company in exchange for a portion of the insurance premium is called reinsurance.
Strategic	Strategic control processes allow managers to evaluate a company's marketing program from a

control	critical long-term perspective. This involves a detailed and objective analysis of a company's organization and its ability to maximize its strengths and market opportunities.
Downsizing	The process of eliminating managerial and non-managerial positions are called downsizing.
Best practice	Best practice is a management idea which asserts that there is a technique, method, process, activity, incentive or reward that is more effective at delivering a particular outcome than any other technique, method, process, etc.
Organizational culture	The mindset of employees, including their shared beliefs, values, and goals is called the organizational culture.
Management development	The process of training and educating employees to become good managers and then monitoring the progress of their managerial skills over time is management development.
Cultural values	The values that employees need to have and act on for the organization to act on the strategic values are called cultural values.
Charter	Charter refers to an instrument or authority from the sovereign power bestowing the right or power to do business under the corporate form of organization. Also, the organic law of a city or town, and representing a portion of the statute law of the state.
Productivity	Productivity refers to the total output of goods and services in a given period of time divided by work hours.
Xerox	Xerox was founded in 1906 as "The Haloid Company" manufacturing photographic paper and equipment. The company came to prominence in 1959 with the introduction of the first plain paper photocopier using the process of xerography (electrophotography) developed by Chester Carlson, the Xerox 914.
Controlling	A management function that involves determining whether or not an organization is progressing toward its goals and objectives, and taking corrective action if it is not is called controlling.
Internationa-ization	Internationalization refers to another term for fragmentation. Used by Grossman and Helpman.
Market position	Market position is a measure of the position of a company or product on a market.
Joint venture	Joint venture refers to an undertaking by two parties for a specific purpose and duration, taking any of several legal forms.
Broker	In commerce, a broker is a party that mediates between a buyer and a seller. A broker who also acts as a seller or as a buyer becomes a principal party to the deal.
Swap	In finance a swap is a derivative, where two counterparties exchange one stream of cash flows against another stream. These streams are called the legs of the swap. The cash flows are calculated over a notional principal amount. Swaps are often used to hedge certain risks, for instance interest rate risk. Another use is speculation.
Implicit contract	An agreement between employer and employees concerning conditions of pay, employment, and unemployment that is unwritten but understood by both parties is called implicit contract.
Loyalty	Marketers tend to define customer loyalty as making repeat purchases. Some argue that it should be defined attitudinally as a strongly positive feeling about the brand.
Psychological contract	A person's set of expectations regarding what he or she will contribute to the organization and what the organization, in return, will provide to the individual is called psychological contract.
Senior executive	Senior executive means a chief executive officer, chief operating officer, chief financial officer and anyone in charge of a principal business unit or function.

Key jobs	Benchmark jobs, used in pay surveys, that have relatively stable content and are common to many organizations is referred to as key jobs.
Compensation package	The total array of money, incentives, benefits, perquisites, and awards provided by the organization to an employee is the compensation package.
Incentive	An incentive is any factor (financial or non-financial) that provides a motive for a particular course of action, or counts as a reason for preferring one choice to the alternatives.
Stock option	A stock option is a specific type of option that uses the stock itself as an underlying instrument to determine the option's pay-off and therefore its value.
Promotion	Promotion refers to all the techniques sellers use to motivate people to buy products or services. An attempt by marketers to inform people about products and to persuade them to participate in an exchange.
Career planning	Process in which individuals evaluate their abilities and interests, consider alternative career opportunities, establish career goals, and plan practical development activities is referred to as career planning.
Evaluation	The consumer's appraisal of the product or brand on important attributes is called evaluation.
Human resource planning	Forecasting the organization's human resource needs, developing replacement charts for all levels of the organization, and preparing inventories of the skills and abilities individuals need to move within the organization is called human resource planning.
Slowdown	A slowdown is an industrial action in which employees perform their duties but seek to reduce productivity or efficiency in their performance of these duties. A slowdown may be used as either a prelude or an alternative to a strike, as it is seen as less disruptive as well as less risky and costly for workers and their union.
Boundaryless organization	A boundaryless organization is an organization not defined or limited by horizontal, vertical, or external boundaries imposed by a predetermined structure. Similar to flat organizations, there is a strong emphasis on teams. Cross-functional teams dissolve horizontal barriers and enable the organization to respond quickly to environmental changes and to spearhead innovation.
Quick response	An inventory management system designed to reduce the retailer's lead-time, thereby lowering its inventory investment, improving customer service levels, and reducing logistics expense is referred to as quick response.
Assault	An intentional tort that prohibits any attempt or offer to cause harmful or offensive contact with another if it results in a well-grounded apprehension of imminent battery in the mind of the threatened person is called assault.
Stretch target	A challenging goal or objective requiring significant effort to achieve is a stretch target.
Inventory turns	In business management, inventory turns measures the number of times capital invested in goods to be sold turns over in a year.
Negotiation	Negotiation is the process whereby interested parties resolve disputes, agree upon courses of action, bargain for individual or collective advantage, and/or attempt to craft outcomes which serve their mutual interests.
Fixture	Fixture refers to a thing that was originally personal property and that has been actually or constructively affixed to the soil itself or to some structure legally a part of the land.
Research and development	The use of resources for the deliberate discovery of new information and ways of doing things, together with the application of that information in inventing new products or

Go to **Cram101.com** for the Practice Tests for this Chapter.

processes is referred to as research and development.

Service business	A business firm that provides services to consumers, such as accounting and legal services, is referred to as a service business.
Annual report	An annual report is prepared by corporate management that presents financial information including financial statements, footnotes, and the management discussion and analysis.
AlliedSignal	AlliedSignal was created through a 1985 merger of Allied Chemical & Dye Corportation and Signal Oil, the company renamed to AlliedSignal on September 19, 1985. The company's involvement in aerospace stems from a previous merger between Signal Oil and the Garrett Corporation in 1968. After that merger, aviation became the company's largest division. In 1999. AlliedSignal acquired Honeywell and took its more-recognizable name.
Six sigma	A means to 'delight the customer' by achieving quality through a highly disciplined process to focus on developing and delivering near-perfect products and services is called six sigma. Originally, it was defined as a metric for measuring defects and improving quality; and a methodology to reduce defect levels below 3.4 Defects Per (one) Million Opportunities (DPMO).
Executive Council	An Executive Council in Commonwealth constitutional practice based on the Westminster system exercises executive power and is the top tier of a government led by a Governor-General, Governor, Lieutenant-Governor or Administrator (all "governors").
Business development	Business development emcompasses a number of techniques designed to grow an economic enterprise. Such techniques include, but are not limited to, assessments of marketing opportunities and target markets, intelligence gathering on customers and competitors, generating leads for possible sales, followup sales activity, and formal proposal writing.
Master black belt	A master black belt is someone who is an expert on Six Sigma techniques and project implementation. They play a major role in training, coaching and in removing barriers to project execution.
Aid	Assistance provided by countries and by international institutions such as the World Bank to developing countries in the form of monetary grants, loans at low interest rates, in kind, or a combination of these is called aid. Aid can also refer to assistance of any type rendered to benefit some group or individual.
Business model	A business model is the instrument by which a business intends to generate revenue and profits. It is a summary of how a company means to serve its employees and customers, and involves both strategy (what an business intends to do) as well as an implementation.
Startup	Any new company can be considered a startup, but the description is usually applied to aggressive young companies that are actively courting private financing from venture capitalists, including wealthy individuals and investment companies.
Business Week	Business Week is a business magazine published by McGraw-Hill. It was first published in 1929 under the direction of Malcolm Muir, who was serving as president of the McGraw-Hill Publishing company at the time. It is considered to be the standard both in industry and among students.
General manager	A manager who is responsible for several departments that perform different functions is called general manager.
Standing	Standing refers to the legal requirement that anyone seeking to challenge a particular action in court must demonstrate that such action substantially affects his legitimate interests before he will be entitled to bring suit.
Human resource management	The process of evaluating human resource needs, finding people to fill those needs, and getting the best work from each employee by providing the right incentives and job environment, all with the goal of meeting the needs of the firm are called human resource

Go to **Cram101.com** for the Practice Tests for this Chapter.

	management.
Resource management	Resource management is the efficient and effective deployment of an organization's resources when they are needed. Such resources may include financial resources, inventory, human skills, production resources, or information technology.
Administration	Administration refers to the management and direction of the affairs of governments and institutions; a collective term for all policymaking officials of a government; the execution and implementation of public policy.
Comprehensive	A comprehensive refers to a layout accurate in size, color, scheme, and other necessary details to show how a final ad will look. For presentation only, never for reproduction.
Empowerment	Giving employees the authority and responsibility to respond quickly to customer requests is called empowerment.
Brief	Brief refers to a statement of a party's case or legal arguments, usually prepared by an attorney. Also used to make legal arguments before appellate courts.
Value added	The value of output minus the value of all intermediate inputs, representing therefore the contribution of, and payments to, primary factors of production a value added.
Strategic management	A philosophy of management that links strategic planning with dayto-day decision making. Strategic management seeks a fit between an organization's external and internal environments.
Theory of the firm	The theory of the firm consists of a number of economic theories which describe the nature of the firm (company or corporation), including its behavior and its relationship with the market.
Clearing system	Clearing system refers to an arrangement among financial institutions for carrying out the transactions among them, including canceling out offsetting credits and debits on the same account.
HarperCollins	HarperCollins is a publishing organization owned by News Corporation. The company found success in 1841 as a printer of Bibles, and in 1848 Collins's son Sir William Collins developed the firm as a publishing venture, specializing in religious and educational books.
Organization model	The Stages of Organization Model provides a system-level language for understanding the evolutionary development of organizations. The model describes seven types of dynamic equilibrium, each of which can provide a coherent basis for action. They represent the increasing complexity possible when people learn the lessons of early stages of activity and incorporate this learning while tackling more advanced challenges.
Profit center	Responsibility center where the manager is accountable for revenues and costs is referred to as a profit center.
Portfolio	In finance, a portfolio is a collection of investments held by an institution or a private individual. Holding but not always a portfolio is part of an investment and risk-limiting strategy called diversification. By owning several assets, certain types of risk (in particular specific risk) can be reduced.
Multinational corporation	An organization that manufactures and markets products in many different countries and has multinational stock ownership and multinational management is referred to as multinational corporation.
Forming	The first stage of team development, where the team is formed and the objectives for the team are set is referred to as forming.
Global matrix	Global Matrix is the largest and oldest non-GDS-affiliated software service provider in the North American retail travel industry. In business for over 35 years, the company's travel

agency support and business management system is used by independent travel agencies in Canada, U.S., and Australia, and forms a unique foundation for the delivery of complete front-, mid-, and back-office functionality.

Communication channel	The pathways through which messages are communicated are called a communication channel.
Channel	Channel, in communications (sometimes called communications channel), refers to the medium used to convey information from a sender (or transmitter) to a receiver.
Contract A	Contract A is a concept applied in Canadian contract law (a Common Law system country) which has recently been applied by courts regarding the fairness and equal treatment of bidders in a contract tendering process. Essentially this concept formalises previously applied precedents and strengthens the protection afforded to Contractors in the tendering process.
Delegation	Delegation is the handing of a task over to another person, usually a subordinate. It is the assignment of authority and responsibility to another person to carry out specific activities.
Export	In economics, an export is any good or commodity, shipped or otherwise transported out of a country, province, town to another part of the world in a legitimate fashion, typically for use in trade or sale.
Core business	The core business of an organization is an idealized construct intended to express that organization's "main" or "essential" activity.
Senior management	Senior management is generally a team of individuals at the highest level of organizational management who have the day-to-day responsibilities of managing a corporation.
Product line	A group of products that are physically similar or are intended for a similar market are called the product line.
Expense	In accounting, an expense represents an event in which an asset is used up or a liability is incurred. In terms of the accounting equation, expenses reduce owners' equity.
Manufacturing costs	Costs incurred in a manufacturing process, which consist of direct material, direct labor, and manufacturing overhead are referred to as manufacturing costs.
Conglomerate	A conglomerate is a large company that consists of divisions of often seemingly unrelated businesses.
Organization development	The process of planned change and improvement of the organization through application of knowledge of the behavioral sciences is called organization development.
Business operations	Business operations are those activities involved in the running of a business for the purpose of producing value for the stakeholders. The outcome of business operations is the harvesting of value from assets owned by a business.
Regular meeting	A meeting held by the board of directors that is held at regular intervals at the time and place established in the bylaws is called a regular meeting.
Customer retention	Customer retention refers to the percentage of customers who return to a service provider or continue to purchase a manufactured product.
Conflict resolution	Conflict resolution is the process of resolving a dispute or a conflict. Successful conflict resolution occurs by providing each side's needs, and adequately addressing their interests so that they are each satisfied with the outcome. Conflict resolution aims to end conflicts before they start or lead to physical fighting.
Vertical integration	Vertical integration refers to production of different stages of processing of a product within the same firm.

Go to **Cram101.com** for the Practice Tests for this Chapter.

Inputs	The inputs used by a firm or an economy are the labor, raw materials, electricity and other resources it uses to produce its outputs.
Corporate Strategy	Corporate strategy is concerned with the firm's choice of business, markets and activities and thus it defines the overall scope and direction of the business.
Status quo	Status quo is a Latin term meaning the present, current, existing state of affairs.
Management control	That aspect of management concerned with the comparison of actual versus planned performance as well as the development and implementation of procedures to correct substandard performance is called management control.
British Airways	British Airways is the largest airline of the United Kingdom. It is also one of the largest airlines in the world, with the greatest number of flights from Europe to North America. Its main bases are London Heathrow (LHR) and London Gatwick (LGW).
World Bank	The World Bank is a group of five international organizations responsible for providing finance and advice to countries for the purposes of economic development and poverty reduction, and for encouraging and safeguarding international investment.
Siemens	Siemens is the world's largest conglomerate company. Worldwide, Siemens and its subsidiaries employs 461,000 people (2005) in 190 countries and reported global sales of €75.4 billion in fiscal year 2005.
PepsiCo	In many ways, PepsiCo differs from its main competitor, having three times as many employees, larger revenues, but a smaller net profit.
Extension	Extension refers to an out-of-court settlement in which creditors agree to allow the firm more time to meet its financial obligations. A new repayment schedule will be developed, subject to the acceptance of creditors.
Organizational environment	Organizational environment refers to everything outside an organization. It includes all elements, people, other organizations, economic factors, objects, and events that lie outside the boundaries of the organization.
Succession planning	Succession planning refers to the identification and tracking of high-potential employees capable of filling higher-level managerial positions.
Supervisor	A Supervisor is an employee of an organization with some of the powers and responsibilities of management, occupying a role between true manager and a regular employee. A Supervisor position is typically the first step towards being promoted into a management role.
Gain	In finance, gain is a profit or an increase in value of an investment such as a stock or bond. Gain is calculated by fair market value or the proceeds from the sale of the investment minus the sum of the purchase price and all costs associated with it.
Mentor	An experienced employee who supervises, coaches, and guides lower-level employees by introducing them to the right people and generally being their organizational sponsor is a mentor.
Tacit knowledge	Knowledge that has not been articulated. Tacit knowledge is often subconscious and relatively difficult to communicate to other people. Tacit knowledge consists often of habits and culture that we do not recognize in ourselves.
Competitiveness	Competitiveness usually refers to characteristics that permit a firm to compete effectively with other firms due to low cost or superior technology, perhaps internationally.
Receiver	A person that is appointed as a custodian of other people's property by a court of law or a creditor of the owner, pending a lawsuit or reorganization is called a receiver.
Alignment	Term that refers to optimal coordination among disparate departments and divisions within a

Go to **Cram101.com** for the Practice Tests for this Chapter.

Go to **Cram101.com** for the Practice Tests for this Chapter.
And, **NEVER** highlight a book again!

firm is referred to as alignment.

Personnel	A collective term for all of the employees of an organization. Personnel is also commonly used to refer to the personnel management function or the organizational unit responsible for administering personnel programs.
A share	In finance the term A share has two distinct meanings, both relating to securities. The first is a designation for a 'class' of common or preferred stock. A share of common or preferred stock typically has enhanced voting rights or other benefits compared to the other forms of shares that may have been created. The equity structure, or how many types of shares are offered, is determined by the corporate charter.
Matching	Matching refers to an accounting concept that establishes when expenses are recognized. Expenses are matched with the revenues they helped to generate and are recognized when those revenues are recognized.
Time Warner	Time Warner is the world's largest media company with major Internet, publishing, film, telecommunications and television divisions.
Process improvement	Process improvement is the activity of elevating the performance of a process, especially that of a business process with regard to its goal.
Contract manufacturing	Contract manufacturing refers to a foreign country's production of private-label goods to which a domestic company then attaches its brand name or trademark; also called outsourcing.
Economics	The social science dealing with the use of scarce resources to obtain the maximum satisfaction of society's virtually unlimited economic wants is an economics.
Artificial intelligence	Computers or computer enhaned machines that can be programmed to think, learn, and make decisions in a manner similar to people is is the subject of artificial intelligence.
Respondent	Respondent refers to a term often used to describe the party charged in an administrative proceeding. The party adverse to the appellant in a case appealed to a higher court.
Venture capital	Venture capital is capital provided by outside investors for financing of new, growing or struggling businesses. Venture capital investments generally are high risk investments but offer the potential for above average returns.
Appeal	Appeal refers to the act of asking an appellate court to overturn a decision after the trial court's final judgment has been entered.
Emerging market	The term emerging market is commonly used to describe business and market activity in industrializing or emerging regions of the world.
Corporate culture	The whole collection of beliefs, values, and behaviors of a firm that send messages to those within and outside the company about how business is done is the corporate culture.
Coercion	Economic coercion is when an agent puts economic pressure onto the victim. The most common example of this is cutting off the supply to an essential resource, such as water.
Knowledge base	Knowledge base refers to a database that includes decision rules for use of the data, which may be qualitative as well as quantitative.
Fragmentation	Fragmentation refers to the splitting of production processes into separate parts that can be done in different locations, including in different countries.
Global platform	Global refers to the home country conditions and competitive advantages from a global strategy that transcend the domicile country. A country is a desirable global platform in an industry if it provides an environment yielding firms domiciled in that country an advantage in competing globally in that particular industry.
Value system	A value system refers to how an individual or a group of individuals organize their ethical

Go to **Cram101.com** for the Practice Tests for this Chapter.

or ideological values. A well-defined value system is a moral code.

Subcontractor   A subcontractor is an individual or in many cases a business that signs a contract to perform part or all of the obligations of another's contract. A subcontractor is hired by a general or prime contractor to perform a specific task as part of the overall project.

CPSIA information can be obtained at www.ICGtesting.com
Printed in the USA
LVOW091505011112

305453LV00001B/101/A